Lecture Notes in Computer Science   6121

Commenced Publication in 1973
Founding and Former Series Editors:
Gerhard Goos, Juris Hartmanis, and Jan van Leeuwen

Editorial Board

David Hutchison
  Lancaster University, UK
Takeo Kanade
  Carnegie Mellon University, Pittsburgh, PA, USA
Josef Kittler
  University of Surrey, Guildford, UK
Jon M. Kleinberg
  Cornell University, Ithaca, NY, USA
Alfred Kobsa
  University of California, Irvine, CA, USA
Friedemann Mattern
  ETH Zurich, Switzerland
John C. Mitchell
  Stanford University, CA, USA
Moni Naor
  Weizmann Institute of Science, Rehovot, Israel
Oscar Nierstrasz
  University of Bern, Switzerland
C. Pandu Rangan
  Indian Institute of Technology, Madras, India
Bernhard Steffen
  TU Dortmund University, Germany
Madhu Sudan
  Microsoft Research, Cambridge, MA, USA
Demetri Terzopoulos
  University of California, Los Angeles, CA, USA
Doug Tygar
  University of California, Berkeley, CA, USA
Gerhard Weikum
  Max Planck Institute for Informatics, Saarbruecken, Germany

Lachlan M. MacKinnon (Ed.)

Data Security and Security Data

27th British National Conference on Databases, BNCOD 27
Dundee, UK, June 29 – July 1, 2010
Revised Selected Papers

 Springer

Volume Editor

Lachlan M. MacKinnon
University of Greenwich
School of Computing and Mathematical Sciences
Old Royal Naval College
Park Row
Greenwich
London SE10 9LS, UK
E-mail: lachlan@ieee.org

ISSN 0302-9743   e-ISSN 1611-3349
ISBN 978-3-642-25703-2   ISBN 978-3-642-25704-9 (eBook)
DOI 10.1007/978-3-642-25704-9
Springer Heidelberg Dordrecht London New York

Library of Congress Control Number: 2011943214

CR Subject Classification (1998): H.4, H.3, H.2, H.2.7-8, K.6.5, I.2.4, I.2.6

LNCS Sublibrary: SL 3 – Information Systems and Application, incl. Internet/Web
and HCI

Typesetting: Camera-ready by author, data conversion by Scientific Publishing Services, Chennai, India

Printed on acid-free paper

Springer is part of Springer Science+Business Media (www.springer.com)

Preface

The BNCOD 2010 Conference was held at the University of Abertay Dundee during June 28–30, 2010. The conference theme was "Data Security—Security Data," and, as well as the usual broad range of papers we would expect at BNCOD, authors were encouraged to submit papers addressing, or at least considering, the conference theme.

Whether this had an influence above and beyond that expected is difficult to tell, but the conference did receive a very large number of non-standard submissions and enquiries, predominantly from authors in Asia. Considerable effort was required on the part of the conference organizers to address all of these inputs, and to attempt to determine genuine inputs from those that were mischievous, sought funding for attendance or even paper production, or saw conference proceedings as some form of vanity publishing.

Although we were eventually able to cut these papers down to a manageable number, we reviewed 42 (mostly through the EasyChair system, which was a boon in producing these proceedings) and accepted 10 full papers and 6 short papers, we were not convinced we had trapped all the problem cases and so changed the publication model to a post-conference one. This proved to be the right decision, as we had a further three no-shows at the conference itself, where the authors advised us at the last minute of their non-attendance for various reasons, but we were aware that they would have required visas for attendance and they had not approached us for letters of support. On that basis, those papers were also withdrawn from the proceedings, so we can say with complete confidence that all the papers contained within these proceedings were presented by one or more of their authors in their prescribed slot in the conference programme in Dundee.

Unfortunately, it does now seem to be necessary to take this approach to maintain the viability of the conference as an academic research event in our discipline. While we would not wish to penalize genuine research authors from any part of the world who wish to engage in dialogue with the community and present and share their work, we do need to discourage those who see the conference fee as a price to pay for a publication, with no intention of attendance or engagement.

Moving away from the problems of identifying genuine authors, once we had done so we had a varied and interesting set of full and short papers, combined with good keynotes and a varied social programme. As in previous years, the conference was preceded by the "Teaching, Learning & Assessment in Databases" workshop, aimed at those researching and reporting novel and high-quality pedagogic activities in the database curriculum, and the Best Paper from that workshop appears later in these proceedings. The conference was also preceded by a PhD Doctoral Consortium, where PhD students at various stages of their studies in a wide variety of data and information systems topics presented short papers on their work. The two Best Papers from that forum also appear at the end of these proceedings.

The conference proper kicked off with a keynote address from Ken Barker of the University of Calgary on the theme of "Valuing Data Privacy While Exposing Data Utility." Ken was provocative, as ever, in proposing that privacy, and more recently data privacy, is more of a desired than achievable goal, and for many users there would be a willingness to trade some measure of data privacy for a value in economic or service terms.

A varied and enjoyable set of conference presentations followed, as can be seen from the contents of these proceedings. The final keynote panel debated the future of the BNCOD conference itself, considering various models in which the database community, particularly in the UK, might become more engaged with the conference, and whether a workshop and symposium model or other forms of model might work more effectively. There was a lively debate and a commitment on the part of the organizers to think about this further for the upcoming conferences in 2011 and 2012.

The conference closed with a short presentation from Alvaro Fernandes, encouraging delegates to attend BNCOD 2011 in Manchester.

Despite the problems in determining genuine submissions, and the failure of some delegates to attend, BNCOD 2010 was a successful and enjoyable event, and I would wish to record my thanks to the conference team, in particular Petra Leimich and Les Ball, for their hard work in making it so.

July 2010   Lachlan MacKinnon

Organization

Organizing Committee

Lachlan MacKinnon (Conference Chair)
Les Ball (Organizing Co-chair)
Petra Leimich (Organizing Co-chair)
Linda Fyfe (Administrator)

Program Committee

Les Ball	University of Abertay Dundee, UK
David Bell	Queen's University Belfast, UK
Sharma Chakravarthy	The University of Texas at Arlington, USA
Richard Cooper	University of Glasgow, UK
Alfredo Cuzzocrea	University of Calabria, Italy
Barry Eaglestone	University of Sheffield, UK
Alvaro Fernandes	The University of Manchester, UK
Mary Garvey	University of Wolverhampton, UK
Georg Gottlob	Oxford University, UK
Alex Gray	Cardiff University, UK
Jun Hong	Queen's University Belfast, UK
Ela Hunt	ETH Zurich, Switzerland
Mike Jackson	Birmingham City University, UK
Anne James	Coventry University, UK
Keith Jeffery	Science and Technology Facilities Council, UK
Graham Kemp	Chalmers University of Technology, Sweden
Jessie Kennedy	Napier University, UK
Petra Leimich	University of Abertay Dundee, UK
Lachlan MacKinnon	University of Greenwich, London, UK
Nigel Martin	Birkbeck College, University of London, UK
Ken Moody	University of Cambridge, UK
David Nelson	University of Sunderland, UK
Moira Norrie	ETH Zurich, Switzerland
Werner Nutt	Free University of Bolzano, Italy
Alex Poulovassilis	Birkbeck College, University of London, UK
Mark Roantree	Dublin City University, UK
Sandra Sampaio	The University of Manchester, UK

Alan Sexton   Birmingham University, UK
Jianhua Shao   Cardiff University, UK
Stratis Viglas   University of Edinburgh, UK
Richard White   Cardiff University, UK
John Wilson   University of Strathclyde, UK

Additional Reviewers

Cappellari, Paolo
Mao, Lu

Table of Contents

TLAD Best Paper

PhD Forum Best Papers

"Valuing" Privacy While Exposing Data Utility

Ken Barker*

Advanced Database Systems and Applications Laboratory,
University of Calgary, Canada

kbarker@ucalgary.ca

Protecting data privacy is an area of increasing concern as the general public has become increasingly impacted by its inability to guarantee that those things we wish to hold private remain private. The concept of privacy is found in the earliest writing of mankind and continues today to be a very high value in modern society. Unfortunately, challenges to privacy have always existed and at times, these challenges have become so strong that any real sense of personal privacy was assumed to unattainable. This occurred in the middle-ages when communal living was normative, at least among the poor, so it was necessary to accept this as a simple matter of fact. This does not mean that privacy was not valued at the time, simply that it was assumed to be unachievable so the absence of it was accepted. A poll in a recent undergraduate/graduate class at the University of Calgary revealed that over half of the students felt that there was no way to protect their privacy in online systems. It was not that they did not value their privacy but simply felt, much like those in the middle-ages, there was nothing they could do about it. In addition, about half of the students felt that there was value in their private information and felt that they would consider trading it for an economic return under certain conditions that varied widely from individual to individual.

Westin has polled users for nearly two decades and his finding reveal three basic types of privacy conscious people [2]. First, *privacy fundamentalists* are cautious about private information and are extremely careful about how it is released and managed (approximately 25%). The second category are *pragmatics* who are willing to make trade-offs between the value for the service provided and the amount of privacy sacrificed for that service (approximately 57%). The third category are those who are *unconcerned* about their private information and represent approximately 18% of those surveyed in the 1991 survey and these remained relatively unchanged when the surveys were run at the end of the 1990s. These findings are relatively consistent with similar surveys undertaken in 2003.

Clearly some people are either naïve or unconcerned about their privacy and are willing to release such information without personal benefit, but this is a minority. Nearly 25% place a very high value on their private information while 59% are clearly pragmatic and are willing to trade privacy for a returned value. An interesting research opportunity presents itself if we can find a way to "value" privacy in such a way that the provider can receive a return for giving their private information to a collector. Subsequently, the collector can receive a value for the collected data either in terms of its

---

* This research is partially support by NSERC Discovery Grant RGP-O10556.

L.M. MacKinnon (Ed.): BNCOD 2010, LNCS 6121, pp. 1–2, 2012.

utility within its own organization or by "re-selling" it in conformance with the criteria specified at the point of collection.

Realizing such a system has several challenges, some of which are the subject of ongoing research but many of which are only beginning to be considered. First, a model capable of valuing data's privacy features can only exist if the characteristics of that privacy are well understood. Our group has produced one such definition [1] but a more restrictive one might be more readily implemented. However, the privacy definition selected must allow the data provider to express how the data is valued in a fairly complete way or those in the privacy fundamentalist category will be reluctant to participate. This must be traded-off against the need to specify privacy in a straight-forward way. A study undertaken in 2007 to assess a user's willingness to provide private data in a survey revealed that by allowing the user to select the level of specificity in their responses; more accurate responses and an increased perception of comfort about the survey resulted [3].

Secondly, a suitable model to value the data must be developed. Several alternatives suggest themselves ranging from a simple static Nashian economic model to a game theoretic scenario where the value proposition is negotiated in a more dynamic way. The former alternative is likely to be more readily understood by naïve users who will be asked to participate but the latter alternative is more likely to allow for individualistic provider preferences. If the privacy model is relatively complete it will be easier to articulate a meaningful value for a piece of data. For example, if the provider is willing to share specific μ-data, a greater value should be returned than if the user is only willing to provide the same data categorically. Similarly if the collector, based on the provider's preferences, is only allowed to re-sell the data in an aggregated way, it will have lesser "value" so the provider cannot expect to realize the same return.

There are many open questions beyond a privacy definition and the selection of an appropriate economic model. Questions include integrating privacy into all aspects of systems that can see private data, providing appropriate ways to allow providers to specify their preferences, resolving conflicts between the collectors and providers, managing diverse provider preferences, and allowing for dynamics such as providers who change their mind. These techniques, once developed, would then have to be tailored to various environments including online provision of services, data collected for retail loyalty programs, B2B data exchange, *etc*. Clearly this is a rich area for future research and the results arising will have wide applicability that will impact on a real need for all online users.

References

1. Barker, K., Askari, M., Banerjee, M., Ghazinour, K., Mackas, B., Majedi, M., Pun, S., Williams, A.: A Data Privacy Taxonomy. In: Sexton, A.P. (ed.) BNCOD 26. LNCS, vol. 5588, pp. 42–54. Springer, Heidelberg (2009)
2. Kumaraguru, P., Cranor, L.F.: Privacy indexes: A survey of westin's studies. Technical Report CMU-ISRI-5-138, Carnegie Mellon University, CMU, Pittsburgh, PA, USA (December 2005)
3. Williams, A., Barker, K.: Controling inference: Avoiding p-level reduction during analysis. Journal of Research and Practice in Information Technology 40(3), 163–185 (2008)

Whither BNCOD? The Future of Database and Information Systems Research

Alasdair J.G. Gray

School of Computer Science, University of Manchester,
Kilburn Building, Oxford Road, Manchester, M13 9PL, UK
A.Gray@cs.man.ac.uk
http://www.cs.man.ac.uk/~graya

Abstract. The British National Conference on Databases (BNCOD), now in its 27th edition, has covered a broad range of database research topics: from the purely theoretical, to more application-oriented subjects. It has proved to be a forum for intellectual debate, and has fostered a sense of community amongst British and overseas database researchers.

Databases have been incredibly successful with most businesses relying on them. However, there are still plenty of challenges that remain to be solved. This paper reflects back on the successes of the BNCOD series, and identifies the challenges that remain, thus showing the continuing importance of the BNCOD conference series.

1 Introduction

Databases and information systems have long been, and continue to be, an active area of research in the UK and the British National Conference on Databases (BNCOD) has played an important part of the intellectual debate amongst British researchers. BNCOD has also provided a forum for overseas researchers, with many participating to the proceedings over the years. In 2008, BNCOD celebrated its 25th edition with a Colloquium on Advances in Database Research [6], which provided the community a chance to look back on past successes.

The results of database research have been widely taken up, with databases forming the cornerstone of virtually all applications upon which businesses rely. For example, eCommerce web sites are driven by databases from which the pages are generated, and customer and stock details stored. Also in science, data values are read and stored in databases for community access, e.g. Sloan Digital Sky Survey[1], UniProt[2]. With this success, some may feel that databases are a problem which has been solved.

This paper, which captures part of the panel session at BNCOD-27, identifies key challenges that face the BNCOD community. Section 2 provides a brief history of BNCOD and the subjects that have been covered. We then identify several open research challenges in Section 3 and present our conclusions in Section 4.

---

[1] http://www.sdss.org/ accessed July 2010.
[2] http://www.uniprot.org/ accessed July 2010.

L.M. MacKinnon (Ed.): BNCOD 2010, LNCS 6121, pp. 3–6, 2012.

Fig. 1. A topic cloud formed from the BNCOD conference session headings 1990 – 2009

2 BNCOD Past

The first BNCOD was held in 1981 and set out the following aim for the conference series:

> "The BNCOD series is meant to focus primarily on British research work, although overseas papers are welcome. ...Its objective is to encourage database research in Britain by bringing together the researchers and other interested parties." [3]

BNCOD has fostered a strong sense of community amongst British database researchers, and provided a vital training ground for PhD students: offering a PhD forum and a friendly environment in which to present a first conference paper. It has also proved to be successful at attracting publications from researchers worldwide.

In recent years there has been a decline in the BNCOD community, although this does not match the situation worldwide where *"[T]he database research community has doubled in size over the last decade"* [1]. The British database research community has diversified into a variety of related research fields which provide their own specialised forums to present and discuss ideas, e.g. bioinformatics with the DILS conference [8], eScience and Grid computing with the eScience conference [4], and the Semantic Web with ESWC [2]. However, the topics of research remain largely database oriented, with the new fields providing motivation and application scenarios for the work.

BNCOD has covered the entire spectrum of database research. Figure 1 presents a topic cloud of the session headings at BNCOD between 1990 and 2009. As will be shown in the next section, many of these topics remain challenges for the database community.

3   Research Challenges

The theme for BNCOD-27 is "data security and security data." As can be seen from Figure 1 *security* and, the closely related, data *privacy* have seen little attention from the British research community. Generally, research projects have seen these as optional details that can be bolted on at a later date. However, with the increasingly digital world in which we live, and the pervasiveness of social networks, these are crucial topics to be addressed.

The most common topic headings over the last 20 years have involved *data* and *databases*. This is not surprising since these are at the heart of database research, and remain central to the research field. There is an ever increasing amount of data being collected, stored, and analysed with exponential growth in the volume of data being experienced in science and industry alike [7,9]. The volumes of data being stored and processed create new challenges of scalability and efficiency, particularly as users increasingly expect instantaneous results. Specifically, this places renewed importance on *query processing* and *optimisation* since these are the major factors which affect *performance* of data management systems for data *retrieval*.

Another major focus of past research has been on data *integration* over *distributed, heterogeneous*, data sets. With the advent of the semantic web, which aims to view the entire web as an interconnected database, these topics take on a renewed importance. However, the semantic web only addresses one aspect of heterogeneity, that of data modelling and interlinking. Issues to resolve the heterogeneity of data format, i.e. relational, RDF, or XML, still remain to be solved. Similarly, querying over multiple sources, including over the semantic web, remains a challenging area where improvements can be made. For example, when querying a distributed set of large sources, the time incurred to move data between sites becomes a significant overhead. Improved mechanisms for moving computation to the data, rather than data to the computation, need to be discovered.

A more recent topic at BNCOD has been data *streams*. This is due to the increasing use of sensor devices to monitor the world around us, e.g. environmental monitoring or patient vital statistics monitoring. Data streams have required a new approach to data management, particularly for query processing, since the data is a potentially infinite sequence of values. Thus, the *store first process later* model of database systems does not work. To date, this work has largely focused on homogeneous data streams in isolation rather than looking at the bigger picture of integrating multiple streaming and stored data sources. Some of the challenges in this area have been outlined in [10,5].

4   Conclusions

We live in an increasingly interconnected world where data from multiple heterogeneous sources needs to be combined and analysed. Users expect to be able to access their data from anywhere, with results being displayed on a plethora of devices including mobile devices. This must be achieved with highly scalable approaches since data is growing at an exponential rate. Finally, security and privacy issues need to be addressed as primary concerns in data management.

The database research community is facing some of its greatest challenges yet. Young researchers can learn from the successes of the past by reading the literature, but new techniques and approaches will be required to overcome these challenges. We live in exciting times!

References

1. Agrawal, R., Ailamaki, A., Bernstein, P.A., Brewer, E.A., Carey, M.J., Chaudhuri, S., Doan, A., Florescu, D., Franklin, M.J., Garcia-Molina, H., Gehrke, J., Gruenwald, L., Haas, L.M., Halevy, A.Y., Hellerstein, J.M., Ioannidis, Y.E., Korth, H.F., Kossmann, D., Madden, S., Magoulas, R., Ooi, B.C., O'Reilly, T., Ramakrishnan, R., Sarawagi, S., Stonebraker, M., Szalay, A.S., Weikum, G.: The claremont report on database research. Commun. ACM 52(6), 56–65 (2009)
2. Aroyo, L., Antoniou, G., Hyvönen, E., ten Teije, A., Stuckenschmidt, H., Cabral, L., Tudorache, T. (eds.): ESWC 2010, Part I. LNCS, vol. 6088, pp. 213–227. Springer, Heidelberg (2010)
3. Deen, S.M., Hammersley, P. (eds.): Proceedings of the First British National Conference on Databases (BNCOD-1), Jesus College, Cambridge, 13-14 July 1982 (1981)
4. Fifth International Conference on e-Science and Grid Computing, e-Science 2009, December 9-11. IEEE Computer Society, Oxford (2009)
5. Gray, A.J.G., Nutt, W., Williams, M.H.: Sources of Incompleteness in Grid Publishing. In: Bell, D.A., Hong, J. (eds.) BNCOD 2006. LNCS, vol. 4042, pp. 94–101. Springer, Heidelberg (2006)
6. Gray, A., Jeffery, K., Shao, J. (eds.): BNCOD 2008. LNCS, vol. 5071, pp. 87–99. Springer, Heidelberg (2008)
7. Howe, D., Costanzo, M., Fey, P., Gojobori, T., Hannick, L., Hide, W., Hill, D.P., Kania, R., Schaeffer, M., Pierre, S.S., Twigger, S., White, O., Rhee, Y.: Big data: The future of biocuration. Nature 455, 47–50 (2008)
8. Paton, N.W., Missier, P., Hedeler, C. (eds.): DILS 2009. LNCS, vol. 5647, pp. 88–95. Springer, Heidelberg (2009)
9. Szalay, A.S.: Scientific publishing in the era of petabye data. JCDL, 261–262 (2008)
10. Tatbul, N.: Streaming data integration: Challenges and opportunities. In: Proceedings of IEEE ICDE International Workshop on New Trends in Information Integration (NTII 2010), Long Beach, California, USA (March 2010)

Whither BNCOD and the UK Database Community

Keith G. Jeffery

Director IT & International Strategy, STFC Rutherford Appleton Laboratory,
Chilton, Didcot, OXON OX11 0QX UK
`keith.jeffery@stfc.ac.uk`

Abstract. The UK database community has a long and eventful history and much is recorded in the proceedings of BNCOD. Despite some notable successes with papers in international journals and conferences, in general the UK community 'punched below its weight' in database research. At the 25th anniversary BNCOD (2008) a special session day brought together well-known international researchers with their perspectives on research directions. This paper attempts to provide directions for the future of database research in a context related to global challenges and evolving requirements.

1 Introduction

After more than 25 years of conferences it is time for BNCOD and the UK database community to take stock. We have accomplished much, but perhaps not as much as we should or could have. Some of the best UK researchers in the field choose to publish elsewhere instead of – rather than in addition to – BNCOD. This reflects the globalisation of research in the last 25 plus years and increasingly the advances made though international cooperation – sometimes with international or jointly organised national funding.

BNCOD started with the aim of sharing experience and research ideas at a time when the technology was evolving fast and undergoing a theory revolution. The original concept of separate national and international conferences hosted in UK was overtaken by events: VLDB, ICDE, ICDT, EDBT and other international conferences which moved from country to country dominated the market leaving BNCOD for national level research discussion. However, quite rapidly BNCOD attracted international contributions – helped by publishing in LNCS - and so became a nationally-hosted international conference. Competition became stiffer and quality higher. Also the programme committees tended to favour academic and theoretical papers over application-driven papers. Nonetheless, BNCOD programme topics matched well the issues in the international database community. BNCOD lost attendance steadily. Associated workshops were successful but most had a limited lifetime. So we reach a point of decision – should BNCOD continue and if so what issues should be addressed. This paper argues BNCOD continues to have a role and that there are important issues that the UK database community can address.

L.M. MacKinnon (Ed.): BNCOD 2010, LNCS 6121, pp. 7–11, 2012.

2   The Past

The early days of BNCOD were marked by intense discussion over the efficacy of Hierarchic, CODASYL and relational DBMS. Data modelling examples were used to illustrate advantages and disadvantages. Programming and user interfaces were discussed. At the time a group of UK universities had secured national funding for a distributed database project – PROTEUS – which linked together the major research centres in database technology in UK. More fundamental work was done on data representation as triples and a triple store project initiated at Birkbeck with IBM. This, and parallel work at Aberdeen and Glasgow led to procedural programming language interface research.

In parallel work on scientific databases with problems of scale, performance and integrity advanced as did work on relating database systems to office automation and coupling structured databases with semi-structured information retrieval systems. Object-Oriented approaches were much discussed. Optimisation of performance and of queries was also a hot topic. Spatial and temporal database development flourished in both theory and practice and the management and representation of provenance was discussed. Work on homogeneous access to heterogeneous distributed databases led to interfacing databases with hypermedia systems and thus to databases and WWW. Deductive database systems and work on integrity constraints and dependencies led to further work on programming languages – this time declarative. These strands came together in work on intelligent agents acting based on metadata describing data, software / services and users.

Given the dominance of relational database technology and WWW, work on web services and database interfaces in a GRIDs (and later CLOUDs) e-infrastructure expanded. Management of streamed data from sensors became a reality. The difficult problem of homogeneous access to heterogeneous data sources was at least partially resolved by utilising human intellect – the concept of Dataspaces. The future internet raises many problems which challenge fundamentally database theory and practice.

3   The Present

The database community is now confronted by a fast-moving world of information systems.

End users are content to spend time browsing information from the shallow web with relatively low recall and relevance and semi-structure.   They expect to be presented with approximately relevant information and using their intellect make choices on what to use or believe. They are content to use their processing capability to perform the processing that is so hard to organise within an IT system, and leave the IT system to reduce an unstructured or semistructured mass of data into something they can manage.

In some application domains – particularly in business information management and in scientific data management - end-users expect not 'tables of results' but graphical representations – and based on structured, validated data that has been reduced using strict algorithms from statistics or data mining.

Thus we have two 'worlds of information' with different characteristics that we need to combine to satisfy most requirements. The end-user also expects the required information (with appropriate recall and relevance) to be presented on the device of choice anywhere, anyhow, anytime (so called 'Martini computing' after the iconic advertisement). They expect not to write programs or even issue commands or queries but to point and click, pull-down and choose or – as a last resort – type a word (e.g. a search term) or better speak it.

4   The Future

The internet is estimated to have 1.5billion fixed connections and 4 billion mobile connections. Data Storage is estimated at 280 Exabytes (280 * 10**18). Processor power continues to follow Moore's Law, recently due to multicore technology. The capacities are expected to increase tenfold in 4 years.

Usage is increasing too. In Asia the estimate is 550 million users representing 14% penetration; in Europe 350 million users representing 50% penetration and in US 250 million users representing 70% penetration. There is still a large increase in users to be accommodated.

This backdrop of sociological, economic and technical development leads to challenges for the database community. These may be characterised as Scalability, Trust, security & privacy, Manageability. Accessibility, Usability and Representativity. They challenge the very fundamentals of database theory and practice within computer science.

4.1   Scalability

Millions of nodes on the internet are collecting data (from sensors or humans) and processing data. How do we manage to specify, control and monitor the integrity of the data? Traditional techniques involving constraints and dependencies just do not scale. How do we represent state? The real word state, and the recorded world state are changing very quickly and locally autonomously. How do we maintain a global stateful representation of the real world? Traditional ACID transactions do not work over even a relatively few nodes in a distributed system and rollback or compensation techniques are overwhelmed by the volume of incoming data. How do we handle streamed data? Since we do not have a static recorded database state traditional validation using constraints and dependencies can at best be partial and preliminary. Similarly with querying; the speed and volume of data acquisition requires a query over a 'window' of the data stream and selection of tuples matching the criteria – but complex data structures (e.g. queries where selection from one stream is conditional upon another) become impossible to handle – yet are exactly what is required for many scientific, environmental, health and sociological applications. Related performance problems occur when particular servers become 'honeypots' providing information in response to popular – sometimes caused by sociological factors – queries. Our protocols and data transfer systems – especially using HTTP and XML are inefficient and have excessive latency. Given all these aspects, how does one provide a quality of service guarantee and how does one maintain service at the appropriate quality? Finally, given the data volumes and the relatively slow intercommunications infrastructure, it becomes necessary to move the code to the data rather than the other way around, with implications in security.

4.2 Trust, Security and Privacy

This topic is dealt with in depth by Lachlan MacKinnon in a companion paper to this.

4.3 Manageability

The scale and complexity of future internet requires automation of management of systems to reduce human error and increase performance. Local optimisation may degrade global optimisation for performance. The requirement is for autonomic systems operating autonomously within parameters set by the system administrator. The autonomicity requires all components (servers, detectors, services, communications, users) to be represented by metadata and agents.

4.4 Accessibility

The requirement is for high-performance, cost-effective networking connections to permit 'Martini computing'. The implication is intelligence in the protocols enveloping the data and software transmitted for compression, routing, security etc. The end-user will wish to use interchangeably desktop, laptop, hand-held devices and will wish them to be configured appropriately for both the user requirements and the context. This implies variable interfaces for different interaction modes (keyboard/nouse, speech, gesture) required by the user being differently-abled (e.g. driving, walking, sitting) and in different contexts (office, internet cafe, climbing up a mountain) with varying security and privacy conditions.

4.5 Usability

The various interaction modes require support to assist the user, ideally by proposing actions to meet the requirements. This implies knowledge-assisted intelligent agents utilising metadata describing the user, context, services etc. The intelligence has to handle different character sets or multimedia representations, language, syntax and semantics with the aim of anticipating, assisting and supporting the end-user.

4.6 Representativity

Examination of existing database systems demonstrates that they do not represent accurately the real world. Problems of validation, integrity and correctness lead to inaccurate data.   Many use hierarchic structures based on primary/foreign keys when in fact the real world is a fully connected network structure.   Similarly, the relationships between entities (objects) in the real world commonly are complex, time-varying and require shared semantics (over a formal syntax) for their description. Representation of incomplete or uncertain information – with additional information on provenance to assist the end-user in judging its relevance to the requirement – is essential.   In this way the system can take over some of the evaluation and selection done now by end-users using their intellect browsing the shallow web.   The requirement is for better data modelling tools and systems to correct and fuse data dealing with incompleteness and uncertainty.

5   Conclusion

There is a feast of challenging issues awaiting the UK database community. Much of the necessary foundational work has been done over the last 25 years or so and the community is well-equipped to face the challenges.

Access Control Using Active Rules

Raman Adaikkalavan[1,*] and Sharma Chakravarthy[2]

[1] Computer and Information Sciences & Informatics,
Indiana University South Bend
raman@cs.iusb.edu
[2] Department of Computer Science Engineering,
The University of Texas At Arlington
sharma@cse.uta.edu

Abstract. Access to only authorized resources is provided by access control mechanisms. Active or Event-Condition-Action rules make the underlying systems and applications active by detecting and reacting to changes. In this paper, we show how active rules can be used to enforce Role-Based Access Control (RBAC) standard. First, we analyze different components of active rules and their mappings for enforcing RBAC standard. Second, we discuss how RBAC standard is enforced using active rules. Finally, we discuss how active rules extend RBAC standard to cater to a large class of applications.

Keywords: ECA Rules, Role-Based Access Control, Event Constraints.

1 Introduction

Role-Based Access Control (RBAC), where object accesses are controlled by roles (or job functions) in an enterprise rather than a user or group, has shown to be a positive alternative to traditional access control mechanisms. RBAC does not provide a complete solution for all access control issues, but with its rich specification [1], it has shown to be cost effective [2] and is used in several domains [3]. ANSI RBAC Standard [4] has four functional components: Core, Hierarchical, Static Separation of Duty and Dynamic Separation of Duty. Existing enforcement techniques are tied to a component, tightly integrated with the underlying system or they just support extensions. Constraints [5, 6] are critical in realizing RBAC over diverse domains, as they provide the flexibility for specifying fine-grained access control policies.

There is consensus in database and other communities on Active or Event-Condition-Action rules as being one of the most general formats for expressing rules in an event-driven application. Active rules and event processing systems [7–18] have been employed successfully in diverse application domains for situation or change monitoring. Existing event specification languages and event detection systems provide well-defined point-based, interval-based and generalized event semantics.

In this paper, we show how the ANSI RBAC standard can be enforced via active rules using a layered approach. We also show how enterprises can move from one RBAC functional component to the other in a seamless manner. In other words, enterprises

---

* This work was supported, in part by, IUSB Faculty Research Grant.

L.M. MacKinnon (Ed.): BNCOD 2010, LNCS 6121, pp. 12–24, 2012.

can move from Core RBAC to Hierarchical RBAC without rewriting events and rules. We then extend the RBAC specification with event-based constraints. We discuss the placement of simple and complex constraints at various granularities. We also show that these event constraints are not affected when the enterprises move from one RBAC component to the other. Finally, we discuss event detection graphs to implement events and rules.

Outline: Events and rules are discussed in Section 2. RBAC is discussed in Section 3. Enforcement using active rules is discussed in Section 4. Event constraints and advantages of our approach are discussed in Section 5. Event detection graph is discussed in Section 6. Section 7 has conclusions.

2   Active Rules

Below, we discuss events and active rules briefly.

2.1   Events

Snoop [9, 10, 14] event specification language, which is a part of the Local Event Detector (LED) [17], is used in this paper. The main motivation to use Snoop is that it supports expressive event specification using *point*-based [14], *interval*-based [10] and *generalized* semantics [7, 9] in various *event consumption modes* [10, 14] and *event detection modes* [7]. LED uses *event detection graphs* to detect events using point-, interval-based and generalized semantics in various consumption and detection modes.

An *event* is "an occurrence of interest" in the real world that can be either *simple* (e.g., depositing cash) or *complex* (e.g., depositing cash, followed by withdrawal of cash). Simple events occur at a point in time (i.e., time of depositing), and complex events occur over an interval (i.e., starts at the time cash is deposited and ends when cash is withdrawn). Simple events are detected at a time point, whereas complex events can be detected either at the *end* of the interval (i.e., point-based semantics) [15, 16] or can be detected *over* the interval (i.e., interval-based semantics) [10, 11, 18]. Each event has a well-defined set of *attributes* based on the *implicit* and *explicit* parameters [9]. *Implicit* parameters contain system- and user-defined attributes such as event name and time of occurrence. *Explicit* parameters are collected from the event itself (e.g., stock price and stock value).

Below, we discuss event specification using the interval-based semantics, represented using $\mathcal{I}$. For more details about event semantics, please refer to [9, 10, 14].

Simple Events: Simple events are the basic building blocks in an event processing system and are derived from various application domains. E.g., data manipulation language and data definition language statements in a DBMS, function call invocation in Object-oriented systems, alarm clock, and increase in stock price.

Definition 1. *An interval-based simple event E occurs atomically at a point $[t]$ on the time line. It is detected over an interval $[t, t']$, where $[t]$ is the start time, $[t']$ is the end time and $(t = t')$[1]. It is defined as $\mathcal{I}(E, [t, t']) \triangleq \exists t = t' \ (E, [t, t'])$;*

---

[1] Simple events have the same start and end time.

Definition 2. *A generalized simple event $G(E)$ can be a point- (G_P) or interval-based (G_I) simple event with conditional expressions based on $\mathcal{I}_{expr}$ and $\mathcal{E}_{expr}$. They are formally defined as $G_I(E, [t, t']) \triangleq \exists t = t' \ (\mathcal{I}(E, [t, t']) \wedge (\mathcal{I}_{expr} \wedge \mathcal{E}_{expr}));$*

Below, we show an event from an Object Oriented system where all function invocations are treated as events. E_1 is the event name and $\mathcal{F}$ is the function name. Formal parameters are explicit parameters, and time of the function call and object that invoked the function are the implicit parameters. Implicit and explicit parameter expressions are represented as $\mathcal{I}_{expr}$ and $\mathcal{E}_{expr}$, respectively. They are discussed in Definition 4.

$$Event \ \ E_1 = (\mathcal{F}(), (\mathcal{I}_{expr} \wedge \mathcal{E}_{expr}));$$

Complex Events: Simple events are often not adequate for modeling real-world scenarios. Complex events are defined by composing more than one simple or complex event using *event operators*. A number of event operators have been proposed in the literature based on several application domains. Using *composition conditions*, an event operator defines how a complex event needs to be composed and detected.

Definition 3. *An interval-based complex event $\mathcal{I}(E)$ occurs and is detected over an interval $[t_s, t_e]$. It is defined as $\mathcal{I}(Eop \ (E_1, \dots E_n), [t_s, t_e]);$*

Definition 4. *A generalized complex event $G(E)$ can be a point- (G_P) or interval-based (G_I) complex event with conditional expressions based on $\mathcal{I}_{expr}$ and $\mathcal{E}_{expr}$. They are formally defined as $G_I(Eop \ (E_1, \dots E_n), (\mathcal{I}_{expr} \wedge \mathcal{E}_{expr}), [t_s, t_e]);$*

- *Eop* represents a n-ary event operator (And, Or, SEQUENCE, NOT, Plus, Periodic, Aperiodic, Periodic*, and Aperiodic*).
- $(E_1, \dots E_n)$ are the constituent events and each one can be simple or complex.
- A complex event occurrence is based on the initiator, detector and terminator events. *Initiator* is the constituent event whose occurrence starts the complex event. *Detector* is the constituent event whose occurrence detects and raises the complex event. *Terminator* is the constituent event that is responsible for terminating the complex event, i.e., no more occurrence of a complex event with the same initiator event is possible. All the operators have initiator and detector events, and some operators have terminator events. In addition, the same constituent event can act as both the detector and terminator event.
- t_s is the start time and t_e is the end time (i.e., time of occurrence).
- $\mathcal{I}_{expr}$ is the expression formed using implicit event parameters. It subsumes existing point- and interval-based semantics. For instance, a binary event operator with events E_1 and E_2 can have $\mathcal{I}_{expr} = E_1.t\_occ \ \theta \ E_2.t\_occ$, where t_occ is the time of event occurrence, and θ can be a relational or set operator based on the domain.
- $\mathcal{E}_{expr}$ is the expression composed using explicit event parameters. Similar to the above expression can be; $\mathcal{E}_{expr} = E_1.A_i \ \theta \ E_2.B_j$, where attributes A_i and B_j have values from the same domain.
- A complex event is detected *iff* the required constituent events occur, and both $\mathcal{I}_{expr}$ and $\mathcal{E}_{expr}$ evaluate to TRUE. Both expressions cannot empty at the same time, as it will detect the complex event always.

Event Modes: In order to avoid unnecessary event detections, *event consumption modes* [10, 14] or contexts such as Recent, Continuous, Chronicle, and Cumulative were defined based on the application domains. *Event detection modes* [7] such as complete, incomplete and failed were defined to detect various types of events.

Below, SEQUENCE ($E_1 \gg E_2$) operator is defined in the unrestricted mode (i.e., no event occurrence is removed after participating in an event detection). This event operator requires event E_1 to occur before event E_2. It is *detected* when E_2 occurs. E_1 is the *initiator* event and E_2 is the *detector* event. It is formally defined in interval semantics as:

$$\mathcal{I}(E_1 \gg E_2, [t_s, t_e]) \triangleq \exists t_s, t_e, t, t'(\mathcal{I}(E_1, [t_s, t]) \wedge \mathcal{I}(E_2, [t', t_e]) \wedge (t_s \leq t < t' \leq t_e))$$

2.2   Active Rules

An event can be associated with multiple rules [12], but a rule can be associated with only one event. Condition and action procedures can be associated/shared between different rules. Rules are executed on an event occurrence and their management involves event detection and rule execution. Rule scheduling involves ordering of rules for execution when several rules are triggered at the same time. Rules can also be nested, i.e., occurrence of an event triggers a rule which in turn detects/raises another event. If an event is not part of a complex event or does not have any rule associated, then that event need not be detected for efficiency. This is possible as rules can be in active or deactive states. An active rule is specified as:

$$R_i = (E_j, (C_1 \ldots C_k), (A_1 \ldots A_n), (AA_1 \ldots AA_p));$$

- Rule R_i – Unique rule name.
- Event E_j – Event associated with the rule. This event *triggers* the rule.
- Condition $C_1 \ldots C_k$ – The set of conditions to be evaluated once the rule is triggered by event E_j.
- Action $A_1 \ldots A_n$ – The set of actions to be triggered when conditions evaluate to TRUE.
- Alternative Action $AA_1 \ldots AA_n$ – The set of actions to be triggered when conditions evaluate to FALSE.

```
addActiveRole(user, session, role) {              //Core RBAC
    IF (user ∈ U && session ∈ S && role ∈ R &&
        session ∈ userSessions(user) &&
        role ∈ sessionRoles(session) &&
        user ∈ assignedUsers(user, role)) {
            addSessionRole(session, role);         //activate role
            return TRUE; }
    ELSE {
            raise error "Access Denied";
            return FALSE; } }
```

Fig. 1. Add Active Role - Core RBAC [4]

3   Role-Based Access Control

Four different sets of functions are provided in the specification (ANSI RBAC Standard [4]) for modeling Core (supports flat roles), Hierarchical (supports role hierarchies), Static Separation of Duty (SSoD) (supports mutually exclusive roles with respect to user assignments) and Dynamic Separation of Duty (DSoD) (provides exclusivity relations with respect to roles that are part of a user's session), respectively. Functions provided by each of the four components include: addRole, deleteRole, addUser, deleteUser, assignUser, deassignUser, createSession, deleteSession, addActiveRole, dropActive-Role, and checkAccess. For example, when a subject tries to activate a role, function $addActiveRole(...)$ is invoked. Figures 1 and 2 display the function definitions from [4] for Core and Hierarchical RBAC, respectively.

Function signatures shown in the figures are the same, but definitions are different. The function definition in Figure 1 checks if the subject has the role assigned, and the definition in Figure 2 checks if the subject has the role authorized via hierarchy. Similarly, all the other functions in the specification have the same signatures but four different definitions. Enterprises implement the component that meets their requirements. In the next section, we will discuss how function signatures can be exploited to enforce all the functional components in a seamless manner using active rules.

```
addActiveRole(user, session, role) {                    //Hierarchical RBAC
    IF (user ε U && session ε S && role ε R &&
        session ε userSessions(user) &&
        role ε sessionRoles(session) &&
        user ε assignedUsers(user, role)) {
            addAuthorizedRole(session, role);    //activate role
            return TRUE; }
    ELSE {
            raise error "Access Denied";
            return FALSE; } }
```

Fig. 2. Add Active Role - Hierarchical RBAC [4]

4   Enforcing Role-Based Access Control Using Active Rules

In this section, we discuss the enforcement of the functional specification discussed in Section 3, using active rules discussed in Section 2. In order to enforce RBAC, active rule components (event, condition, action, alternative action) have to be mapped to RBAC components (users, roles, access requests). First we need to identify simple events for RBAC, and then the other components. Using active rules, RBAC specification can be extended with additional capabilities as discussed in this section and the next. The use of complex events is also analyzed in the next section.

As discussed in Section 2, any occurrence of interest can be defined as an event. The main objective of identifying simple events is to show the adequacy of events to represent occurrence of interest in RBAC. In order to find the occurrence of interest in

RBAC, we need to identify the operations that can be carried out. In RBAC, operations are carried out by users or subjects that have a set of roles. All operations are carried out using the functions (e.g., addActiveRole) specified in the RBAC standard. These are termed as role-dependent operations. Other operations (e.g., system clock) that are not part of RBAC, are termed as role-independent operations.

Simple events can be based on both role-dependent and role-independent operations. As discussed in Section 2.1, each function invocation can be treated as an event in Object-oriented systems. Thus, function signature of each role-dependent operation from the functional specification can be defined as a simple event, and each invocation can be captured as that event. Additionally, explicit and implicit event parameters need to be identified. Formal parameters of the functions can be considered as the explicit parameters, and other system generated values can be treated as implicit parameters.

Let us define an event based on the RBAC function $addActiveRole(...)$ from Figures 1 and 2. Formal parameters ($user$, $session$ and $role$) can act as the explicit event parameters.

Event E_{AAR} (defined below) is raised when $addActiveRole(...)$ is invoked, i.e., when a user tries to activate a role. However, appropriate rules have to be created to implement or invoke appropriate function definitions allowing authorized users to activate roles. For example, rule R_{AAR} defined below handles role activations for Core RBAC.

Event $E_{AAR} = addActiveRole(user, session, role)$;
RULE [R_{AAR}
      EVENT E_{AAR}
      CONDITION   "Core RBAC AAR Function Definition from Figure 1"
      ACTION   "Allow Activation"
      ALT ACTION raise error "Access Denied Cannot Activate"   ]

Rule R_{AAR} is triggered when event E_{AAR} is raised. Once the rule is triggered, conditions are checked. In our example, function definition that handles role activations in Core RBAC is implemented in the Condition part. Allowing or denying activation is mapped to Action and Alternative Action parts, respectively. With Core RBAC, if the user is assigned to the role, Condition part will return TRUE and the user will be allowed to activate the role.

Though the above approach allows the enforcement of functional specification of one RBAC component, it is not sufficient. If the enterprise chooses to use Hierarchical instead of Core, then the active rule or the Condition part has to be rewritten. In order to overcome this, we create another layer based on the function signatures to exploit the functionality of active rules. For example, modified rule R_{AAR1} defined below is similar to the rule defined above. The main difference is the association of a function call in the Condition part rather than the function definition itself. So whenever the user is trying to activate a role, event E_{AAR} is raised, which in turn triggers rule R_{AAR1}, which in turn invokes the function $\_addActiveRole(user, session, role)$. This function can implement the definition shown in Figure 1 or Figure 2. This allows the enterprise to choose Core, Hierarchical, SSoD, or DSoD seamlessly without rewriting the rule or the Condition part.

RULE [R_{AAR1}
      EVENT E_{AAR}
      CONDITION $< call > \_addActiveRole(user, session, role)$
      ACTION   "Allow Activation"
      ALT ACTION raise error "Access Denied Cannot Activate"   ]

The above approach allows us to enforce all components of RBAC seamlessly; however, it still does not utilize the capabilities of active rules completely. With active rules, Condition part can include multiple complex conditions. This can be exploited to extend RBAC with additional constraints required by an enterprise. For example, a condition such as "any role can be activated only between 8 a.m. and 5 p.m." can be enforced using the Condition part. Another example involving prerequisite roles, "role b can be activated only if role a is activated," can also be enforced. In order to support extensions (discussed in Section 5), rule R_{AAR1} shown above can be rewritten as shown below.

RULE [R_{AAR2}
      EVENT E_{AAR}
      CONDITION   /*Enterprise Specific Constraints*/
                        $< call > \_addActiveRole(user, session, role)$
      ACTION   "Allow Activation"
      ALT ACTION raise error "Access Denied Cannot Activate"   ]

Whenever a user tries to activate a role, event E_{AAR} is raised and rule R_{AAR2} is triggered. In the Condition part, enterprise specific constraints are checked. If those constraints are satisfied, then function $\_addActiveRole(user, session, role)$ is invoked. If the Condition part returns FALSE, then Alternative Actions are executed.

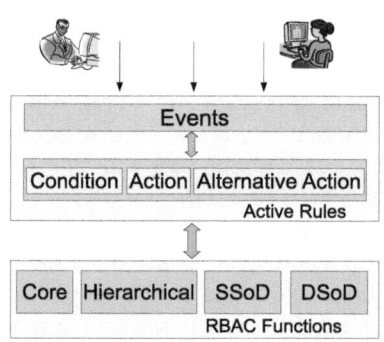

Fig. 3. Enforcing ANSI RBAC Specification Using Active Rules

Layered approach shown in Figure 3 supports all the four components of ANSI RBAC, in a seamless manner. For example, when the function $\_addActiveRole$ (user, session, role) is invoked from the Action part, it can invoke the function with definition from Core RBAC (Figure 1), Hierarchical (Figure 2), SSoD, or DSoD. This is possible mainly due to the RBAC functional specification, as all the components use the same functions and function signatures with different function definitions. Enterprises choose the component that meets their requirements.

5   Advantages and Extensions to RBAC

Using active rules not only provides seamless support for the standard, but also extends it using enterprise specific constraints based on events. Our approach generalizes constraint specification, since location, time, and any other occurrence of interest can be captured as an event. Complex events further extend the specification. Below, we discuss various extensions provided by our approach and their advantages.

5.1   Enterprise Specific Constraints Using the Condition Part

All user operations in RBAC are captured as events, and are permitted only if they satisfy: (1) standard RBAC specification; and (2) tailor-made constraints. An enterprise wants to *"allow users to activate roles from their computing devices only if they are connected to the enterprise network (161.162.) either physically or using VPN."* This policy can be enforced by modifying rule R_{AAR2} defined in Section 4 as shown below. The modified rule R_{AAR3} checks whether the IP Address of the user device starts with "161.162." using function *checkIP*, which returns a Boolean value. Thus, users are allowed to activate roles only from those IP Addresses. Only if the context constraint is satisfied, function $\_addActiveRole(user, session, role)$ is invoked. In other words, users must first satisfy the constraints in the Condition part and then the requirements of RBAC components to activate any role.

RULE [R_{AAR3}
    EVENT E_{AAR}
    CONDITION $< call > checkIP($"161.162."$)$ /*Enterprise Specific*/
                $< call > \_addActiveRole(user, session, role)$
    ACTION   "Allow Activation"
    ALT ACTION raise error "Access Denied Cannot Activate"   ]

When the enterprise wants to move from Core to Hierarchical RBAC, for example, only the definition used in $\_addActiveRole(user, session, role)$ changes, but the constraints specified in the Condition part are untouched and the rule is *not* modified. Similar to the above, other complex constraints based on time, locations, context, content, etc. and their combinations can be specified using the Condition Part.

5.2   Enterprise Specific Constraints Using Implicit and Explicit Expressions

In addition to specifying enterprise specific constraints in the Condition part, constraints can be specified using implicit (I_{expr}) and explicit (E_{expr}) expressions. Constraints specified using these expressions are checked after the function is invoked but before the event is raised (i.e., before triggering any associated rules), whereas the Condition part constraints are checked after the event is raised (i.e., after the rule is triggered). In other words, the former is part of the event and the latter is part of the rule. The former cannot be replaced by the latter and vice versa, as it will affect complex event processing and can detect *complex events* incorrectly.

Both I_{expr} and E_{expr} can be effectively used for specifying tailor-made constraints. Below, we define events based on *addActiveRole(...)* from the RBAC specification.

Event $E_1 = (addActiveRole(user, session, role))$;

Event $E_2 = (addActiveRole(user, session, role), (role = \text{``}Manager\text{''}))$;

Event $E_3 = (addActiveRole(user, session, role), (user = \text{``}Jane\text{''}))$;

Event $E_4 = (addActiveRole(user, session, role), ((user = \text{``}Jim\text{''})$
$$\wedge (role = \text{``}CEO\text{''})));$$

Event E_1 is the same as E_{AAR} defined in Section 4 and has no additional constraints.

Assume, an enterprise wants to *"restrict users trying to activate a sensitive role"*. The enterprise cannot use the general rule R_{AAR3}, as it is for all activations (i.e., event E_1). A new event with E_{expr} and a new rule can be used to model this policy. For example, event E_2 shown above is raised if someone tries to activate role *"Manager"*. A new rule $R_{AARManager}$ can be created with additional constraints in the Condition Part and RBAC functions in the Action part. Thus, anyone trying to activate role *"Manager"* will raise event E_2, which in turn will trigger rule $R_{AARManager}$.

On the other hand, if the enterprise wants to *"place additional restrictions on user Jane irrespective of the role being activated"*, it cannot use the general rule R_{AAR3}. In this case, E_3 shown above can be used, which is raised only for user *"Jane"*. A new rule $R_{AARJane}$ can be created to specify additional constraints using the Condition Part.

Event E_4 is a combination of both subject- and role-level operations and is the most restrictive. If the enterprise wants to relax additional context constraints specified in rule R_{AAR3} for a particular user in a particular role, it can use event E_4. This event is raised only when user *"Jim"* tries to activate the role *"CEO"*. A new rule $R_{AARJimCEO}$ can be created to relax the restrictions.

In addition, other events can be created based on needs of the enterprise using the implicit and explicit expressions. However, events have to be prioritized so that the system triggers only the required events. For example, when user *"Jane"* is trying to activate a role, she invokes function *addActiveRole(...)*. This can trigger events E_1 to E_4 as all of them are based on the same function signature. Since *"Jane"* is activating, events E_1 and E_3 will be raised. It can also trigger event E_2 if she tries to activate role *"Manager"*. Thus, events need to be prioritized so that only one of them will be triggered. Assume that the enterprise assigns the following priorities (low to high): general, role-level, subject-level, subject- and role-level. If *"Jane"* is trying to activate a role, only event E_3 is triggered.

5.3   Enterprise Specific Constraints Using Complex Events

Even though specification of constraints using the Condition part and I_{expr} and E_{expr} are necessary, they are not sufficient in many situations. Below, we discuss two policies and how they are enforced by complex events using event operators.

Policy 1 (Drop Active Role). *Allow user* Jane *to be active in a role for only two hours.*

This policy places a duration-based constraint. As it requires deactivating user *"Jane"* from any active role after two hours, we need to associate this constraint with event E_3

defined in Section 5.2. There are two steps involved; the first step requires to know when two hours have elapsed, and the second is deactivating the role itself. Snoop complex event operator PLUS detects an event after ΔT time. Thus, using the PLUS operator with E_3 and two hours, we can capture the first requirement.

$$\text{Event } E_{DARJane} = \text{PLUS}(E_3, 2 \text{ hours});$$

Whenever *"Jane"* activates a role, an instance of $E_{DARJane}$ is started. Two hours after the start, event $E_{DARJane}$ is raised. For example, if *"Jane"* has activated a role at 9 a.m. and another at 9:15 a.m., then event $E_{DARJane}$ will be detected once at 11 a.m. and again at 11:15 a.m. Once event $E_{DARJane}$ is detected, the role can be deactivated by using the rule shown below. In the rule, role is dropped from *"Jane's"* active role set by invoking the function $\_dropActiveRole(user, session, role)$.

```
RULE  [ R_DARJane
        EVENT       E_DARJane
        CONDITION   < call > _dropActiveRole(user, session, role)
        ACTION      "Drop Role"
        ALT ACTION  /* None */   ]
```

Policy 2 (Prerequisite Role). *Allow user* Tom *to activate any role only* after Jim *has activated role* Nurse.

Activation of role *"Nurse"* by user *"Jim"* is modeled using event $E_{AARJimNurse}$ and rule $R_{AARJimNurse}$. This event is similar to event E_4 defined in Section 5.2. Event E_{AARTom} (similar to event E_3 defined in Section 5.2) and rule R_{AARTom} handle role activations for user *"Tom"*. Rule R_{AARTom} is shown below.

```
RULE  [ R_AARTom
        EVENT       E_AARTom
        CONDITION   < call > _addActiveRole(user, session, role)
        ACTION      "Allow Activation"
        ALT ACTION  raise error "Access Denied Cannot Activate"   ]
```

Activation of *"Tom"* has to be restricted in order to meet the policy requirements (i.e., event E_{AARTom} should not trigger rule R_{AARTom}). Sequence complex event operator discussed in Section 2.1 can be used to enforce this. Below, we define a Sequence event E_{P2}, and re-associate rule R_{AARTom} with the new Sequence event.

$$\text{Event } E_{P2} = (E_{AARJimNurse} \gg E_{AARTom});$$

```
RULE  [ R_AARTom
        EVENT       E_P2
        CONDITION   < call > _addActiveRole(user, session, role)
        ACTION      "Allow Activation"
        ALT ACTION  raise error "Access Denied Cannot Activate"   ]
```

Event E_{P2} is raised only when the second event follows the first event. Let us assume that *"Jim"* has activated role *"Nurse"*. This will initiate the event E_{P2}. When Tom tries to activate a role, it will detect event E_{P2}, which is initiated by $E_{AARJimNurse}$ as the role activation constraints are satisfied. This will trigger rule R_{AARTom}, which allows the role activation, if *"Tom"* has the required permissions. On the other hand, assume that user *"Tom"* tries to activate a role, but *"Jim"* has not activated the role *"Nurse"*.

In other words, the policy constraint is not satisfied. In this case, the detector occurs albeit the initiator has not initiated event E_{P2}. This can be captured using an incomplete rule [7], which in turn returns a "Denied" message.

All the above policies require complex constraints and are enforced using complex events. Similarly, other complex policies can be enforced using other event operators mentioned in Section 2 and their combinations.

6   Implementation

In this section, we discuss how events and rules are implemented, since enforcement mechanisms are equally important in order to employ the specified policies.

Event detection graphs (EDGs), part of the Local Event Detector [17], keep track of event occurrences. EDGs record event occurrences as and when they occur, and keep track of the constituent event occurrences over the time interval they occur. EDGs are acyclic graphs, where each complex event is a *connected tree*. In addition, simple events that have the same function signature or events that appear in more than one complex event are shared. In Figure 4, the complex event is a binary event operator (e.g., AND), thus having two child events and each of them represents a simple event. Similarly, the internal node represents a complex event. The EDG as a whole represents a complex event. Although the leaf nodes in Figure 4 are simple events, they can be complex events as well.

In order to facilitate the propagation of events as they occur, each node in the EDG (see Figure 4) has several lists that allow the propagation of events to parent nodes and

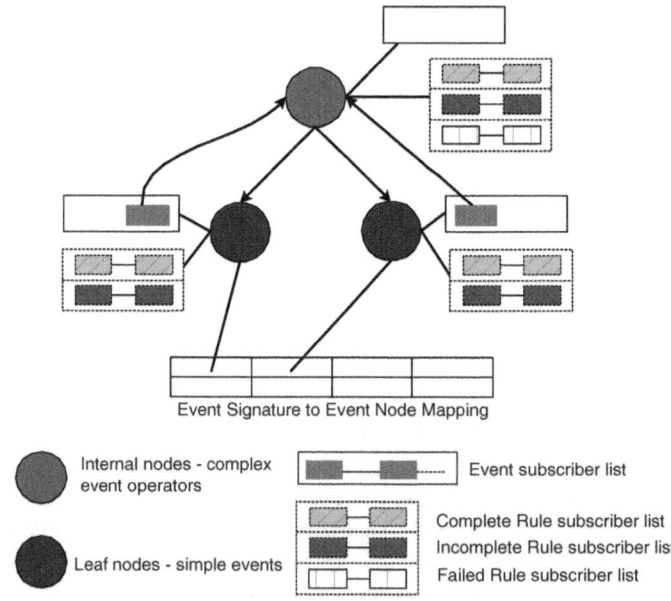

Fig. 4. Event Detection Graph

triggering of rules. All the nodes can detect events and trigger rules based on event expressions, event consumption modes, event detection modes, point-based, interval-based, and generalized event semantics, priorities, etc., discussed in Section 2. When a simple event occurs, it should be propagated to the internal node if it is a part of that complex event. Similarly, internal nodes also propagate when they are the sub-events of another complex event. Thus, when a user tries to activate a role in RBAC, appropriate events are detected and rules are triggered.

7 Conclusions

Layered approach introduced in this paper enforces RBAC standard and supports tailor-made constraints at different granularities or levels: 1) Condition part, 2) implicit and explicit expressions, and 3) other events using complex event operators. Our approach does not modify the RBAC standard as opposed to the existing systems. All RBAC components (Core, Hierarchical, SSoD and DSoD) and associated constraints are supported. Enterprises can move from one component to another without changing or rewriting any of the event-based constraints or active rules.

Our approach allows the modeling of current constraints in role-based access control models and extends them using event constraints. Events and active rules allow the modeling of various constraints that cannot be modeled using current access control models. We have shown diverse policies involving various types of constraints and how they are modeled using events and rules. Finally, we discussed event detection graphs that follow a bottom-up data flow paradigm, for enforcing access control. These graphs are efficient as they allow the sharing of complex events and simple events.

References

1. Sandhu, R.S., Coyne, E., Feinstein, H., Youman, C.: Role-Based Access Control Models. IEEE Computer 29(2), 38–47 (1996)
2. The Economic Impact of Role-Based Access Control, NIST (2002), http://www.nist.gov/director/prog-ofc/report02-1.pdf
3. Role-Based Access Control Case Studies and Experience, NIST, http://csrc.nist.gov/rbac/RBAC-case-studies.html
4. RBAC Standard, ANSI INCITS 359-2004, International Committee for IT Standards (2004)
5. Chen, F., Sandhu, R.S.: Constraints for role-based access control. In: Proc. of the ACM Workshop on RBAC, p. 14. ACM Press, New York (1996)
6. Strembeck, M., Neumann, G.: An integrated approach to engineer and enforce context constraints in RBAC environments. ACM TISSEC 7(3), 392–427 (2004)
7. Adaikkalavan, R., Chakravarthy, S.: When to Trigger Active Rules?. In: Proc. of the CO-MAD, Mysore, India (December 2009)
8. Demers, A.J., Gehrke, J., Panda, B., Riedewald, M., Sharma, V., White, W.M.: Cayuga: A general purpose event monitoring system. In: Proc. of the CIDR, pp. 412–422 (2007)
9. Adaikkalavan, R., Chakravarthy, S.: Event Specification and Processing For Advanced Applications: Generalization and Formalization. In: Wagner, R., Revell, N., Pernul, G. (eds.) DEXA 2007. LNCS, vol. 4653, pp. 369–379. Springer, Heidelberg (2007)
10. Adaikkalavan, R., Chakravarthy, S.: SnoopIB: Interval-Based Event Specification and Detection for Active Databases. DKE 59(1), 139–165 (2006)

11. Carlson, J., Lisper, B.: An Interval-Based Algebra for Restricted Event Detection. In: Larsen, K.G., Niebert, P. (eds.) FORMATS 2003. LNCS, vol. 2791, pp. 121–133. Springer, Heidelberg (2004)
12. Paton, N.W.: Active Rules in Database Systems. Springer, New York (1999)
13. Widom, J., Ceri, S.: Active Database Systems: Triggers and Rules. Morgan Kaufmann Publishers, Inc. (1996)
14. Chakravarthy, S., Krishnaprasad, V., Anwar, E., Kim, S.-K.: Composite Events for Active Databases: Semantics, Contexts, and Detection. In: Proc. of the VLDB, pp. 606–617 (1994)
15. Gatziu, S., Dittrich, K.R.: Events in an Object-Oriented Database System. In: Proc. of the Rules in Database Systems (September 1993)
16. Gehani, N.H., Jagadish, H.V., Shmueli, O.: Composite Event Specification in Active Databases: Model & Implementation. In: Proc. of the VLDB, pp. 327–338 (1992)
17. Chakravarthy, S., Anwar, E., Maugis, L., Mishra, D.: Design of Sentinel: An Object-Oriented DBMS with Event-Based Rules. IST 36(9), 559–568 (1994)
18. Galton, A., Augusto, J.: Two Approaches to Event Definition. In: Hameurlain, A., Cicchetti, R., Traunmüller, R. (eds.) DEXA 2002. LNCS, vol. 2453, pp. 547–556. Springer, Heidelberg (2002)

Providing Group Anonymity Using Wavelet Transform

Oleg Chertov and Dan Tavrov

Faculty of Applied Mathematics, National Technical University of Ukraine,
"Kyiv Polytechnic Institute", 37 Peremohy Prospekt, 03056 Kyiv, Ukraine
{chertov,kmudisco}@i.ua

Abstract. Providing public access to unprotected digital data can pose a threat of unwanted disclosing the restricted information.

The problem of protecting such information can be divided into two main subclasses, namely, individual and group data anonymity. By group anonymity we define protecting important data patterns, distributions, and collective features which cannot be determined through analyzing individual records only.

An effective and comparatively simple way of solving group anonymity problem is doubtlessly applying wavelet transform. It's easy-to-implement, powerful enough, and might produce acceptable results if used properly.

In the paper, we present a novel method of using wavelet transform for providing group anonymity; it is gained through redistributing wavelet approximation values, along with simultaneous fixing data mean value and leaving wavelet details unchanged (or proportionally altering them). Moreover, we provide a comprehensive example to illustrate the method.

Keywords: wavelet transform, group anonymity, statistical disclosure control, privacy-preserving data mining.

1 Introduction

The problem of preserving privacy has become pressing in the recent years, and this fact doesn't seem to change in the nearest future. That is mainly due to the rapid growth of digital data [1], and the enhancement of public access to collected information. The latter means that with an additional permission one can easily get access to the great variety of primary data such as information on patients' hospital treatment (so-called Clinical Data Repositories [2]), electronic commerce results in big automated collections of consumer data, microfiles with large census (or other sociological surveys) data samples etc. The most fundamental project is without a doubt IPUMS-International [3]. Within it, more than 279 million person records collected from 130 censuses held in 44 countries (at the moment this paper is being written) are accessible for the researchers. Of course, this information is totally de-identified. To preserve its privacy, special data anonymity methods need to be used. Moreover, this is often a subject to legal regulation. E.g., in the USA, to comply with the Health Insurance Portability and Accountability Act of 1996 (HIPAA) [4] and the Patient Safety and Quality Improvement Act of 2005 (PSQIA) [5], organizations and

L.M. MacKinnon (Ed.): BNCOD 2010, LNCS 6121, pp. 25–36, 2012.
© Springer-Verlag Berlin Heidelberg 2012

individuals don't have to reveal their medical data without preceeding privacy protection in any case. Besides, some consumer information transfer shouldn't lead to the individual persons' public profiling, and is a subject of a strict regulation. For instance, see Directive on privacy and electronic communications [6] to learn more about such regulations in the EU.

So, the overall accessible information amount growth, emerging of various (and often cross-referencing) sources to get it, developing of the data mining methods for finding out implicit data patterns, and necessity of following appropriate regulation rules issue more and more challenges to respond to before publishing the data.

Works on privacy protection in publicly accessed data can be considered as a part of privacy-preserving data mining field.

Usually, the first thing to define is microdata which mean information on respondents (e.g., persons, households, or companies). Respectively, a microfile is a set of microdata reduced to one file that consists of attributive records describing each respondent. Statistical disclosure control (SDC) methods aim at receiving new, protected microdata basing on the original ones. But, such a procedure should meet following conditions [7, p. 399]:

- Disclosure risk is low or at least adequate to protected information importance.
- Both original and protected data, when analyzed, yield close, or even equal results.
- The cost of transforming the data is acceptable.

These requirements are equivalent to an assertion that the informational and financial losses during microdata transformation have to be acceptable, and the level of disclosure risk has to be adequate. In other words, the microdata distortion should be small enough to preserve data utility but sufficient enough to prevent exposing the private information on *individuals* (or *groups of individuals*) within the released data.

We can mark out following SDC methods that are heavily used in practice:

- *randomization* – a noise is added to the data to mask records' attribute values [8];
- *microaggregation* – a set of original records is partitioned into several groups such way that the records in a group are similar. In addition, there are at least k records in each group. The average value over each group is computed for every attribute. Then this value is used to replace each of the original ones [9];
- *data swapping* – transforming the microfile by exchanging values of confidential attributes among individual records [10];
- *non-perturbative methods* – protecting data without altering them. These methods are based on suppression and generalization (recoding). Suppression means removing some data from the original set, whereas recoding is data enlargement [11].

Apart from these ones, matrix decomposition [12] and factorization [13] techniques have also been used for distorting numeric sets of data (in the applications of privacy-preserving data mining). And, of course, using wavelet transform (WT) seems to be a perspective approach as well. E.g., we can use discrete WT to decompose primary data into an approximation and details with corresponding coefficients. After that, we can suppress the high-frequency detail coefficients to gain data distortion.

But, all the methods mentioned above are designed to provide data anonymity of individuals. At the same time, a problem of providing data anonymity of a respondent group remains open [7]. By *anonymity of a group* (or simply *group anonymity*) we define protecting important data distributions, patterns and features that cannot be revealed by analyzing individual records only. Providing group anonymity means performing specific primary data rearrangements which guarantee preserving privacy of a particular attribute values' distribution (for a determined respondent group). E.g., we could possibly want to protect military personnel regional distribution, or to hide the information on how the drugs are spread among different ethnic groups.

These tasks only seem to be easy-to-solve. Of course, we might swap values standing for the "Region of work" attribute between military base officers and those civilians with other attribute values similar. As a result, we would possibly conceal the base location. But, there is huge downside: such data swapping can badly influence the overall data utility.

In general, providing group anonymity implies deliberate modifying the respondents' distribution over specific attribute values. But, the data utility must be necessarily preserved. By such a utility we understand ratios between some respondent groups, or other appropriate relative values.

Let's consider one typical example. Real regional distribution of military and special service officers can be totally confidential. But, information on their distribution by age or, say, number of family members can be an interesting subject to sociological researches.

In this paper, we propose using WT to find some balance between modifying primary data and preventing loss of their utility. But, we suggest using it in a way opposite to the one applied for providing individual anonymity (see [14]). To protect data, we redistribute WT approximation values. To prevent utility loss, we fix the data mean value and leave WT details unchanged (or alter them only proportionally). In this case, ratios between various attribute values ranges will persist. Let's take [15] as an illustration. In Russia, 44 public opinion polls (1994-2001) showed that WT details actually reveal hidden time series features which are significant for near- and medium-term social processes forecasting.

The rest of this paper is arranged as follows. We provide a brief review of the related work in Section 2. The basics of our wavelet-based method for providing group anonymity are presented in Section 3. Experimental results of applying the method to a model example are discussed in Section 4. Finally, a brief conclusion is given in Section 5.

2   Related Work

There exist two main approaches to completing the task of protecting the confidential information. The classical one lies in encrypting the data or protecting them using different means like restricting public access. The main target of this approach is to disable (complicate) obtaining the data. In the paper, we do not consider it. We examine another one that provides SDC methods instead.

In the past decade, there has been published various literature on data anonymity (consult the anonymity bibliography from the Free Haven Project [16]).

We can divide all SDC methods into two large classes, namely, randomization methods and group-based anonymization methods.

The randomization methods [8, 17] are simple techniques which can be easily implemeted while collecting the data. It is possible because the noise being added to a record is independent of the other records' values. In addition, these methods serve well at preserving data utility, especially patterns and association rules. But, their advantages give rise to their main downsides. Provided there are other sources of information with publicly available records intersecting with the data to be masked, privacy can be violated with a great possibility [18]. In particular, this is the case with the outlier records which can easily be distinguished among the other ones in the same area [19].

A typical example of the group-based anonymization is so-called k-anonymity [20]. Its main idea is to ensure that every attribute values combination corresponds to at least k respondents in the dataset. To achieve that, different methods can be used, mentioned in [9, 10, 11] being the most popular.

For the last 4-5 years, WT has also been used for providing data anonymity, though it has widely been used mainly in signal processing [21, 22] before. Paper [23] presents a good overview of applying wavelets to data mining in general.

Paper [24] was the first work to introduce WT into preserving data anonymity. It proposed a new data-modification algorithm for revealing data patterns without revealing the data themselves. But, the wavelet-perturbed dataset has different dimensions in the transformed space, if to compare with the original one. Later, a method [14] free of this disadvantage was introduced. In [25], the same authors improved it with simultaneous privacy- and statistics-preserving. They showed that normalizing the data guarantees the persistance of their mean value and standard deviation. Another technique proposed in [14, 25] reduces the high-frequency "noise" hidden in the original data entries by thresholding WT detail coefficients. Thus, the respondent anonymity can be achieved.

But, all these methods guarantee individual anonymity only. To solve the problem of providing group anonymity stated in [7], we introduce a novel wavelet-based method. We tend to achieve anonymity by redistributing approximation values, but we also try to save data utility by fixing the details. Figuratively speaking, we change the relief of a restricted area but try to preserve local data distribution.

3   Theoretic Background

3.1   General Definitions

Let the microfile data be organized in a table similar to Table 1. Here, m stands for a number of respondents, q stands for a number of attributes, w_j stands for the jth attribute, r_i stands for the ith record, z_{ij} stands for a microfile data element.

Table 1. Microfile data

	w_1	w_2	...	w_q
r_1	z_{11}	z_{12}	...	z_{1q}
r_2	z_{21}	z_{22}	...	z_{2q}
...	...	...	...	...
r_m	z_{m1}	z_{m2}	...	z_{mq}

Solving group anonymity problems implies redistributing elements z_{ij} according to some purpose. Let us formally set a corresponding task.

We will denote by S_v a subset of a Cartesian product $w_{v_1} \times w_{v_2} \times ... \times w_{v_l}$ of Table 1 columns. Here, v_i, $i = \overline{1,l}$ are integers. We will call an element $s_k^{(v)} \in S_v$, $k = \overline{1,l_v}$, $l_v \leq l$ a *vital value combination* because such combinations are vital for solving our task. Respectively, each element of $s_k^{(v)}$ will be called *a vital value,* and w_{v_j} will be called *a vital attribute.*

Group anonymity is gained through redistributing records with specific vital value combinations. E.g., to redistribute "Middle-aged women" we need to take "Age" and "Sex" as vital attributes.

We will also denote by S_p a subset of microfile data elements z_{ip} corresponding to the pth attribute, $p \neq v_i$ $\forall i = \overline{1,l}$. Elements $s_k^{(p)} \in S_p$, $k = \overline{1,l_p}$, $l_p \leq l$ will be called *parameter values*, whereas p^{th} attribute will be called *a parameter attribute.* We call it this way becaues we will use it to divide microfile records into categories.

For instance, having taken "Region" as a parameter attribute, we obtain groups of residents living in particular area.

Thus, providing group anonymity actually means redistributing records with particular vital value combinations over various parameter values.

Having defined attributes, we need to calculate the number of microfile records with a specific pair of a vital value combination and a parameter value. In many cases, absolute numbers do not provide important information on data distribution features and are not representative. Thus, modifying them can guarantee data privacy but surely leads to siginificant loss of data utility.

On the other hand, redistributing ratios sounds like a much better idea. That's why we need to divide the absolute numbers by the overall number of records in the same group. E.g., to protect "Middle-aged women", we can divide their quantity by the overall number of "Women", or "Middle-aged people", or even "People" in general (coming from a particular task to be completed). Obtained ratios can be gathered in an array $c = (c_1, c_2, ..., c_n)$ which we will call *a concentration signal.*

According to Section 1, we need to construct a new concentration signal $\tilde{c} = (\tilde{c}_1, \tilde{c}_2, ..., \tilde{c}_n)$ by redistributing the wavelet approximation of signal c. At the same time, we need to preserve data utility by fixing the signal mean value ($\sum_{i=1}^{n} c_i = \sum_{i=1}^{n} \tilde{c}_i$) and wavelet details (or altering these details only proportionally).

In the next subsections, we will examine an appropriate method.

3.2 Wavelet Transform Basics

In this subsection we will revise general wavelet theory results necessary for the subsequent explanations. For a detailed information, refer to [22].

Let us call an array $s = (s_1, s_2, ..., s_n)$ of discrete values a signal. Let a high-pass wavelet filter be denoted as $h = (h_1, h_2, ..., h_t)$, and a low-pass wavelet filter be denoted as $l = (l_1, l_2, ..., l_t)$.

If to denote a convolution by $*$, and a dyadic downsampling by $\downarrow_{2n}$, we can perform signal s one-level wavelet decomposition as follows:

$$a_1 = s *_{\downarrow_{2n}} l; \quad d_1 = s *_{\downarrow_{2n}} h .$$ (1)

In (1), a_1 is an array of approximation coefficients at level 1, whereas d_1 is an array of detail coefficients at the same level 1.

Also, we can apply (1) to a_1 receiving approximation and detail coefficients at level 2. In general, to obtain approximation and detail coefficients at any level k, we need to apply (1) to the approximation coefficients at level k-1 :

$$a_k = a_{k-1} *_{\downarrow_{2n}} l = (\underbrace{(s *_{\downarrow_{2n}} l)...*_{\downarrow_{2n}} l}_{k \ times}); d_k = a_{k-1} *_{\downarrow_{2n}} h = (\underbrace{((s *_{\downarrow_{2n}} l)...*_{\downarrow_{2n}} l}_{k-1 \ times}) *_{\downarrow_{2n}} h) .$$ (2)

Any signal s can always be presented as a following sum:

$$s = A_k + \sum_{u=1}^{k} D_u .$$ (3)

In (3), A_k denotes an approximation at level k, and D_u denotes a detail at level u. They can be obtained from the corresponding coefficients as follows:

$$A_k = (\underbrace{(a_k *_{\uparrow_{2n}} l)...*_{\uparrow_{2n}} l}_{k \ times});$$ (4)

$$D_k = (\underbrace{((d_k *_{\uparrow_{2n}} h) *_{\uparrow_{2n}} l)...*_{\uparrow_{2n}} l}_{k-1 \ times}) .$$ (5)

In (4) and (5), a_k and d_k are being dyadically upsampled (which is denoted by $\uparrow_{2n}$) first, and then they are convoluted with an appropriate wavelet filter.

When the length of s is odd, performing dyadic downsampling becomes ambiguous. To get over this collision, we need to somehow make the signal length even. It can be done either by removing an element from the signal, or by adding a new one to it. Since removing elements always involves loss of data, adding a new sample is a lot more acceptable. In our opinion, extending the signal symmetrically (either leftwards or rightwards) seems to be the most adequate solution.

3.3   Modifying Approximations and Fixing Details

As we mentioned in Subsection 3.1, the approximation A_k needs to be modified somehow. Coming from (4) and (5), the approximation depends only on the approximation coefficients, and the details depend only on the detail ones. Therefore, preserving the detail coefficients at level k preserves the details at any level below k. Respectively, by modifying approximation coefficients at level k we can modify the approximation at level k.

There exist two totally different approaches to transforming A_k. We called the first one an extremum transition approach. Applying it means performing such a modification that the resultant approximation's extremums totally differ from the initial ones. The other approach is called an "Ali Baba's wife" approach. Its name sends us back to the collection of the Middle Eastern and South Asian stories and folk tales "One Thousand and One Nights". One of the tales says that Ali Baba's wife marked all the houses in the neighborhood with the same symbol the thieves used to mark Ali Baba's house with. Having done that, she saved Ali Baba from an inevitable death. In terms of our paper, it means we do not eliminate existing extremums but add several alleged ones.

But, nobody can predict how changing the approximation coefficients will change the approximation without additional information. That's why we need to get such information about the signal.

3.4   Applying Wavelet Reconstruction Matrices to Modifying Approximations

It is known that WT can be performed using matrix multiplications [22]. In particular, we can rewrite (4) as follows:

$$A_k = M_{rec} \cdot a_k \,. \tag{6}$$

We will call M_{rec} a wavelet reconstruction matrix (WRM). It can be obtained consequently multiplying appropriate upsampling and convolution matrices.

Now, let us apply WRM to solving our main task. As it was mentioned before, we need to find new approximation coefficients $\tilde{a}_k$. The structure of M_{rec} always makes it possible to find appropriate solution (an illustrative example will be showed in the next section). After having chosen new coefficients, we can obtain a new approximation $\tilde{A}_k$ using (6). Then, we need to add $\tilde{A}_k$ and all the signal c details. As a result, we get a new concentration signal $\tilde{c}$.

According to Subsection 3.2, when the signal length is odd, we need to symmetrically extend it. In this case, it is necessary to ensure that the resultant signal

$\tilde{c}$ is also a symmetric extension of any other odd-length signal. This means border signal elements have to be equal. We can always achieve that by fixing the difference between appropriate approximation values.

Besides, some $\tilde{c}$ elements can turn out to be negative. Since ratios cannot be negative, we have to make all $\tilde{c}$ elements positive (e.g., by adding to each of them a reasonably large value). But, in return we will get the signal with a completely different mean value. The only opportunity to overcome this problem is to multiply the signal by an appropriate value. Due to the algebraic properties of the convolution, both details' and approximation's elements will also be multiplied by the same value. This means the details will be changed proportionally, which totally suits our task definition requirements.

4   Experimental Results

To show the proposed algorithm in action and stress on its main features, we took the UK Census-2001 microfile provided by [3] as the data to analyze. The microfile contains information on more than 1,8 million respondents. For our sake, we decided to set a task of protecting the scientific professionals and technicians distribution over the regions of the UK. The importance of such a task is obvious. Maximums in an appropriate concentration signal can possibly lead to exposing the restricted scientific research centers which weren't supposed to be revealed. But, by adding alleged maximums to the signal we can guarantee that such centers will not be found out.

According to Subsection 3.1, we have to define both parameter and vital attributes and values. Since we intend to change regional distribution of scientists, we took "REGNUK" (which is an abbreviation of "Region of the UK") as a parameter attribute. Each value of this attribute stands for a particular region, making a total of 16 regions. Although, in the data extract provided by [3], there is no information on the "North", "East Anglia" and "Rest of South East" regions. Therefore, we were able to choose only 13 values left as parameter ones.

We also took "OCC" (which means "Occupation") as a vital attribute. This attribute values are three-digit numbers standing for various occupations and activities. But, since we're concerned in redistributing people of science only, we took just two vital values, i.e., "211" (for "Science Professionals") and "311" (for "Science and engineering technicians").

The next step is to build up a concentration signal. We counted up all the respondents with "Occupation" value "211" or "311" and a parameter value representing every region of the UK. These quantities are presented in Table 2 (the fourth row). Afterwards, we divided them by the overall number of employed people in each region.

We got the following concentration signal:

$$c = (0.0143, 0.0129, 0.0122, 0.0140, 0.1149, 0.0141,$$

$$0.0142, 0.0128, 0.0077, 0.0100, 0.0159, 0.0168, 0.0110).$$

In the paper, we present all the numeric data with 4 decimal numbers, but all the calculations were carried out with a higher proximity.

As we can see, the penultimate concentration is maximal. Further on, we will try to hide this maximum using "Ali Baba's wife" approach.

Since the resultant signal is of an odd length, we needed to add an additional element to it. We decided to symmetrically extend our signal leftwards.

Then, we used the second order Daubechies low-pass wavelet filter $l \equiv \left(\dfrac{1+\sqrt{3}}{4\sqrt{2}}, \dfrac{3+\sqrt{3}}{4\sqrt{2}}, \dfrac{3-\sqrt{3}}{4\sqrt{2}}, \dfrac{1-\sqrt{3}}{4\sqrt{2}} \right)$ to perform one-level wavelet decomposition (2) of c :

$a_1 = (a_1(1), a_1(2), a_1(3), a_1(4), a_1(5), a_1(6), a_1(7)) =$
$= (0.0188, 0.0186, 0.0184, 0.0189, 0.0180, 0.0135, 0.0223).$

The WRM for such a signal is as follows:

$$M_{rec} = \begin{pmatrix} 0.8365 & 0 & 0 & 0 & 0 & 0 & -0.1294 \\ 0.2241 & 0.4830 & 0 & 0 & 0 & 0 & 0 \\ -0.1294 & 0.8365 & 0 & 0 & 0 & 0 & 0 \\ 0 & 0.2241 & 0.4830 & 0 & 0 & 0 & 0 \\ 0 & -0.1294 & 0.8365 & 0 & 0 & 0 & 0 \\ 0 & 0 & 0.2241 & 0.4830 & 0 & 0 & 0 \\ 0 & 0 & -0.1294 & 0.8365 & 0 & 0 & 0 \\ 0 & 0 & 0 & 0.2241 & 0.4830 & 0 & 0 \\ 0 & 0 & 0 & -0.1294 & 0.8365 & 0 & 0 \\ 0 & 0 & 0 & 0 & 0.2241 & 0.4830 & 0 \\ 0 & 0 & 0 & 0 & -0.1294 & 0.8365 & 0 \\ 0 & 0 & 0 & 0 & 0 & 0.2241 & 0.4830 \\ 0 & 0 & 0 & 0 & 0 & -0.1294 & 0.8365 \\ 0.4830 & 0 & 0 & 0 & 0 & 0 & 0.2241 \end{pmatrix}.$$

According to (6), we obtained a signal approximation:
$A_1 = (0.0129, 0.0132, 0.0131, 0.0130, 0.0130, 0.0132, 0.0134, 0.0129,$
$0.0126, 0.0106, 0.0090, 0.0138, 0.0169, 0.0141).$

Also, we got a signal detail at level 1 according to (5):
$D_1 = (0.0014, 0.0011, -0.0003, -0.0008, 0.0010, -0.0017, 0.0007,$
$0.0013, 0.0002, -0.0029, 0.0011, 0.0021, -0.0007, -0.0031).$

To ensure that the difference between the first two approximation values will persist, we had to fix elements $a_1(1)$, $a_1(2)$, and $a_1(7)$, because the other 4 coefficients don't influence the first two approximation values when performing (6).

Taking into consideration the M_{rec} elements in different rows, we can always pick such coefficients $\hat{a}_1$ that multiplication (6) yields different maximums in the resultant approximation. For example, if to take $\hat{a}_1 = (0.0188, 0.0186, -2, 0, 1, -5, 0.0223)$ we receive new maximal values in the 3rd, the 9th, and (as we intended to) the 13th

approximation elements. This particular choice isn't a unique one. In general, one can pick any other coefficients depending on the desired outcome.

So, in our case we got a new approximation:

$$\hat{A}_1 = (0.0129, 0.0132, 0.0131, -0.9618, -1.6754, -0.4483, 0.2588,$$
$$0.4830, 0.8365, -2.1907, -4.3120, -1.1099, 0.6657, 0.0141).$$

Having added old details to a new approximation, we got a new concentration signal:

$$\hat{c} = \hat{A}_1 + D_1 = (0.0143, 0.0143, 0.0129, -0.9626, -1.6744, -0.4500,$$
$$0.2595, 0.4843, 0.8367, -2.1935, -4.3109, -1.1078, 0.6656, 0.0110).$$

As we can see, some signal elements are negative. To make them all strictly positive, we added to each signal element 6.3109 (actually, we could add any other value large enough to make the signal positive):

$$\breve{c} = (6.3252, 6.3252, 6.3238, 5.3484, 4.6365, 5.8609, 6.5704,$$
$$6.7952, 7.1476, 4.1174, 2.0000, 5.2031, 6.9765, 6.3220).$$

The only necessary condition we haven't met yet is the equality of corresponding mean values. For that sake, we multiplied $\breve{c}$ by a coefficient $\sum_{i=2}^{14} c_i / \sum_{i=2}^{14} \breve{c}_i = 0.0023$.

Here, we took into consideration only 13 last signal elements because the first one was added to make signal length even, and doesn't contain any necessary information.

The resultant signal is presented in Table 2 (the last row).

The last step is to obtain new quantities. We have done that by multiplying new ratios by a total number of employed people in each region. As quantities can be only integers, we had to round them afterwards (see Table 2, the sixth row).

Table 2. Quantities and ratios distributed by regions

Column number	1	2	3	4	5	6	7
Region code	11	13	14	21	22	31	33
Employed	48591	129808	96152	83085	101891	108120	161395
Scientists (initial)	695	1672	1176	1163	1171	1524	2294
Signal c (initial)	0.0143	0.0129	0.0122	0.0140	0.1149	0.0141	0.0142
Scientists (final)	699	1867	1170	876	1358	1616	2495
Signal c (final)	0.0144	0.0144	0.0122	0.0105	0.0133	0.0149	0.0155

Column number	8	9	10	11	12	13	Mean
Region code	40	51	52	60	70	80	
Employed	97312	54861	86726	99890	55286	33409	
Scientists (initial)	1246	422	871	1589	927	369	1163
Signal c (initial)	0.0128	0.0077	0.0100	0.0159	0.0168	0.0110	0.0129
Scientists (final)	1582	514	395	1182	877	480	1162.4
Signal c (final)	0.0163	0.0094	0.0045	0.0118	0.0159	0.0144	0.0129

Though the resultant data completely differ from the initial ones, we preserved both mean value and wavelet decomposition details.

It is important to note that rounding the quantities may lead to some changes in wavelet decomposition details. Though, in most cases they are not very significant.

All that is left to fulfil is to construct a new microfile. We can always do that by changing vital values of different records according to the received quantities.

It is obvious that picking different vital and parameter attributes, or even different WRMs, doesn't restrict the possibility of applying the method under review to providing group anonymity.

5 Conclusion and Future Research

In the paper, we attracted attention to the problem of providing group anonymity while preparing microdata. In response to this new challenge, we introduced a totally novel wavelet-based method for providing group anonymity in collective data.

It is significant to state that the proposed method might be combined with those for providing individual anonymity without any restrictions. Thus, it can be implemented in a real-life privacy-preserving data mining system.

We beleive that the current paper cannot suggest answers to all the questions and problems arising. In our opinion, there exist many other kinds of group anonymity tasks to study in the future.

Apart from it, we can distinguish the following problems:

- It is important to introduce group anonymity measure.
- Using different wavelet bases leads to different WRMs, so it is interesting to study the opportunities they provide when modifying approximation coefficients.

References

1. Gantz, J.F., Reinsel, D.: As the Economy Contracts, the Digital Universe Expands. An IDC Multimedia White Paper (2009),
   http://www.emc.com/collateral/demos/microsites/idc-digital-universe/iview.htm
2. Mullins, I., Siadaty, M., Lyman, J., Scully, K., Garrett, C., Miller, W., Muller, R., Robson, B., Apte, C., Weiss, S., Rigoutsos, I., Platt, D., Cohen, S., Knaus, W.: Data Mining and Clinical Data Repositories: Insights from a 667,000 Patient Data Set. Computers in Biology and Medicine 36(12), 1351–1377 (2006)
3. Minnesota Population Center. Integrated Public Use Microdata Series International,
   https://international.ipums.org/international/
4. Health Insurance Portability and Accountability Act of 1996 (HIPAA). Public Law 104-191, 104th Congress, August 21 (1996), http://www.hipaa.org/
5. Patient Safety and Quality Improvement Act of 2005 (PSQIA). Federal Register 73(266) (2001)
6. Directive 2002/58/EC of the European Parliament and of the Council of 12 July 2002. Official Journal of the European Communities L 201, 37–47 (July 31, 2002)

7. Chertov, O., Pilipyuk, A.: Statistical Disclosure Control Methods for Microdata. In: International Symposium on Computing, Communication and Control, pp. 338–342. IACSIT, Singapore (2009)
8. Agrawal, R., Srikant, R.: Privacy-Preserving Data Mining. In: ACM SIGMOD International Conference on Management of Data, pp. 439–450. ACM Press, Dallas (2000)
9. Domingo-Ferrer, J., Mateo-Sanz, J.M.: Practical Data-oriented Microaggregation for Statistical Disclosure Control. IEEE Transactions on Knowledge and Data Engineering 14(1), 189–201 (2002)
10. Fienberg, S., McIntyre, J.: Data Swapping: Variations on a Theme by Dalenius and Reiss. Technical Report, National Institute of Statistical Sciences (2003)
11. Domingo-Ferrer, J.: A Survey of Inference Control Methods for Privacy-Preserving Data Mining. In: Aggarwal, C.C., Yu, P.S. (eds.) Privacy-Preserving Data Mining: Models and Algorithms, pp. 53–80. Springer, New York (2008)
12. Xu, S., Zhang, J., Han, D., Wang, J.: Singular Value Decomposition Based Data Distortion Strategy for Privacy Protection. Knowledge and Information Systems 10(3), 383–397 (2006)
13. Wang, J., Zhong, W.J., Zhang, J.: NNMF-based Factorization Techniques for High-accuracy Privacy Protection on Non-negative-valued Datasets. In: IEEE Conference on Data Mining, International Workshop on Privacy Aspects of Date Mining, pp. 513–517. IEEE Computer Society, Washington (2006)
14. Liu, L., Wang, J., Lin, Z., Zhang, J.: Wavelet-Based Data Distortion for Privacy-Preserving Collaborative Analysis. Technical Report No. 482-07, Department of Computer Science, University of Kentucky, Lexington (2007)
15. Davydov, A.: Wavelet-analysis of the Social Processes. Sotsiologicheskie issledovaniya 11, 89–101 (2003) (in Russian),
http://www.ecsocman.edu.ru/images/pubs/2007/10/30/0000315095/012.DAVYDOV.pdf
16. The Free Haven Project, http://freehaven.net/anonbib/full/date.html
17. Evfimievski, A.: Randomization in Privacy Preserving Data Mining. ACM SIGKDD Explorations Newsletter 4(2), 43–48 (2002)
18. Kargupta, H., Datta, S., Wang, Q., Sivakumar, K.: Random-data Perturbation Techniques and Privacy-preserving Data Mining. Knowledge and Information Systems 7(4), 387–414 (2005)
19. Aggarwal, C.C.: On Randomization, Public Information and the Curse of Dimensionality. In: 23rd International Conference on Data Enginering, pp. 136–145. IEEE Computer Society, Washington (2007)
20. Sweeney, L.: k-anonymity: a Model for Protecting Privacy. International Journal on Uncertainty, Fuzziness and Knowledge-Based Systems 10(5), 557–570 (2002)
21. Mallat, S.: A Wavelet Tour of Signal Processing. Academic Press, New York (1999)
22. Strang, G., Nguyen, T.: Wavelet and Filter Banks. Wellesley-Cambridge Press, Wellesley (1997)
23. Li, T., Li, Q., Zhu, S., Ogihara, M.: A Survey on Wavelet Applications in Data Mining. ACM SIGKDD Explorations Newsletter 4(2), 49–68 (2002)
24. Bapna, S., Gangopadhyay, A.: A Wavelet-based Approach to Preserve Privacy for Classification Mining. Decision Sciences Journal 37(4), 623–642 (2006)
25. Liu, L., Wang, J., Zhang, J.: Wavelet-based Data Perturbation for Simultaneous Privacy-Preserving and Statistics-Preserving. In: 2008 IEEE International Conference on Data Mining Workshops, pp. 27–35. IEEE Computer Society, Washington (2008)

Efficient Model Selection for Large-Scale Nearest-Neighbor Data Mining

Greg Hamerly and Greg Speegle

Baylor University, Waco, TX 76798, USA
{greg_hamerly,greg_speegle}@baylor.edu

Abstract. One of the most widely used models for large-scale data mining is the k-nearest neighbor (k-nn) algorithm. It can be used for classification, regression, density estimation, and information retrieval. To use k-nn, a practitioner must first choose k, usually selecting the k with the minimal loss estimated by cross-validation. In this work, we begin with an existing but little-studied method that greatly accelerates the cross-validation process for selecting k from a range of user-provided possibilities. The result is that a much larger range of k values may be examined more quickly. Next, we extend this algorithm with an additional optimization to provide improved performance for locally linear regression problems. We also show how this method can be applied to automatically select the range of k values when the user has no *a priori* knowledge of appropriate bounds. Furthermore, we apply statistical methods to reduce the number of examples examined while still finding a likely best k, greatly improving performance for large data sets. Finally, we present both analytical and experimental results that demonstrate these benefits.

Keywords: data mining, k nearest neighbor, optimal parameter selection.

1 Introduction

The nearest neighbor algorithm is a powerful tool for finding data similar to a query example. It is popular because it is simple to understand and easy to implement, has good theoretical properties and flexible modeling assumptions, and can operate efficiently in low dimensions with indexes [7,13,3] and in high dimensions via approximations [1,25]. The nearest neighbor algorithm is used in applications such as bioinformatics [17], multimedia databases [3], collaborative filtering [33] and many others. In fact, the k-nearest neighbor (k-nn) algorithm was chosen as one of the top 10 data mining algorithms in ICDM 2006 [32].

Before using k-nn, a practitioner must select the size of the neighborhood such that all neighbors are considered similar. The best size will depend on the application and the data. For k-nn, the neighborhood size is k, the number of nearby examples that are part of the neighborhood. In other contexts, the neighborhood size is the radius r of a sphere centered at the query example, and examples contained in the sphere are neighbors of the query example.

L.M. MacKinnon (Ed.): BNCOD 2010, LNCS 6121, pp. 37–54, 2012.
© Springer-Verlag Berlin Heidelberg 2012

The choice of k has a large impact on the performance and behavior k-nn models. A small k allows simple implementation, permits efficient queries, and enjoys provable theoretical properties [4]. However, larger values of k tend to produce smoother models and are less sensitive to label noise. Ferrer-Troyano et al. [6] show that for some data sets the prediction error varied greatly depending on the value selected for k. Thus, the choice of k must be carefully made for the task at hand.

While the model selection problem is important, there has been little published research on selecting a good k for k-nn-based prediction models. Typically a practitioner tries several different k values, using cross-validation to measure prediction loss for each k, and chooses a k which has sufficiently small loss. This can be a very slow task on large datasets and when there are many possible k values. Thus, the focus of this work is on automating, accelerating, and extending this method of selecting k based on cross-validation in varying contexts.

In this paper, we provide algorithms for efficiently determining the best k (the one having the least prediction loss) under diverse situations. First, we consider the type of data analysis to be performed, classification or constant regression versus linear regression. While the first two types are easy to optimize, we show how to efficiently determine the best k when using linear regression. Second, we consider the case where the maximum possible best k (denoted K^*) is initially unknown, and show how to efficiently determine the appropriate K^*. Finally, we consider the case where the data set is extremely large. Statistical methods allow us to analyze a small fraction of the data with a high confidence of selecting a k with an estimated loss very close to that of the best k.

Section 2 contains related work on efficient k-nn search, optimal k selection, and efficient cross-validation. In Section 3, we present two algorithms for finding the best k within a user-specified range. The first is the naïve algorithm, which is presented for comparison purposes. The second incorporates a known optimization to provide clear benefits for some data mining applications. We provide explanation and analysis of these benefits. In Section 4, we show how this optimization does not provide the same benefits for locally linear regression problems, but additional techniques can be applied to achieve the same speedup. In Section 5, we consider the case of environments without *a priori* knowledge of an upper bound on k. Under these circumstances, it is possible for the naïve algorithm to *outperform* the optimized algorithm. We present a technique with asymptotic running time better than the naïve algorithm. Section 6 contains a methodology to apply statistical methods (BRACE [19]) to greatly reduce the number of examples examined in cross-validation on large data sets. Section 7 gives experimental evidence of the effectiveness of our proposed algorithms. In Section 8 we conclude with a discussion of our findings in this work, and future work.

2   Related Work

Cross-validation is a simple and popular method to estimate the loss of a model in a way that maximizes the use of training data. Rather than just train on one subset of the data and estimate loss on the remaining part, cross-validation tries multiple train/test splits to get an average loss. Cross-validation was popularized by Stone [26] and Geisser [8]. Two common types of cross validation are leave-one-out (LOOCV) and m-fold (or k-fold as it's more commonly called). In m-fold cross-validation we partition the training data into m folds, train a model on $m-1$ of the folds and then estimate loss by making predictions on the held-out fold. This is repeated m times, holding out a different fold each time. LOOCV is a particular type of m-fold cross-validation where m is the number of examples in the training set.

LOOCV has been shown to be optimal in the sense of minimizing the squared prediction error [16]. Ouyang et al. [23] recently showed asymptotic results for k-nn model selection using cross-validation, in the context of least-squares regression. Cross-validation can be computationally costly, since it requires training m models. In Section 3, we exploit the properties of LOOCV to efficiently perform k-nn model selection. In the remainder of this section, we review previous work on speeding up k-nn queries, model selection for k-nn, and speeding up cross-validation.

2.1   Speeding Up k-nn

The vast majority of work on k-nn involves improving the query efficiency of finding nearest neighbors. The simplest solution requires $O(nd)$ time to perform a linear scan on the dataset and $O(n \log k)$ to maintain the k nearest neighbors with a distance-ordered priority queue. Indexing techniques reduce to this time when d is large, due to the curse of dimensionality [15]. Both memory- and disk-based indexes have been developed to help with specific types of queries, including k-d trees [7], R-trees [13] and metric trees [28].

In order to avoid the curse of dimensionality, dimension reduction techniques such as principal components analysis have been applied [18]. Other efficient approaches have been developed, including approximate solutions [25,1] and techniques such as locality sensitive hashing [11]. All of these techniques can be used in conjunction with the algorithm improvements, as these issues are orthogonal to this work.

There are several papers on using locally adaptive methods for neighborhood size [30,14,29]. This paper is concerned with finding a globally-best k. Although there is an obvious application of the technique in this paper to locally adaptive k-nn, applying the optimization in this environment is ongoing research.

2.2   Selecting k for k-nn

Cover and Hart [4] proved that there exists a distribution for which no choice of k is better than $k = 1$. They also showed that the error rate of a 1-nn classifier is at most twice the Bayes' rate (the theoretical lower bound). Obviously, $k = 1$ is not always the best solution, as Devroye et al. [5] discuss the asymptotic prediction error bounds of nearest neighbor classifiers as $n \to \infty$ and $k/n \to 0$.

From an applied perspective, Ferrer-Troyano et al. [6] present a comparison of k-nn over various UCI datasets, showing that finding a 'best' k can be difficult. They observe that larger values of k produce smaller errors on some datasets, but low values of k are similar on other datasets. Additionally, some examples could not be classified correctly for any value of k. They do not mention an efficient way to determine the best k.

Olsson [22] studied the impact of training size on the best k for text retrieval problems. On large training sets a broad set of k values were similar, while small training sets required careful selection of k. The paper uses an algorithm similar to Algorithm 1, presented in Section 3, for finding the optimal k in each case. As an aside, our techniques in Section 5, would improve the performance of their work.

Loop reordering is mentioned briefly in [10] as an efficient means to perform many k-nn searches over the same data. The authors of Weka [31] implement the loop reordering presented in Section 4. However, this paper significantly extends these works by analyzing the efficiency gains, extending the technique to additional decision models, discovering novel algorithms resulting from the loop reordering, determining reasonable bounds for k when the maximum is not known, and using statistical techniques to efficiently approximate k for very large data sets.

2.3   Speeding Up Cross-Validation

Several techniques have been developed to improve the performance of cross-validation. Mullin and Sukthankar [21] developed an efficient method of calculating the 'complete cross-validation' error. Complete cross-validation considers all possible divisions of the data into training and test data, for a fixed training data size. Their approach uses combinatorics to determine the number of training sets that would correctly classify a test example. Similar to our approach, their optimization comes from a view centered on the entire data set, rather than on the training sets. Their approach is only directly applicable to binary classification tasks, not for multiclass or regression problems.

Moore and Lee [19] used LOOCV to compare the accuracies of many different learning models and to select a best model in terms of minimal loss. Their approach looks at each example in turn, computing its loss for every model in contention. Whenever a model is statistically unlikely to be the best, it is eliminated from consideration (called *racing*). Likewise, if two models are statistically similar, one is dropped from the competition (called *blocking*). Combining these yields their BRACE algorithm, which can usually select a best model without having to compute the cross-validation loss for every example. We show how the BRACE method can be used to select the likely best k in Section 6.

Blockeel and Struyf [2] use a technique similar to the loop reordering of this paper for efficient cross-validation during the decision tree induction process. They apply each test only once per test example and store the results for each possible training set that contains that example. This generates a $O(m)$ speedup (where m is the number of folds). Unfortunately, in some cases, other factors

Algorithm 1. Naive K-nn LOOCV(K^*, λ, X, Y)

1: **for** $k = 1$ to K^* **do**
2:　　loss$(k) \leftarrow 0$
3:　　**for** $i = 1$ to n **do**
4:　　　　$N \leftarrow$ KnnQuery$(k, x_i, X - \{x_i\})$
5:　　　　$s \leftarrow 0$
6:　　　　**for all** $j \in N$ **do** {Sum neighbor labels}
7:　　　　　　$s \leftarrow s + y_j$
8:　　　　$\hat{y} \leftarrow s/k$ {Prediction is average of labels}
9:　　　　loss$(k) \leftarrow$ loss$(k) + \lambda(\hat{y}, y_i)$
10: **return** $\text{argmin}_k \text{loss}(k)$

Algorithm 2. Optimized K-nn LOOCV(K^*, λ, X, Y)

1: loss$(k) \leftarrow 0$ for $1 \le k \le K^*$
2: **for** $i = 1$ to n **do**
3:　　$N \leftarrow$ KnnQuery$(K^*, x_i, X - \{x_i\})$
4:　　Sort(N) {by increasing distance from x_i}
5:　　$s \leftarrow 0;\quad k \leftarrow 1$
6:　　**for all** $j \in N$ **do** {From nearest to furthest}
7:　　　　$s \leftarrow s + y_j$
8:　　　　loss$(k) \leftarrow$ loss$(k) + \lambda(y_i, s/k)$
9:　　　　$k \leftarrow k + 1$
10: **return** $\text{argmin}_k \text{loss}(k)$

dominate the cost of the execution so that overall performance is not always improved. Blockeel and Struyf have also proposed methods of parallelizing cross-validation for more general inductive logic programming tasks [27].

Racine [24] showed how to reduce the computation necessary for cross-validation of globally linear models, using incremental update techniques. His work was specifically for 'h-block' cross-validation, which is where observations close in time are assumed to be dependent, and observations that are far apart in time are assumed independent. In h-block cross-validation, making a prediction on an observation at time t involves leaving out the examples at times $t - h$ through $t + h$. We show in Section 4 how to use the optimized algorithm for efficiently updating linear models in Racine's work.

3   Efficient Cross-Validation for Selecting k

To serve as the basis for improved best k selection, we first present Algorithm 1, a naïve algorithm for best k selection using LOOCV. The algorithm selects a value of k from a range of values $\{1 \ldots K^*\}$.

- $\mathcal{X}, \mathcal{Y}$ – Domain, range of prediction problem.
- n – Number of training examples.
- $X = \{x_1, \ldots, x_n \mid x_i \in \mathcal{X}\}$ – Training examples.
- $Y = \{y_1, \ldots, y_n \mid y_i \in \mathcal{Y}\}$ – Training labels.
- K^* – Maximum reasonable value of k.
- KnnQuery $: k \times \mathcal{X} \times \mathcal{X}^{n-1} \to \mathcal{Z}^k$ – Search algorithm that finds the k nearest neighbors of a query example from a dataset with $n - 1$ examples (the query example being held out).

Algorithm 1 runs in $O\left(n \sum_{k=1}^{K^*} Q(k,n) + nK^{*2}\right)$ time, where $Q(k,n)$ is the running time for finding the k nearest neighbors in a database with n rows. The summation is not in closed form because $Q(k,n)$ depends on the search algorithm used, which has not yet been specified (see Table 1 for specific examples). We expect that in most applications the calls to KNNQUERY will dominate this algorithm's running time. Making a k-nn prediction on held-out x_i requires the following steps:

1. Finding the k nearest neighbors of x_i from $X - \{x_i\}$ (line 4). In practice, to avoid actually removing x_i from the search space, we request the $k+1$ nearest neighbors of x_i and discard x_i from the result set.
2. Building a model based on those neighbors, and making a prediction for x_i (in this case, constant regression, lines 5-9 average the labels of the k nearest neighbors).

These two steps are **computationally wasteful**, since the cross-validation repeats these computations over multiple values of k. For a single held-out example x_i, the innermost loop computes the $k = 1$ nearest neighbors, then the $k = 2$ nearest neighbors, etc., as well as summing the labels for these nearest neighbor sets. Obviously, the nearest neighbors for $k = m$ includes the $k = m - 1$ nearest neighbors. Thus, it should be sufficient to search for the K^* nearest neighbors of each held-out example **only once**, and derive necessary information for all smaller k. This simple observation has been previously exploited (e.g. in Weka) and provides a speedup for constant regression and classification that will be the basis of our further optimizations.

3.1   Optimized LOOCV to Select k

Three changes to Algorithm 1 enable a large potential speedup. These key changes are (1) reordering the nesting of the two outermost loops, (2) searching for all K^* nearest neighbors at once, and (3) computing label predictions and loss for each value of k in an incremental fashion. The result is shown in Algorithm 2.

Algorithm 2 will generally greatly outperform Algorithm 1 because it calls KNNQUERY only once (instead of K^* times) per held-out example. The algorithm uses the K^* neighbors to construct the predictions (and losses) for all $k \leq K^*$ nearest neighbors. To do this incrementally, it considers the K^* neighbors of the held-out example in order of increasing distance from the example. Thus, Algorithm 2 requires a sort which Algorithm 1 does not. All these transformations incur a negligible amount of extra memory over Algorithm 1.

Algorithm 2 runs in $O\left(nQ(K^*,n) + nK^* \log(K^*)\right)$ time. The term $nQ(K^*,n)$ comes from executing KNNQUERY n times, once per held-out example. The term $K^* \log(K^*)$ comes from the call to SORT, which is also called once for each held-out example. As before, $Q(k,n)$ represents the running time for the k-nn query algorithm. In the following subsection, we investigate the difference in running time between Algorithms 1 and 2 for particular k-nn query algorithms.

Table 1. Running time comparison for Algorithms 1 and 2 for two different k-nn implementations

k-nn query	$Q(k,n)$	Algorithm 1	Algorithm 2	**Speedup**
Linear scan	$n\log(k)$	$O(n^2 K^* \log(K^*))$	$O(n^2 \log(K^*))$	$O(K^*)$
Tree-based search	$k\log(n)$	$O(n\log(n)K^{*2})$	$O(n\log(n)K^*)$	$O(K^*)$

3.2 Algorithm Analyses for Specific Q

There are many ways to implement the KNNQUERY algorithm. Significant research has gone into speeding up k-nn queries under different assumptions or conditions, such as low dimension indexes [7,13,28], approximate answers [25,1,15,11], high-dimensional data [18,15], etc. While there are many possible implementations, we consider the running times of two typical representatives for comparison under our proposed cross-validation algorithm. Table 1 shows an analysis of the running times of Algorithms 1 and 2 when using either a linear scan algorithm or an efficient tree-based index search for KNNQUERY.

The linear scan examines all $n-1$ examples from $X - \{x_i\}$ and keeps track of the k nearest neighbors using a priority queue ordered by distance from the query example. This leads to a running time of $Q(k,n) = O(n\log(k))$. It may seem inefficient to scan all examples, but most indexing methods degrade to this behavior in high dimensions, due to the curse of dimensionality.

Searching a tree-based index, such as a k-d tree, can often be much more efficient than linear scan, especially in low dimensions and clustered data. It saves work by pruning branches of the tree based on its current estimate of the furthest nearest neighbor. Like the linear scan, it also maintains a priority queue of nearest neighbors. Our empirical evidence strongly suggests that for uniform data distribution, a simple k-d tree search will yield an *expected* running time of $O(k\log(n))$ for exact search of the k nearest neighbors.

For each analysis, we start from the running times of Algorithms 1 and 2 and use the appropriate form of $Q(k,n)$. The analyses simplify to the given forms under the natural assumption that $n \gg k$. In both cases, Algorithm 2 gives a speedup of $O(K^*)$ over Algorithm 1. This speedup is conserved over more costly k-nn implementations, as long as $Q(k,n)$ is polynomial in k and n.

4 Locally Linear Regression Problems

The loop reordering optimization proposed in Section 3 is simple and mentioned elsewhere [10,31]. It provides benefits for selecting k under different scenarios: constant regression (as already demonstrated), binary classification, and multiclass classification. However, the beauty of this algorithm (and the contribution of this paper), becomes more evident when it is applied in less obvious cases where it affords advantages not possible under the naïve cross-validation algorithm. One such application is locally-linear regression.

We can use k-nearest neighbor search in combination with a linear regression model to form a locally-linear regression model. This model adapts its regression coefficients based on the location of the desired prediction. Making a prediction on a query example requires finding its nearest neighbors, fitting a linear model to the neighbors, and using the model to make a prediction at the query example.

Consider adapting Algorithms 1 and 2 for finding an appropriate k for the locally-linear regression task. Let $X_k \in \mathbb{R}^{k \times d}$ represent the matrix of d attributes from each of the k nearest neighbors, and let $Y_k \in \mathbb{R}^k$ represent the column vector of output values for those neighbors. Estimating model coefficients for the locally linear model via least-squares requires finding $\hat{\beta}_k = (X_k^T X_k)^{-1} X_k^T Y_k$, which can be computed in $O(kd^2)$.

Algorithms 1 and 2 make the same number of model predictions, namely nK^*. Thus, computing $\hat{\beta}$ in $O(kd^2)$ for each model prediction adds a term of $O(nK^{*2}d^2)$ to the run time of both algorithms. While Algorithm 2 is still faster, it does not maintain an $O(K^*)$ speedup, since this additional term is *added* to both algorithms' run times. Nevertheless, the optimization unlocks further possibilities for speedup.

We can improve the performance of Algorithm 2 by incrementally calculating $\hat{\beta}_{k+1}$ from the partial calculations for $\hat{\beta}_k$, and the $(k+1)$st neighbor, rather than calculating it from scratch from all $k+1$ nearest neighbors. Racine [24] used this approach for global linear regression. To initialize this process, prior to the loop, we calculate the value of $\hat{\beta}_d$ (for the first d neighbors). We retain the two parts used to compute $\hat{\beta}_d$, i.e. $(X_d^T X_d)^{-1}$ and $X_d^T Y_d$, and update them during each iteration.

In particular, $X_{k+1}^T X_{k+1} = X_k^T X_k + x^T x$, where x is the $(k+1)$st nearest neighbor, and $x^T x$ is a $d \times d$ matrix of rank 1. The key observation is that the Sherman-Morrison formula [12, p. 50] allows us to calculate the inverse of $X_{k+1}^T X_{k+1}$ from $x^T x$ and the (already-computed) inverse of $X_k^T X_k$ in only $O(d^2)$ operations, which is asymptotically faster than taking the inverse of $X_{k+1}^T X_{k+1}$ directly.

The other part used in calculating $\hat{\beta}_k$, namely $X_k^T Y_k$, can be updated with the $(k+1)$st nearest neighbor to form $X_{k+1}^T Y_{k+1}$ in $O(d)$ time. Putting together these two parts, we can compute $\hat{\beta}_{k+1}$ incrementally more efficiently than computing it from the original matrices. This reduces the cost of estimating the linear model coefficients to $O(nK^*d^2)$. Thus, with incremental computation of $\hat{\beta}$, Algorithm 2 maintains a speedup of $O(K^*)$ over Algorithm 1. This additional speedup due to the Sherman-Morrison formula is not possible in Algorithm 1. In fact, this algorithm demonstrates one of the fundamental properties for improving performance with Algorithm 2– incremental evaluation of the prediction error.

The model we have discussed is linear in the coefficients of the model. Thus, we can apply this locally-linear regression speedup to any basis expansion model that is linear with respect to the estimated coefficients. For example, this speedup applies directly to polynomial regression.

5   Execution under Unknown K*

Algorithms 1 and 2 both require K^* as input. However, in some applications a reasonable upper bound on k is unknown. For instance, in [22], the best k is determined when no improvement in the error has been seen for 15 iterations. Fortunately, it is straightforward to modify both algorithms to dynamically determine an appropriate value for K^*. We first introduce a predicate called *nextk()*, which examines the results of cross-validation thus far and returns true as long as a larger value of k is worth examining. In later analysis we assume the running time of *nextk()* is negligible.

5.1   Modifications to Determine K*

We modify Algorithm 1 to dynamically determine K^* by substituting 'while *nextk()* do' in place of 'for $k = 1$ to K^* do'. This supports both the case where K^* is known in advance and the case where it must be determined dynamically. For example, in [9], $K^* = \sqrt{n}$, so *nextk()* would return true while $k \leq \sqrt{n}$. Alternatively, in [22], where K^* is unknown, *nextk()* would return true as long as $k \leq \operatorname{argmin}_i \operatorname{loss}(i) + 15$.

In Algorithm 2, it is assumed that K^* is known. Therefore, our approach is to wrap the algorithm in an outer loop which chooses K^*, runs Algorithm 2, and then consults *nextk()* to determine if K^* is large enough. If not, the outer loop doubles K^* and repeats. This wrapper can start with any value of K^* that prior knowledge suggests; otherwise, it starts with $K^* = 1$. We investigate the efficiency of this wrapper under two conditions: the initial guess for K^* is too high, or too low. If the initial K^* is exactly right, then Algorithm 2 keeps the same $O(K^*)$ speedup over Algorithm 1.

For the remainder of this section, when referring to Algorithms 1 and 2, we mean the modified versions of these algorithms that dynamically determine K^* by using *nextk()*, as described above. We define K_N^* (K_O^*) to be the maximum value of k considered in Algorithm 1 (2). Note that $K_N^* \leq K_O^*$, since K_N^* increments by one until *nextk()* returns false, but K_O^* doubles each time.

5.2   When K* Is Larger Than Necessary

If K_O^* is chosen to be larger than necessary, then Algorithm 2 wastes computation. In particular, KNNQUERY searches for more neighbors than necessary. Until *nextk()* returns false, however, Algorithm 1 performs more k-nn lookups than Algorithm 2. Thus, there is a break-even point between the two algorithms.

Using Table 1, with tree-based search, Algorithms 1 and 2 have running times of $O(n \log(n) K_N^{*2})$ and $O(n \log(n) K_O^*)$, respectively. This suggests that as long as $K_O^* = O(K_N^{*2})$, Algorithm 2 is the best choice. Even if K_O^* is too large, it is unlikely to be a factor of K_N^* too large in practice.

If KNNQUERY is a linear scan, the running times for Algorithms 1 and 2 are $O(n^2 K_N^* \log(K_N^*))$ and $O(n^2 \log(K_O^*))$. In this case, Algorithm 2 will perform better as long as the initial value of $K_O^* = O(K_N^{*K_N^*})$, which is likely to be true in practice unless an initial guess is grossly too large.

5.3   When K* Is Too Small

When the initial guess of K_O^* is too small, all of the work performed by Algorithm 2 is wasted; K_O^* must be doubled and the process restarted. We double K_O^* because the penalty for guessing too high is small. Eventually, we reach the case where $K_O^* \geq K_N^*$. Assuming that K_O^* starts at 1, the number of times that Algorithm 2 must double K_O^* is $t = \lceil \log_2(K_N^*) \rceil$. With the tree-based search, Algorithm 1 requires $O(n \log(n) K_N^{*2})$ time, and Algorithm 2 requires $O(n \log(n) \sum_{i=0}^{t} 2^i) = O(n \log(n) K_N^*)$ time. Note that this analysis gives the same result as the analysis of Algorithm 2 in Table 1. This analysis suggests that Algorithm 2 is still asymptotically faster than Algorithm 1, even when searching for K_O^*.

When using a linear scan, Algorithm 1 has a running time of $O(n^2 K_N^* \log(K_N^*))$, while Algorithm 2 now requires $O(\sum_{i=0}^{t} n^2 \log(2^i)) = O(n^2 \log^2(K_N^*))$ time. Clearly, the wrapped version of Algorithm 2 should outperform Algorithm 1, even when K^* is unknown.

If K_N^* is large, larger initial values of K_O^* will improve the performance of Algorithm 2 (over choosing $K_O^* = 1$). A larger guess avoids lost work on too-small K_O^* values. For example, in [22], the desired R-precision influences best k selection. For high R-precision, the initial guess for K^* should be 64, while for lower R-precision, an initial guess of 16 would find the best k with less work. Other optimization techniques, including parallelization across different values for K_O^*, are part of our ongoing research.

6   Statistical Methods for Large Data Sets

Although the optimized algorithm improves the performance for finding the best k by a factor of K^*, the dominant term in the running time is the number of times KNNQUERY must be called. Clearly, reducing the number of queries could greatly improve the running time of the optimized algorithm over large data sets.

Selecting the best k can be thought of as selecting the best model from a set of K^* models. As such, the BRACE algorithm [19] can be combined with Algorithm 2 to determine when there is a low probability that any other model will have a lower loss than the selected value of k. We denote this new algorithm as Alg 2+BRACE. BRACE eliminates models which are unlikely to be the best by regular statistical comparisons. Models may be eliminated before seeing all the examples. BRACE assumes that model losses are distributed independently throughout the dataset. As a result, the best k returned by Alg 2+BRACE may not be the same as under the Algorithm 2, but it is likely to have a very similar loss value.

Alg 2+BRACE requires two parameters to determine the likelihood the chosen model is the best. Larger values for these parameters yield quicker results, but with greater probability that the selected model does not have the lowest loss. The hypothesis test error rate δ indicates the probability of making an error on eliminating a model. The loss indifference parameter γ defines the range of loss values within which two models are considered similar. Alg 2+BRACE works as follows:

- Start with an initial K^*.
- For each k maintain a status (active/inactive) and two sufficient statistics: the sum of prediction losses, and the sum of the squared prediction losses (on examples seen thus far).
- After each interval of t examples, compare each pair of active k values using hypothesis tests. If some k is unlikely to have significantly lower loss than another, mark k as inactive.
- If two values of k are determined to have similar loss, mark the greater k as inactive
- Reduce K^* to the largest active k.
- Stop if only one k is active or all examples have been examined. Choose the active k with minimum loss.

This algorithm has the potential for computational savings by reducing K^* whenever possible, and also by stopping before examining the entire training set. However, it does introduce overhead in the hypothesis testing and, to a much lesser extent, in the maintenance of additional statistics. The hypothesis testing is between all pairs of models, resulting in $O(K^{*2})$ model comparisons. The hypothesis tests can be applied after the examination of each example, but the number of models eliminated per example is typically very small. Thus, we introduce an interval, t, as the number of examples processed before the hypothesis testing is applied. Optimal selection of t is ongoing work.

Experimental results (Section 7.3) indicate this overhead can be significant for small data sets, causing Alg 2+BRACE to be slower than Algorithm 2. However, with an application specific well-chosen t and large data sets, the savings far outweigh the overhead.

7   Experimental Results

We now consider the running time of Algorithms 1 and 2 under various conditions. We report three categories of experiments: when K^* is known; when K^* is unknown; and when applying the BRACE algorithm. When K^* is known, we compare the running times of these algorithms on several classification and regression datasets, including using the Sherman-Morrison improvement. When K^* is unknown, we compare both the linear scan and tree-indexed approaches. For BRACE, we use one very large regression dataset, allowing us to compare it directly with algorithm without BRACE. The datasets we used are (see also Table 2):

Magic04 is a binary classification dataset from the UCI repository with 19,020 examples, each having 10 features. This data comes from a Monte Carlo simulation of high-energy gamma particles. The task is to predict whether a record indicates a gamma particle or background noise.

Table 2. A summary of the experiments according to dataset, size, task, and implementation. The two implementations are ANN tree-based index search [20], and linear scan which examines every example. Note that we test sine10d on two different tasks.

	dataset	n	d	# predictions	task	KNNQUERY
K^* known	magic04	19,020	10	19,020	binary classification	tree index (ANN)
(section 7.1)	sine10d	10,000	10	10,000	locally constant regression	tree index (ANN)
	sine10d	10,000	10	10,000	locally linear regression	tree index (ANN)
	Netflix	480,189	17,770	100,480,507	locally constant regression	linear scan
K^* unknown	sine4d	10,000	4	10,000	locally constant regression	tree index (ANN)
(section 7.2)	sine32d	10,000	32	10,000	locally constant regression	linear scan
BRACE (7.3)	sine2d	10e3 - 10e7	2	10e3 - 10e7	locally constant regression	tree index (ANN)

SineXd represents a set of similar synthetic regression datasets having $2 \leq X \leq 32$ features. Each feature is drawn from the $[0, 1]$ uniform distribution. Denoting feature j of example i as x_{ij}, we generate the label for x_i as $y_i = \sin(\sum_{j=1}^{X} x_{ij}^2) + \epsilon$, where $\epsilon \sim \mathcal{N}(0, 0.05)$.

Netflix is a large, sparse regression dataset. It contains 480,189 users who have provided 100,480,507 ratings of 17,770 movies. The goal is to predict a user's movie rating, based on ratings other similar users gave that movie. User similarity is based on Pearson correlation between the ratings on movies both users have rated (excluding the query movie). Each rating requires a k-nn query for prediction.

Our primary focus is on running time rather than prediction accuracy. Thus, these large datasets which cover a wide range of prediction tasks are sufficient for showing the speedups of the proposed methods.

Our experiments run on a four-core, 3 GHz Intel Xeon with 8 GiB of RAM running Linux 2.6. We use the Approximate Nearest Neighbor (ANN) library [20] as a k-d tree search algorithm for k-nn queries on low-dimensional datasets. For high-dimensional datasets, we use a linear scan algorithm, and on the Netflix dataset we optimize the fact that there are multiple similar k-nn queries per user. Further, we parallelized the Netflix experiment across four processors. For experiments comparing known and unknown K^*, we report only running times, since both algorithms produce the same cross-validation results. Figure 3 reports the differences in best k reported using Alg 2+BRACE.

7.1   Experiments with Known K*

Figure 1 shows the relative speedup of Algorithm 2, defined as the time for Algorithm 1 divided by the time for Algorithm 2. Each experiment performed LOOCV for varying values of K^*. Clearly, the optimization gives vast improvements in running time in each task, allowing searches over much larger values of k much more quickly. For instance, we could search with $K^* = 250$ with Algorithm 2 in less time than it takes Algorithm 1 to search with $K^* = 30$.

For the locally linear regression experiment, we implemented two versions of Algorithm 2 – one that recomputed the linear model each time, and one that

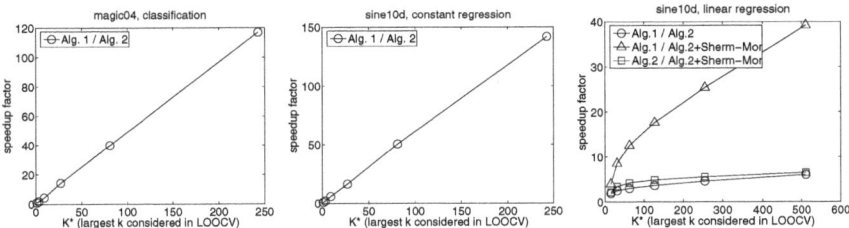

Fig. 1. These graphs show the relative speedup of Algorithm 2 over Algorithm 1 for three datasets. Each line shows speedup: the time of the slower algorithm divided by that of the faster algorithm. Speedup is linear with K^* for classification, constant regression, and linear regression with the Sherman-Morrison incremental evaluation.

used the Sherman-Morrison incremental calculations discussed in Section 4. The Sherman-Morrison optimization yields significant additional speedup, and is not possible with the original algorithm.

We ran the parallel optimized algorithm on the Netflix dataset with $K^* = 500$ in 78 wall-clock hours (310 CPU hours). This was with a linear scan-based k-nn algorithm; a highly optimized algorithm should be able to easily handle the entire dataset even more quickly. For a fixed k, there are over 100 million rating predictions to make. Trying $K^* = 500$ predictions per user rating meant that the algorithm actually made 50 billion predictions in that time – approximately 180,000 predictions per wall-clock second. We did not run the naïve algorithm on this dataset, which we predict would take about 2.2 wall-clock years (based on relative speeds observed in other experiments).

7.2   Experiments with Unknown K*

For the algorithms in Section 5, we verify the analysis with experiments on both low dimensional data with effective indexes and high dimensional data using a linear scan. In all cases, 10,000 examples are used. Table 2 reports additional details of the experiments.

Figure 2 reports the results of our experiments. Each line represents a different initial guess for K_O^* (1, 8, 32 and 128). The x-axis represents the range of values for K_N^*. A point on the line represents the speedup of Algorithm 2 over 1. Note the jagged lines for most initial guesses – the drops correspond to those points where Algorithm 2 restarts with a larger K^*, so the work up to that point is wasted. As predicted, the better the initial guess, the better the performance gain.

As K_N^* increases, even vaguely reasonable guesses for K_O^* give significant speedup. The middle graph provides greater detail of the rectangle in the left graph, showing those conditions which allow Algorithm 1 to outperform Algorithm 2. Points below the line speedup=1 (middle graph only) indicate these conditions, e.g., an initial guess of a very large K_O^* results in poor performance, if K_N^* actually is small. However, an initial guess of $K_O^* = 1$ performs at least

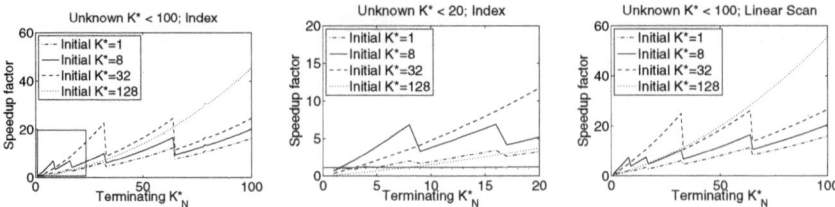

Fig. 2. The running time of Algorithm 1 divided by the running time of Algorithm 2 for various ranges of K_N^*. The task is constant regression. The data have 4 dimensions (indexed search) or 32 dimensions (linear scan). Each line is a different initial guess for K_O^*. The rectangle in the left graph is blown up to give the middle graph. Note that the initial guess of 128 outperforms a guess of 32 when $K_N^* \geq 33$. This is exactly the point where a new K_O^* is required. This implies that the best performance comes from an intelligent, sufficiently large initial guess.

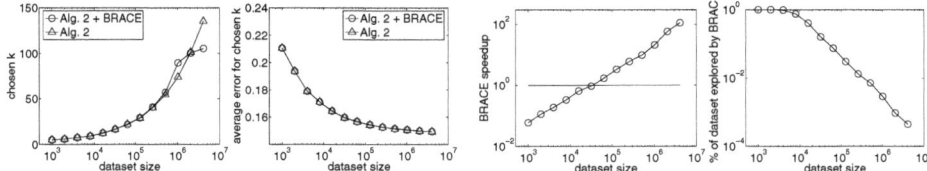

Fig. 3. The left plot shows the k chosen by Algorithm 2 with and without BRACE on the sine2d dataset for varying n. The right graph shows average LOOCV error for both algorithms (the lines overlap).

Fig. 4. The left plot shows the speedup of using BRACE with Algorithm 2. The right plot shows the percentage of examples that BRACE examines. Both are on a log-log scale. The speedup plot shows a line at speedup=1. For large datasets using BRACE gives 100-fold speedup.

as well as the Algorithm 1 under all conditions *except* when $K_N^* = 3$. In the right graph, the performance gains are even higher because the linear scan k-nn search is even more costly (relative to other cross-validation calculations) than an indexed search.

7.3 Experiments with BRACE

We perform a number of experiments combining the BRACE algorithm with Algorithm 2 to see how much further the model selection process can be accelerated. We compare Algorithm 2 for selecting k in k-nn search with the Alg 2+BRACE version. We use 0.001 for both BRACE parameters γ and δ, and compare models every 10 examples. We show average performance over 20 synthetically generated versions of the sine2d dataset. Alg 2+BRACE produces an extremely fast model selection algorithm for k-nearest neighbor search. While the two versions do not always choose the same k, the chosen k gave nearly the same loss, so that the average loss Alg 2+BRACE is always within 0.003 of the best loss.

Figure 3 shows the results over various dataset sizes of the chosen k and the resulting losses, which are indistinguishable due to overlap.

Figure 3 shows that the LOOCV-selected k increases as n increases. The reason for this is as n increases the density of samples across the domain increases, and so does the expected number of neighbors within a fixed radius of any point. Nearby neighbors in regression tend to have the same labels, so using more neighbors in a denser space is beneficial. In this experiment the best k for small n is still a good k for larger n in terms of providing low loss, it's just that an even larger k provides even lower loss for large n.

Despite giving nearly equal losses, Alg 2+BRACE was much faster for large datasets. Figure 4 shows the computational speedup as well as the percentage of the total dataset that Alg 2+BRACE examined. Recall that Alg 2+BRACE stops execution early if it determines a single best k, so on large datasets it usually will stop before it has examined all the examples. Indeed, the second plot shows that as n increases, the percentage of the dataset examined drops dramatically. The details are even more surprising – as n increases, the total number of examples that BRACE examines initially increases, and then actually decreases. While this might seem counter-intuitive, there's a good reason.

On this dataset (and likely most regression datasets) the best k is positively related to n. When comparing two model's estimated losses, BRACE's hypothesis tests use both the difference and the variance of the difference. This variance tends to go down as more examples are examined, at a rate of $1/\sqrt{i}$ for i examples. When k is large, regression noise tends to average out, resulting in lower prediction variance. When the best k is small, BRACE has a difficult time differentiating between the various k values because their predictions tend to have high variance. Thus BRACE must examine many examples until the estimator variance is low enough to cause a significant test, thus eliminating a model. When the best k is large, small values of k are quickly eliminated because their errors are significantly larger. Then, deciding among different large values of k proceeds quickly, because the variance between them is low. BRACE's indifference parameter γ helps speed up this process significantly by eliminating near-identical models.

8   Conclusion

We present detailed analysis and experimental evidence for improving k-nn model selection. Given a maximum reasonable k value, called K^*, the optimized algorithm is $O(K^*)$ faster than the naïve algorithm for leave-one-out cross-validation. This speedup holds for both indexed and linear-scan k-nn queries. The optimization enables additional performance enhancements, such as using the Sherman-Morrison formula for incremental calculations in locally linear regression tasks.

When K^* is not known *a priori*, we present an algorithm to efficiently find it, given a stopping criterion. It starts with an initial guess for K^* and doubles K^* if the criterion has not been met. This adaptive version still has asymptotic running time less than the naive algorithm.

Finding the k-nn for very large datasets is computationally demanding. The BRACE algorithm [19] can be combined with Algorithm 2 to both reduce the number of examples examined and K^*. The resulting algorithm provides dramatic additional speedup for large data sets.

Although the results we have shown in this paper are significant, additional issues include:

- Search for K^* with a number of parallel processes which use different K^* values (using powers of two). All machines terminate when any finds a satisfactory K^*.
- Leave-one-out cross validation is easy to optimize, but m-fold and h-block cross-validation appear more difficult. This is especially true when using indexes such as k-d trees.
- In this work we considered the problem of finding a single best k. We would like to apply this optimization to locally adaptive k-nn problems [30].
- When the underlying dataset is changing, as in a large dynamic database, the question arises of how to efficiently maintain the best k.
- A key to efficiency in the optimized algorithm is the fact that nearest-neighbor models are nested. We would like to explore speedups in other similarly structured models.

Although the basic ideas behind Algorithm 2 are straightforward and known, their implications are significant and underexploited. The optimization allows far more values of k to be considered in the same amount of time. It also allows further optimizations such as Sherman-Morrison, and it surprisingly outperforms Algorithm 1 in the case where K^* is unknown. Finally, BRACE provides significant additional speedup by avoiding examining all examples. Combined, these ideas provide a powerful tool for practitioners to automatically perform k-nn model selection easily and efficiently.

References

1. Arya, S., Mount, D., Netanyahu, N., Silverman, R., Wu, A.: An optimal algorithm for approximate nearest neighbor searching in fixed dimensions. Journal of the ACM 45(6), 891–923 (1999)
2. Blockeel, H., Struyf, J.: Efficient algorithms for decision tree cross-validation. In: International Conference on Machine Learning, pp. 11–18 (2001)
3. Böhm, C., Berchtold, S., Keim, D.A.: Searching in high-dimensional spaces: Index structures for improving the performance of multimedia databases. ACM Computing Surveys 33(3), 322–373 (2001)
4. Cover, T., Hart, P.: Nearest neighbor pattern classification. IEEE Transactions on Information Theory 13(1), 21–27 (1967)
5. Devroye, L., Györfi, L., Lugosi, G.: A Probabilistic Theory of Pattern Recognition. Springer, Heidelberg (1996)
6. Ferrer-Troyano, F.J., Aguilar-Ruiz, J.S., Riquelme, J.-C.: Empirical Evaluation of the Difficulty of Finding a Good Value of k for the Nearest Neighbor. In: Sloot, P.M.A., Abramson, D., Bogdanov, A.V., Gorbachev, Y.E., Dongarra, J., Zomaya, A.Y. (eds.) ICCS 2003. LNCS, vol. 2658, pp. 766–773. Springer, Heidelberg (2003)

7. Friedman, J.H., Bentley, J.L., Finkel, R.A.: Two algorithms for nearest-neighbor search in high dimensions. ACM Transactions on Mathematical Software 3(3), 209–226 (1977)
8. Geisser, S.: The predictive sample reuse method with applications. Journal of the American Statistical Association 70(350), 320–328 (1975)
9. Ghosh, A., Chaudhuri, P., Murthy, C.: On visualization and aggregation of nearest neighbor classifiers. IEEE Transactions on Pattern Analysis and Machine Intelligence 27(10), 1592–1602 (2005)
10. Ghosh, A.K.: On nearest neighbor classification using adaptive choice of k. Journal of Computational and Graphical Statistics 16(2), 482–502 (2007)
11. Gionis, A., Indyk, P., Motwani, R.: Similarity search in high dimensions via hashing. In: International Conference on Very Large Data Bases, pp. 518–529 (1999)
12. Golub, G.H., Van Loan, C.F.: Matrix Computations, 2nd edn. Johns Hopkins University Press (1996)
13. Guttman, A.: R-trees: A dynamic index structure for spatial searching. In: ACM International Conference on Management of Data, pp. 47–57 (1984)
14. Hastie, T., Tibshirani, R.: Discriminant adaptive nearest neighbor classification. IEEE Transactions on Pattern Analysis and Machine Intelligence 18(6), 607–616 (1996)
15. Indyk, P., Motwani, R.: Approximate nearest neighbors: Towards removing the curse of dimensionality. In: ACM Symposium on Theory of Computation, pp. 604–613 (1998)
16. Li, K.-C.: Asymptotic optimality for c_p, c_l, cross-validation, and generalized cross-validation: Discrete index set. The Annals of Statistics 15(3), 958–975 (1987)
17. Li, L., Weinberg, C., Darden, T., Pederson, L.: Gene selection for sample classification based on gene expression data: Study of sensitivty to choice of parameters of the ga/knn method. Bioinformatics 17(12), 1131–1142 (2001)
18. Lin, K.-I., Jagadish, H., Faloutsos, C.: The TV-tree: An index structure for high-dimensional data. The International Journal on Very Large Databases 3(4), 517–542 (1994)
19. Moore, A., Lee, M.S.: Efficient algorithms for minimizing cross validation error. In: International Conference on Machine Learning, pp. 190–198 (1994)
20. Mount, D.M., Arya, S.: ANN: A library for approximate nearest neighbor searching (2006), http://www.cs.umd.edu/~mount/ANN/
21. Mullin, M., Sukthankar, R.: Complete cross-validation for nearest neighbor classifiers. In: International Conference on Machine Learning, pp. 639–646. Morgan Kaufmann (2000)
22. Olsson, J.S.: An analysis of the coupling between training set and neighborhood sizes of the knn classifier. In: SIGIR, pp. 685–686 (2006)
23. Ouyang, D., Li, D., Li, Q.: Cross-validation and non-parametric k nearest-neighbor estimation. Econometrics Journal 9, 448–471 (2006)
24. Racine, J.: Feasible cross-validatory model selection for general stationary processes. Journal of Applied Econometrics 12(2), 169–179 (1997)
25. Shakhnarovich, G., Indyk, P., Darrell, T. (eds.): Nearest-Neighbor Methods in Learning and Vision. MIT Press (2006)
26. Stone, M.: Cross-validatory choice and assessment of statistical predictions. Journal of the Royal Statistical Society, Series B 36(2), 111–147 (1974)
27. Struyf, J., Blockeel, H.: Efficient Cross-Validation in ILP. In: Rouveirol, C., Sebag, M. (eds.) ILP 2001. LNCS (LNAI), vol. 2157, pp. 228–239. Springer, Heidelberg (2001)

28. Uhlmann, J.K.: Satisfying general proximity/similarity queries with metric trees. Applied Mathematics Letters 4, 175–179 (1991)
29. Wang, J., Neskovic, P., Cooper, L.N.: Neighborhood size selection in the k-nearest-neighbor rule using statistical confidence. The Journal of the Pattern Recognition Society 39(3), 417–423 (2006)
30. Wettschereck, D., Dietterich, T.G.: Locally adaptive nearest neighbor algorithms. Advances in Neural Information Processing Systems 6, 184–191 (1994)
31. Witten, I.H., Frank, E.: Data Mining: Practical Machine Learning Tools and Techniques (1999)
32. Wu, X., Kumar, V., Quinlan, J.R., Ghosh, J., Yang, Q., Motoda, H., McLachlan, G.J., Ng, A., Liu, B., Yu, P.S., Zhou, Z.-H., Steinbach, M., Hand, D.J., Steinberg, D.: Top 10 algorithms in data mining. Knowledge and Information Systems 14(1), 1–37 (2008)
33. Xue, G.-R., Lin, C., Yang, Q., Xi, W., Zeng, H.-J., Yu, Y., Chen, Z.: Scalable collaborative filtering using cluster-based smoothing. In: SIGIR, pp. 114–121 (2005)

EXPLORE: A Novel Decision Tree Classification Algorithm

Md Zahidul Islam*

School of Computing and Mathematics, Charles Sturt University, Locked Bag 588,
Boorooma Street, Wagga Wagga, NSW 2678, Australia
zislam@csu.edu.au
http://csusap.csu.edu.au/~zislam/

Abstract. Decision tree algorithms such as See5 (or C5) are typically used in data mining for classification and prediction purposes. In this study we propose EXPLORE, a novel decision tree algorithm, which is a modification of See5. The modifications are made to improve the capability of a tree in extracting hidden patterns. Justification of the proposed modifications is also presented. We experimentally compare EXPLORE with some existing algorithms such as See5, REPTree and J48 on several issues including quality of extracted rules/patterns, simplicity, and classification accuracy of the trees. Our initial experimental results indicate advantages of EXPLORE over existing algorithms.

Keywords: Data Mining, Classification Algorithm, Decision Tree.

1 Introduction

Advances in information processing technology and storage capacity have enabled collection of huge amount of data for various data analyses. Data mining techniques such as classification and clustering are often applied on these data sets to extract hidden information. In this study, we consider a data set as a two dimensional table where rows are individual records and columns are the attributes. We consider that a data set can have mainly two types of attributes; numerical (such as Age and Salary) and categorical (such as Educational qualification and Country of Origin).

A data set can have any number of numerical and categorical attributes. In order to produce a decision tree, one of the categorical attributes is considered as the class attribute that classifies or labels the records, and all other attributes are considered as classifier attributes. A decision tree algorithm is used to explore the logic rules (patterns) that represent relationships between various classifier attributes and the class attribute. It produces a decision tree having nodes and leaves as shown in Figure 1. The rectangles are nodes and the ovals are leaves which are numbered from 1 to 7 in the figure. Each node tests an attribute. If the

---

* This work was supported by author's CSU Small Grant at Charles Sturt University, Australia.

L.M. MacKinnon (Ed.): BNCOD 2010, LNCS 6121, pp. 55–71, 2012.
© Springer-Verlag Berlin Heidelberg 2012

attribute tested in a node (i.e. the test attribute of a node) is numerical (such as Income) then typically there are two edges from the node. One of the edges is labeled "$> c$" while the other edge is labeled "$<= c$", where c is a constant drawn from the domain of that attribute. The constant "c" is also known as the splitting point for the attribute Income. On the other hand, if the attribute is categorical (such as Country) then there are typically a few edges from the node, each labeled by a categorical value drawn from the attribute domain. The edges protruding from a node typically divide the data set into mutually exclusive partitions.

Each leaf of the tree has a class value associated with it. In a homogeneous leaf all the records belonging to the leaf have the same class value. However, in a heterogeneous leaf the records have different values for the class attribute [4], [2]. In Figure 1, Leaf 1 has 70 records. All of the records belonging to the leaf have Toyota as the value of the class attribute "Car Make", in the training data set i.e the data set where the tree has been obtained from. However, Leaf 6 is a heterogeneous leaf having 12 records out of which 7 do not have Holden as the class value.

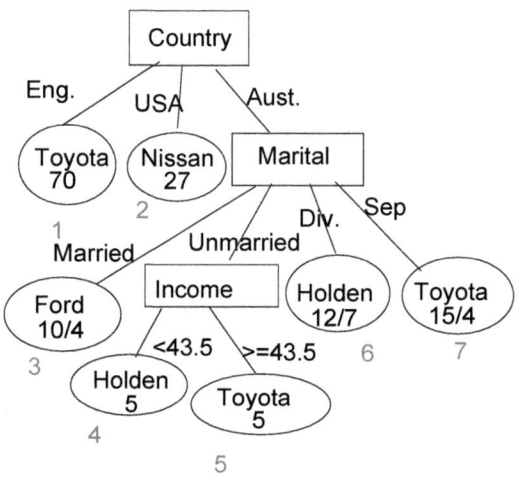

Fig. 1. An example decision tree obtained from a synthetic data set called MCSD

A decision tree is typically used for knowledge discovery as it explores patterns (logic rules) from a data set. It can also be used to predict the class of an unlabeled record. For example, a decision tree can be built from a health data set having attributes on various health information (such as blood pressure and cholesterol) and a class attribute, say Diagnosis of Disease. The logic rules produced by the decision tree can then be used to predict the class value (diagnosis) of a new patient based on his/her health information.

See5 [8], [9] is one of the most commonly used decision tree algorithms. In this study we propose EXPLORE: a novel decision tree classification technique, which is a modification of See5 algorithm. The main focus of the proposed algorithm is to extract some hidden patterns that are generally overlooked by existing algorithms.

EXPLORE extends the See5 algorithm by introducing new splitting criteria for both numerical and categorical test attributes while searching for the best test attribute of a node. It also uses a new measure called Ultimate Gain Ratio instead of Gain Ratio that is used in selection of a test attribute. We explain the properties of EXPLORE in detail in Section 3. However, in short, for a numerical attribute a data set is divided into two partitions based on the best window (instead of just a splitting point) of the numerical values. This splitting criterion allows to capture patterns involving a window of values of a numerical attribute. For example, in a data set if there is a specific tendency (such as buying a particular product) within the people having age between 20 and 30 years then EXPLORE aims to pick the pattern clearly by choosing the numerical window (20 to 30) for attribute "Age" in the logic rule. Traditional algorithms may find it difficult to extract the pattern by splitting Age into two partitions such as greater than 30 and less than 30. However, a similar approach of using numerical window was taken by an existing technique [1] in the context of association rule mining.

The second property of EXPLORE is related to categorical attributes. For a categorical attribute it divides a data set into two partitions based on an attribute value instead of all values of the attribute. For example, if it is strongly evident from a data set that all academics are inquisitive and people of any other profession are equally divided between inquisitive and non-inquisitive group then traditional algorithms would not generally extract the pattern involving academics and being inquisitive. Traditional algorithms would rather choose another attribute $A=\{a_1,a_2\}$ where say 70% people having a_1 are inquisitive and say 70% people having a_2 are not inquisitive. However, EXPLORE aims to extract the pattern involving the academics as the pattern is very strong. Another property of EXPLORE is that it favours a pattern involving a bigger segment. EXPLORE uses Ultimate Gain Ratio instead of just Gain Ratio that is used in some existing algorithms.

If a data set has some patterns involving a window of numerical values and/or a categorical value (instead of all values of an attribute) then EXPLORE can be very useful to extract such hidden patterns from the data set. We have experimentally compared EXPLORE with several existing algorithms including See5, J48 and REPTree on various issues such as quality of extracted pattern, simplicity of the obtained tree, accuracy and significance of the patterns. Our initial experimental results indicate clear advantages of EXPLORE over some existing algorithms, in this context.

In the next section we give a brief introduction to See5 algorithm. In Section 3 we present various steps of our decision tree algorithm. Experimental results have been presented in Section 4. Section 5 provides concluding remarks and future research plan.

2   Background Study

There are many classification algorithms in the literature [8], [9], [5], [6], [2]. Since, our proposed algorithm (EXPLORE) is similar to See5, we briefly introduce See5 in this section before we present EXPLORE in the next section.

See5 is an entropy based decision tree algorithm that takes a divide and conquer approach. Using the following notations we illustrate the basic steps of See5 for constructing a decision tree [8], [9], [2].

D - whole data set.

T - an attribute with n number of mutually exclusive outcomes T_1, T_2, ... T_n.

c - number of classes i.e. the domain size of the class attribute.

$p(D, j)$ - proportion of records in D belonging to the jth class.

$D_i \subseteq D$ - the partition of the data set where all records have T_i for the attribute T.

$|D_i|$ - size (number of records) of the partition D_i.

See5 first calculates the entropy (i.e. the uncertainty about the class value of a record) of the whole data set (D) as follows.

$$I(D) = -\sum_{j=1}^{c} p(D, j) log_2(p(D, j)).$$ (1)

If T is a categorical attribute, See5 in the next step calculates entropy within a segment (of the data set) where all records have T_i for T. It calculates the entropy as follows.

$$I(D_i) = -\sum_{j=1}^{c} p(D_i, j) log_2(p(D_i, j)).$$ (2)

Therefore, the weighted entropy of the whole data set when attribute T is tested at the first node is as follows.

$$I(D, T) = -\sum_{i=1}^{n} \frac{|D_i|}{|D|} \times I(D_i).$$ (3)

However, if T is a numerical attribute (instead of a categorical attribute) having a domain $[l, u]$ then the records are first re-arranged so that values of T are placed in ascending or descending order. The data set is then divided into two partitions D_1 and D_2 based on a splitting point p so that the domain of T in D_1 is $[l, p]$ and D_2 is $[p + 1, u]$, where $p + 1$ means the next higher value to p in the domain. $I(D, T)$ is then calculated as follows.

$$I(D_i) = -\sum_{j=1}^{c} p(D_i, j) log_2(p(D_i, j)), for 1 \leq i \leq 2.$$ (4)

$$I(D,T) = -\sum_{i=1}^{2} \frac{|D_i|}{|D|} \times I(D_i). \tag{5}$$

$I(D,T)$s are calculated for all possible splitting points of a numerical attribute T. Finally, the minimum $I(D,T)$ is considered as the $I(D,T)$ of T and the splitting point that produces the minimum $I(D,T)$ is considered as the best splitting point of T.

The reduction of entropy, as a result of choosing an attribute T (numerical or categorical) as a test attribute, is considered as the gain of information for the attribute. The gain is calculated as follows.

$$Gain(D,T) = I(D) - I(D,T). \tag{6}$$

$Gain(D,T)$ of an attribute T is influenced by the domain size of T and will be maximal when there is only one record in each subset D_i. Therefore, the above mentioned information gain calculation favours the attributes with bigger domain sizes over those having smaller domain sizes. In order to minimize this undue favour, gain ratio (instead of information gain) of the attribute is used for the selection of the test attribute for the node. Gain ratio is calculated as follows.

$$GainRatio(D,T) = \frac{I(D) - I(D,T)}{Split(D,T)}. \tag{7}$$

The split information of an attribute $Split(D,T)$ generally increases when an attribute has bigger domain size. Split information of each attribute is calculated as follows.

$$Split(D,T) = -\sum_{i=1}^{k} \frac{|D_i|}{|D|} \times log_2 \frac{|D_i|}{|D|}, \tag{8}$$

where the domain size of T, $|T| = k$.

Finally, out of all non-class attributes the one having the highest gain ratio is chosen as the root node of the decision tree. If the chosen attribute T is a categorical attribute having the domain size $|T| = k$ then the data set D is divided into k mutually exclusive partitions $D_1, D_2 \ldots \ldots D_k$. On the other hand if the chosen attribute T is a numerical attribute with domain $[l, u]$ then the data set D is divided into two partitions D_1 and D_2 using the best splitting point of T.

Once the test attribute for the root node of a decision tree is chosen, the same processes (as explained above) are repeated recursively on each partition of the data set until a termination condition is met. Examples of user defined termination conditions can be having the same class value for all records within a partition, lack of enough records in a partition, and not having a gain ratio greater than a threshold [8,9]. Suitable termination conditions can be chosen to obtain a useful decision tree.

3   Our Technique

The proposed decision tree classification technique (EXPLORE) is a modifications of the existing See5 algorithm. We first mention the main properties of
EXPLORE as follows, and then explain each of them in detail.

1. For a numerical attribute, EXPLORE divides a data set into two partitions
   using the best window instead of a splitting point.
2. For categorical attributes, it chooses the test attribute of a node based on an
   attribute value instead of all values of the attribute.
3. It uses Ultimate Gain Ratio (UGR, explained later) instead of the Gain Ratio.
4. It can use a minimum window size to ensure statistical significance of the
   result. (Some existing algorithms also have similar property.)
5. It can use a user defined threshold for Ultimate Gain Ratio (UGR) as a
   termination condition. (Some existing algorithms also have similar threshold
   based property.)

**Property 1: For a numerical attribute, EXPLORE divides a data set
into two partitions using the best window instead of a splitting point.**
    While testing a numerical attribute as the test attribute of a node, EXPLORE
divides the data set into two partitions based on the best window of the numerical attribute, instead of the best splitting point (as explained in Section 2). For
example, if the domain of a numerical attribute T is $[l, u]$, EXPLORE looks for
the window $W = [w_1, w_2]$, where $l \leq w_1 \leq w_2 \leq u$, producing the maximum
information gain. It then divides the data set into two mutually exclusive partitions where in one partition the domain of T is $[w_1, w_2]$ and in the other partition
the domain is $\subseteq [l, u]$, but not $\subseteq [w_1, w_2]$. We explain the process as follows.
    Let us assume that the domain of a numerical attribute "Age" is [20,60]. First
$LocalI(D_{[20]})$, the entropy in the segment of the data set where for all records
Age=20, is calculated as follows.

$$LocalI(D_{[20]}) = -\sum_{j=1}^{c} p(D_{20}, j) log_2(p(D_{20}, j)). \qquad (9)$$

The weighted entropy $wLocalI(D_{[20]})$ is then calculated as follows.

$$wLocalI(D_{[20]}) = \frac{LocalI(D_{20})}{log_2(log_2|D_{20}|)}. \qquad (10)$$

Weighted entropy takes the segment size into consideration to favour a pattern
with bigger size i.e greater significance. However, note that $LocalI(D_{20})$ is di-
vided by $log_2(log_2|D_{20}|)$ (instead of just $|D_{20}|$) in order to reduce the effect of
the size on weighted entropy. A justification of using $log_2(log_2|D_i|)$ is given later
while describing Property 3.
    We now similarly calculate all weighted entropies $wLocalI(D_{[20,w_2]})$ for all pos-
sible windows $[20, w_2]$ where, $20 \leq w_2 \leq 60$. Note that $wLocalI(D_{[20,w_2]})$ is the
weighted entropy in the segment of the data set where for all records Age $= [20, w_2]$.

Let us call these weighted entropies as Weighted Local Entropies for various windows starting from Age=20. We then pick the minimum of these entropies and call it as the Global Entropy $(GlobalI(D_{20}))$ for the best window starting from Age=20. For example, if $wLocalI(D_{[20,32]})$ is the minimum of all weighted local entropies then,

$$GlobalI(D_{20}) = wLocalI(D_{[20,32]}). \qquad (11)$$

$GlobalI(D_{20})$ is actually the best window starting from Age=20. Similarly, $GlobalI(D_{21})$, $GlobalI(D_{22})$, ... $GlobalI(D_{60})$ are calculated. Finally, we pick the minimum of all of these global entropies. Let us assume that $GlobalI(D_{38})$ is the minimum of all $GlobalI(D_i)$ where $20 \leq i \leq 60$. Now, if $GlobalI(D_{38}) = wLocalI(D_{[38,46]})$ then it means that the window [38,46] for Age is the best window as it produces the minimum global entropy. Therefore, we consider $I(D, Age) = wLocalI(D_{[38,46]}) \times log_2(log_2 |D_{[38,46]}|)$. Hence, if the attribute "Age" is chosen as the test attribute for the node, EXPLORE divides the data set into two mutually exclusive partitions (any record belongs to either of the partitions) where in one partition a record has Age = 38, 39, 40, ... or 46 (i.e. the domain of Age is [38,46]) and in the other partition no record has Age = 38, 39, 40 ... or 46.

A decision tree algorithm typically aims to maximize the information gain in every step where it chooses a test attribute for a node. We argue that for a numerical attribute, there can be a pocket or window which produces a segment of the data set having a low entropy and therefore, produces a high information gain. If we split a numerical attribute into two partitions where in one partition there will be all values from bottom to the split point and in another partition the values from the split point to the top (as it is done in traditional approaches) then we may miss the window that produces the maximum information gain. Also note that while calculating $I(D, Age)$ we only consider the segment having the minimum entropy, instead of the both segments and taking the weighted average of their entropies as in Equation 5. We aim to pick a test attribute having the minimum entropy (among all attributes) within the segment defined by the best numerical window of the attribute. Therefore, we do not dilute the minimum entropy of the segment partitioned by the best numerical window of an attribute by taking an weighted average of entropies. The entropy of a numerical attribute $I(D, T)$ is based on a partition only.

Property 2: For categorical attributes, EXPLORE chooses the test attribute of a node based on an attribute value, instead of all values of the attribute.

See5 calculates entropy of a data set, $I(D, T)$ by calculating the weighted average of the entropies for each value of a categorical attribute T (see Equation 2 and Equation 3). We argue that due to the averaging out process we may miss an attribute value which has a very low entropy. For example, let us consider two categorical attributes $A = \{a_1, a_2\}$ and $B = \{b_1, b_2, b_3\}$. Let us denote the entropy of a segment D_{a_1} where all records have $A = a_1$ by $I(D, a_1)$.

Let us assume that $I(D, a_1) = 0.3$, $|D_{a_1}| = 50$, $I(D, a_2) = 0.9$ and $|D_{a_2}| = 50$. Also assume that $I(D, b_1) = I(D, b_2) = I(D, b_3) = 0.5$, $|D_{b_1}| = |D_{b_2}| = 33$ and $|D_{b_3}| = 34$. Using Equation 3 we get $I(D, A) = 0.6$ and $I(D, B) = 0.5$. Therefore, See5 picks B as the test attribute as $I(D, B) < I(D, A)$. Due to the averaging out process we loose the best pattern involving $A = a_1$ that produces the lowest entropy $I(D, a_1) = 0.3$. EXPLORE aims to extract such natural patterns. Therefore, EXPLORE picks attribute A (instead of attribute B) as the test attribute and divides the data set into two partitions regardless of the domain size of A. One partition contains all records having $A = a_1$ and the other partition contains records with $A \neq a_1$. We argue that with this approach EXPLORE increases the information gain in every step. Therefore, we expect to produce shallower trees and extract natural patterns of a data set.

Property 3: It uses Ultimate Gain Ratio (UGR) instead of the Gain Ratio.

The conventional calculation of gain ratio (Equation 7) does not take the size (number of records) of a segment into consideration. We argue that if a segment is much bigger than another segment then it is worthwhile to choose the bigger segment even if it has a slightly lower gain ratio. Choosing a bigger segment we aim to discover a more significant pattern. Therefore, EXPLORE uses a new measure called Ultimate Gain Ratio (UGR) by modifying the equation of gain ratio. For example, let us consider two categorical attributes $A = \{a_1, a_2\}$ and $B = \{b_1, b_2, b_3\}$. If the $GainRatio(D, a_1) = 1.2$, $|D_{a_1}| = 30$, $GainRatio(D, b_1) = 0.95$ and $|D_{b_1}| = 200$ then we argue that due to the bigger segment size it might be worthwhile to choose B (despite its slightly smaller gain ratio) as the test attribute and split the data set into two partitions where in one partition $B = b_1$ and in the other partition $B \neq b_1$. We now explain Ultimate Gain Ratio calculation as follows.

Since EXPLORE chooses a test attribute based on the best value, instead of all values of the attribute, it calculates $Gain(D, T_i)$ instead of $Gain(D, T)$ as follows.

$$Gain(D, T_i) = I(D) - I(D_i). \tag{12}$$

Hence, it calculates the $GainRatio(D, T_i)$ instead of $GainRatio(D, T)$ as follows.

$$GainRatio(D, T_i) = \frac{I(D) - I(D_i)}{Split(D, T)}. \tag{13}$$

The conventional calculation of gain ratio (Equation 13) does not take the size of the segment (partition) into consideration. Therefore, we introduce a new term called Ultimate Gain Ratio (UGR) which is calculated as follows.

$$UGR(D, T_i) = GainRatio(D, T_i) \times log_2(log_2|D_i|). \tag{14}$$

Note that gain ratio is multiplied by $log_2(log_2|D_i|)$ (instead of just $|D_i|$) in order to balance the influence of the size on UGR while taking the size into consideration to favour a pattern with bigger segment size. In order to discover

Table 1. Test on a suitable UGR calculation

Gain Ratio	Size	UGR				
		$sqrt\ |D_i|$	$log_{10}\ |D_i|$	$log_{10}\ (log_{10}|D_i|)$	$log_2\ |D_i|$	$log_2\ (log_2|D_i|)$
1.2	30	6.57	1.77	0.20	5.88	2.75
0.4	200	5.66	0.92	0.14	3.06	1.17
0.5	200	7.07	1.15	0.18	3.82	1.47
0.6	200	-	1.15	0.21	4.58	1.76
0.75	200	-	1.72	-	5.73	2.20
0.80	200	-	1.84	-	6.11	2.34
0.90	200	-	-	-	-	2.64
0.95	200	-	-	-	-	2.78

the best multiplying factor we compare various possible factors such as $|D_i|$, $\sqrt{(|D_i|)}$, $log_{10}|D_i|$, $log_{10}(log_{10}|D_i|)$, $log_2|D_i|$, and $log_2(log_2|D_i|)$ as illustrated in the Table 1. Column 3 to 7 are the various options that could be used to multiply Gain Ratio by for calculating UGR. Column 3 to 7 of Row 3 shows the values of UGR calculated using various multipliers, when Gain Ratio of a partition (segment) is 1.2 and the size (no. of records) of the partition is 30. In the following rows of the table we examine the UGR values for various Gain Ratios of another segment having 200 records. It shows that if we use $\sqrt{(|D_i|)}$ to calculate UGR then the UGR for the segment having Gain Ratio only 0.5 is greater than the UGR of the segment having Gain Ration 1.2, due to size differences between the segments (see Column 3 of Row 3, Row 4 and Row 5). Therefore, we consider that influence of size on UGR calculation is too high if we use $\sqrt{(|D_i|)}$ as a multiplier. We can see from Table 1 that the use of $log_2(log_2|D_i|)$ minimizes the influence of size the most.

Property 4: EXPLORE can use a minimum segment size (number of records in a segment) to ensure statistical significance of the result.

EXPLORE can also use a minimum segment size in order to maintain a statistical significance. If a segment has high UGR but fails to fulfill the user defined size EXPLORE disregards the segment. This property can be optional and a user can choose whether to use the property or not. We note that some existing techniques also use similar property.

Property 5: EXPLORE can use a user defined threshold for Ultimate Gain Ratio as a termination condition.

EXPLORE can use a user defined threshold of UGR as a termination condition of the tree generation process. This will restrict further partitioning at a point if UGR of all of the possible partitions are less than the threshold value. On the other hand, we can also allow a tree to fully grow and then use pruning. Growing and pruning a tree may slow down the process but is often more reliable, since a fully grown tree explores possible partitions more thoroughly [8].

4   Experimental Results

We use a synthetic data set called MCSD having five categorical attributes Country = {USA, Australia, England}, Profession = {Scientist, Academic, Engineer}, Marital Status = {Married, Unmarried, Divorced, Separated}, Status = {Good, Bad} and Car Make = {Toyota, Ford, Holden, Nissan}. The data set also has a numerical attribute Income = [20,150]. The synthetic data set has been created with some predefined rules/patterns (similar to CSD data set [3]). An example of the patterns is that all records having Car = Holden, and Status = Good have Income within the range [90,100]. Another example is that 30% of the total records having Car = Toyota and Status = Good also have the values for the attribute Income within the range [90,100].

We now introduce the properties of MCSD. Each record of the data set has been created as follows.

```
Country of Origin   = A value is generated using the following
                      probability distribution:
40% probability for each of USA and England, 20% probability for Australia;

if (Country of Origin = USA or England){
   Profession = A value is generated using the following
              probability distribution:
   95% probability for Scientist, 3% probability for Academic,
   2% probability for Engineer;
   Car Make = A value is generated using the following
            probability distribution:
   40% probability for each of Toyota and Ford, 20% probability for Nissan;
   if(Country of Origin = USA) {
       if (Car Make = Toyota or Ford) Status = Good;
       else Status = Bad;}
   if(Country of Origin = England){
       if(Car Make = Nissan or Ford) Status = Good;
       else Status = Bad; }
} // end of if (Country of Origin = USA or England)

else if (Country of Origin = Australia){
  Profession = A value is generated using the following
             probability distribution:
  40% probability for Engineer, 30% probability for each of Academic & Scientist;
  if (Profession = Engineer){
     Car Make = A value is generated using the following
              probability distribution.
     50% probability for each of Toyota and Holden;
     Status = Bad; }
  else if (Profession = Scientist or Academic){
     Car Make = A value is generated with 25% probability for
     each of the four possible values (Toyota, Nissan, Ford, Holden);
     if (Profession = Scientist) Status = Bad;
     else Status = Good; }
} // end of else if (Country of Origin = Australia)
```

```
if (Status = Good and Car Make = Toyota){
    30% probability, Income = A random value within [90,100],
    40% probability, Income = A random value within [20,90],
    30% probability, Income = A random value within [100,150]; }

else if (Status = Good and Car Make = Holden){
    Income = a random value within [90,100]; }

else if (Status = Good and Car Make = Ford or Nissan){
    58% probability, Income = A random value within [20,90],
    42% probability, Income = A random value within [100,150]; }

else Income = A random value within[20,150];

if(Status = Bad and Car Make = Ford or Nissan and Country = Australia)
    Marital Status = Married;

else if(Status = Bad){
    Marital Status = A value is generated using the following
                    probability distribution:
    33.33% probability for each of Unmarried, Divorced, and Separated; }

else{
    Marital Status = A value is generated using the following
                    probability distribution:
    25% probability for each of Married, Unmarried, Divorced, and Separated;}
```

We apply EXPLORE on MCSD to classify attribute Car. A user defined threshold of 0.15 for UGR is used as the termination condition as explained in Property 5 of Section 3. We also apply See5 (commercial software), J48, and REPTree decision tree algorithms (available from Weka [7]) on MCSD. The obtained decision trees are carefully examined and compared.

Figure 2 shows the decision tree obtained from MCSD using EXPLORE to classify the attribute Car. The logic rules obtained by EXPLORE have been processed to create the tree. If two consecutive nodes test the same attribute then those two nodes have been merged in the figure for better representation. For example, consider the leaves 5, 6 and 7. The last node tested for these leaves is Marital Status. EXPLORE first divided the data set at this node level into two partitions where in the first partition we had $\{Status = Bad\} \wedge \{Country = Australia\} \wedge \{Profession \neq Engineer\} \wedge \{MaritalStatus = Separated\} \Rightarrow \{Car = Toyota\}$ and in the second partition we had $\{Status = Bad\} \wedge \{Country = Australia\} \wedge \{Profession \neq Engineer\} \wedge \{MaritalStatus \neq Separated\} \Rightarrow Car = \{Toyota, Holden, Ford, Nissan\}$. EXPLORE then further divided the data set of the second partition into two partitions where in one partition Marital Status is equal to Married and in the other partition it is equal to Unmarried or Divorced. Therefore, EXPLORE ends up with two consecutive nodes testing the attribute Marital Status. We have merged these two

66   M.Z. Islam

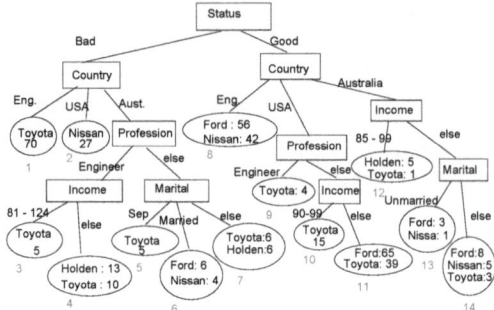

Fig. 2. A decision tree obtained from MCSD using our algorithm

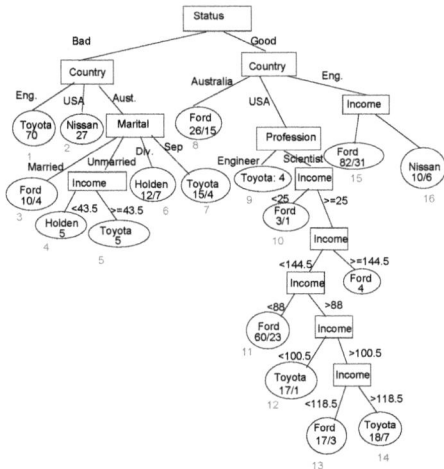

Fig. 3. A decision tree obtained from MCSD using REPTree

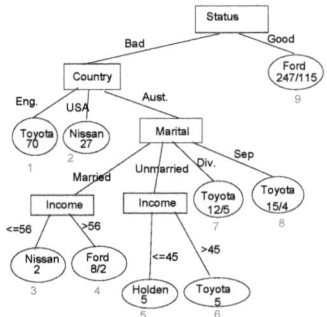

Fig. 4. A decision tree obtained from MCSD using J48

Table 2. Issues and Factors Used in Comparison of Various Algorithms

Issues	Factors
Quality of extracted patterns.	Number of logic rules involving a categorical attribute having only one useful value.
	Number of logic rules with numerical windows (direct)
	Number of logic rules with numerical windows (implied)
Simplicity of the tree	Max Depth
	Average Depth per Leaf
	Total Depth for All Leaves
	Average number of nodes per logic rule having a numerical window.
Performance	Classification Accuracy
Significance of logic rules	Number of leaves having $\geq$ 70 records.
	Number of leaves having $\geq$ 90 records.

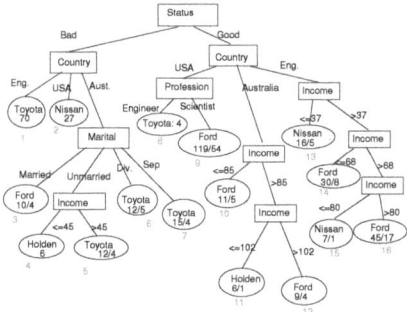

Fig. 5. A decision tree obtained from MCSD using See5

nodes for better representation (see Figure 2). Such merging is of course considered as a part of the EXPLORE algorithm. The decision tree obtained from MCSD using EXPLORE, REPTree, J48 and See5 are shown in Figure 2, 3, 4 and 5.

Our decision tree (Figure 2) shows some advantages over existing trees. It extracts some patterns that are either not extracted by other trees or extracted in a complex form. For example, the pattern extracted in Leaf 3 of our tree (Figure 2) is not extracted by any other trees obtained by the REPTree, J48 or See5 algorithms. In the logic rule for Leaf 3 of our tree a numerical window from 81 to 124 for the attribute Income is used at the last node. No other trees extracted the pattern involving the numerical window for the leaf. Moreover, at the node which is one level above the last node, our tree tests the categorical attribute Profession. Note that out of three possible values (Engineer, Scientist and Academic) of the attribute only the value Engineer helps in better classification by reducing the entropy more than any other values of any attributes. Therefore, EXPLORE picks the pattern involving the value Engineer. However, the pattern

Table 3. Comparison of various decision tree algorithms

Factors	Decision Tree Algorithms			
	EXPLORE Fig. 2	REPTree Fig. 3	J48 Fig. 4	See5 Fig. 5
Number of logic rules involving a cat. attr. having only one useful value.	4 (4) L:3, L:4 L:9, L:13	0 (1)	0 (1)	0 (1)
Number of logic rules with num. windows (direct)	3 (4) L: 3, L: 10, L: 12	0 (1)	0 (1)	0 (1)
Number of logic rules with num. windows (direct or implied)	3 (4) L: 3, L: 10 L: 12	2 (2) L: 12, L: 13	0 (1)	3 (4) L: 11, L: 14 L: 15
Max Depth	4 (4)	8 (1)	4 (4)	5 (2)
Avg. Depth per leaf	3.43 (3)	4.38 (1)	3 (4)	3.43 (3)
Total Depth for all leaves	48 (3)	70 (1)	27 (4)	55 (2)
Avg. number of nodes per logic rules having a num. window	3.67 (4)	7.5 (2)	N/A (1)	4.33 (3)
Classification Accuracy	72% (3)	74% (4)	68% (1)	72% (3)
No. of logic rules having ≥ 70 records.	3 (4) L:1, L: 8 L: 11	2 (3) L: 1, L: 15	2 (3) L: 1 L: 9	2 (3) L: 1 L: 9
No. of logic rules having ≥ 90 records.	2 (4) L:8, L: 11	0 (1)	1 (3) L: 9	0 (1)
Total Score	37	17	23	23

is not extracted by any other trees. EXPLORE extracts another pattern (Leaf 13) of similar type involving a value Unmarried of the attribute Marital Status. This pattern is also not extracted by any other trees.

Another example of advantages of EXPLORE can be the numerical window (90 to 99) of the attribute Income in the logic rule for Leaf 10 (Figure 2). We note that the pattern involving the numerical window (90 to 99) was created through the MCSD data generation process. EXPLORE identifies the pattern very accurately. The tree obtained by EXPLORE requires only 4 nodes (levels) to reach the leaf. However, to extract the same pattern REPTree requires 7 or 8 nodes as shown in Leaf 12 and Leaf 13 of Figure 3. Moreover, REPTree does not extract the pattern directly as EXPLORE does. We can only discover the pattern through a very careful study of the obtained tree. Such a careful study of a tree may not be performed by a user every time. The pattern is not extracted at all by J48 and See5 as shown in Figure 4 and Figure 5. EXPLORE also extracts similar patterns in the logic rules for some other leaves such as Leaf 12 and Leaf 9. These patterns are also either not extracted by other trees or extracted in a complex form as shown in Figure 3, Figure 4 and Figure 5.

In Table 3, we present a quantitative comparison of various decision tree algorithms through the trees obtained from MCSD data set. The algorithms are compared on several issues. The issues are quality of extracted patterns, simplicity of the obtained trees, accuracy and significance of patterns. Each of these issues is then evaluated through a number of factors (see Table 2). For example, quality of extracted patterns of a tree is evaluated through Number of logic rules involving a categorical attribute that has only one useful value for classification, and Number of logic rules involving a numerical window (direct and implied). The simplicity of a tree is evaluated through the Max Depth (the maximum number of nodes used in the logic rule of any single leaf) of a tree, Average Depth per Leaf, Total Depths of All Leaves, and Average Number of Nodes Used per Logic Rule Involving a Numerical Window. The performance of a tree is measured by its Classification Accuracy. In order to explore the significance of logic rules we compare the trees based on the number of leaves having more than or equal to 70 and 90 records (see Table 2).

We now discuss the observations presented in Table 3. The tree obtained by EXPLORE has ten logic rules (for Leaf 3 to 7, Leaf 9 to 11, and Leaf 13 to 14), involving a categorical attribute that has only one useful value for classification (see Figure 2). In this case the attributes are Profession and Marital Status, and their useful values are Engineer and Unmarried, respectively. We can see from the first row of Table 3 that out of the ten logic rules four (for Leaf 3, Leaf 4, Leaf 9 and Leaf 13) directly involve a single value of an attribute. It is also clear from the table that none of the existing trees are capable of extracting any such patterns. Therefore, in a data set if there is a pattern involving only one value of a categorical attribute C, where the value increases the gain ratio for classification better than any other values of any attributes and all other values of C are not good enough for classification purpose then the pattern is generally not extracted by the existing trees, even if it has high confidence and support. However, the experiments presented in this study indicate that unlike existing algorithms EXPLORE can extract such patterns very well. The figures in parentheses in Table 3 are scores of the algorithms based on their performances for the factors. We introduce the figures within parentheses in more detail at the end of this section.

The second row of Table 3 shows that the tree obtained by EXPLORE has three logic rules (for Leaf 3, Leaf 10 and Leaf 12), which directly involve a numerical window. It reveals that patterns involving a numerical window of an attribute can be effectively extracted by EXPLORE. Existing algorithms do not extract any such patterns directly. Often similar patterns can be extracted by existing decision trees indirectly. A user needs to study the trees carefully in order to discover the indirect patterns. It is quite possible that a user will often miss them out. However, EXPLORE extracts and presents them in a very effective way. Moreover, Row 3 shows that EXPLORE performs better than REPTRee and J48 even if we consider indirect pattern extraction. Additionally, by reducing the user defined threshold for UGR to a value lower than 0.15 (that we have used in the experiments for EXPLORE) we can easily extract more of patterns involving numerical windows. For example, the leaves Leaf 13 to Leaf 16 of Figure 5 are extension of Leaf 8 of Figure 2. Leaf 8 of Figure 2 could be further split or extended by choosing a lower UGR threshold. The advantage of EXPLORE is that it picks such patterns directly (without requiring careful study by a user) and quickly involving low number of nodes to reach such a pattern as evident in Row 7 of Table 3. Through a careful observation of Table 3 we argue that EXPLORE performs better than existing trees in extracting good quality patterns (logic rules) in this context. However, we can say that See5, REPTree and J48 come 2nd, 3rd and 4th in terms of good quality pattern extraction.

Careful observation of Row 4 to Row 7 reveals that in terms of simplicity J48 perhaps perform similar to EXPLORE when EXPLORE performs clearly better than REPTree and See5. We can see from Row 8 that EXPLORE performs the second best (along with See5) in terms of classification accuracy. Row 9 and 10 reveal that EXPLORE extracts the largest number of significant sized patterns.

To wrap up the comparison we assign a score to an algorithm for each factor of Table 3. If an algorithm performs the best for a factor then it scores 4 and if it performs the worst then it scores 1. The second and third best performing algorithms score 3 and 2, respectively. If two algorithms perform jointly the best then both of them score 4 but the next best performing algorithm scores 2 (instead of 3) for the factor. For coming up with the worst possible performance an algorithm gets the least possible score which is 1. The score of an algorithm for a factor is presented within brackets in Table 3. For example, EXPLORE scores 4 for the factor presented in Row 1. The last row of the table shows the total score of each algorithm. According to the factors we consider, EXPLORE scores the highest (37) indicating its clear superiority over other three algorithms that score 23, 23 and 17, respectively.

5   Conclusion

In this study we present EXPLORE, a novel classification algorithm which is a modification of See5. The modifications are mainly made in order to improve the capability for extracting some interesting patterns that are generally missed out by existing algorithms. We also present experimental results and quantitative comparison of EXPLORE and a few existing algorithms such as See5, REPTree and J48. The algorithms are compared on several factors in order to evaluate the quality of an extracted pattern, simplicity of an obtained tree, performances of a tree and significance of a logic rule.

Our experimental results indicate advantages of EXPLORE over other existing algorithms in extracting hidden patterns, involving both numerical and categorical attributes, that are often missed out by existing decision tree algorithms. EXPLORE performs the best in extracting those interesting patterns. In terms of simplicity, EXPLORE and J48 appear to be better than See5 and REPTree. EXPLORE performs the second best in terms of classification accuracy. It also extracts the most number of significant sized patterns. In order to draw a conclusion of the comparison, we assign a score to an algorithm for each factor based on its performance and a scoring rule. EXPLORE scores 37 in total while See5, J48 and REPTree score 23, 23 and 17, respectively. Our future research plans include further development of the algorithm and carrying out extensive experiments on several data sets, both natural and synthetic.

References

1. Fukuda, T., Morimoto, Y., Morishita, S., Tokuyama, T.: Data mining using two-dimensional optimized association rules: Scheme, algorithms, and visualisation. ACM SIGMOD 25(2), 13–23 (1996)
2. Han, J., Kamber, M.: Data Mining Concepts and Techniques. Morgan Kaufmann Publishers, San Diego (2001)
3. Islam, M.Z.: Privacy Preservation in Data Mining through Noise Addition. PhD thesis, School of Electrical Engineering and Computer Science, The University of Newcastle, Australia (June 2008)
4. Islam, M.Z., Brankovic, L.: Noise addition for protecting privacy in data mining. In: Proceedings of of the 6th Engineering Mathematics and Applications Conference (EMAC 2003), Sydney, Australia, vol. 2, pp. 85–90 (2003)
5. Kohavi, R.: Scaling up the accuracy of naive-bayes classifiers: a decision-tree hybrid. In: Proceedings of the Second International Conference on Knowledge Discovery and Data Mining (1996)
6. Kohavi, R., Quinlan, R.: Decision tree discovery. In: Handbook of Data Mining and Knowledge Discovery, pp. 267–276. University Press (1999)
7. WEKA:The University of Waikato. Weka 3: Data mining software in java, http://www.cs.waikato.ac.nz/ml/weka/ (visited on 12.08.09)
8. Ross Quinlan, J.: C4.5: Programs for Machine Learning. Morgan Kaufmann Publishers, San Mateo (1993)
9. Ross Quinlan, J.: Improved use of continuous attributes in c4.5. Journal of Artificial Intelligence Research 4, 77–90 (1996)

Comparing the Performance of Object and Object Relational Database Systems on Objects of Varying Complexity

Reza Kalantari* and Christopher H. Bryant

School of Computing, Science and Engineering, Newton Building,
University of Salford, Salford, Greater Manchester, M5 4WT, UK
me@reza-kalantari.com, C.H.Bryant@salford.ac.uk

Abstract. This is the first published work to compare the performance of object and object relational database systems based on the object's complexity. The findings of this research show that the performance of object and object relational database systems are related to the complexity of the object in use. Object relational databases have better performance compared to object databases for fundamental database operations, with the exception of insert operations, on objects with low and medium complexity. For objects with high complexity, the object relational databases have better performance for update and delete operations.

1 Introduction

When object oriented programming languages such as Java, C++ and Smalltalk became popular in the 1980s, application developers found a mismatch between their applications' needs and Relational Database Management Systems (RDBMSs). The mismatch led to the invention of Object Database Management Systems (ODBMSs). In fact, ODBMSs are an extension of object oriented programming into the world of databases and they benefit from using object programming languages. Despite the fact that ODBMSs are very suitable for some specific applications, developers encountered major problems when using them in place of RDBMSs such as a lack of a universal standard, complex query optimization and poor support for large scale business information systems. These drawbacks made developers generate another type of database system, namely Object Relational Database Management Systems (ORDBMSs). The main objective of ORDBMSs was to achieve the benefits of both the relational and the object models and, in fact, ORDBMSs combine the features of RDBMSs with the best ideas of ODBMSs. ORDBMSs store data in tables but the main difference between ORDBMSs and RDBMSs is that ORDBMSs have object-oriented features. The standard programming language for ORDBMSs is OR-SQL which is also known as SQL3. Many well known database vendors such as IBM and Oracle have released the object relational version of their database management systems [2].

---

* To whom correspondence should be addressed.

L.M. MacKinnon (Ed.): BNCOD 2010, LNCS 6121, pp. 72–83, 2012.
© Springer-Verlag Berlin Heidelberg 2012

The success or failure of an application directly depends on the performance of the database system in use. Therefore performance is a vital factor for the selection of database systems in real-time applications. A variety of different ideas about the performance of ODBMSs and ORDBMSs have been published. While [8] states ODBMSs are known to be rich in functionality but poor in performance, [7] believe that the performance of object databases is far better than hybrid ORDBMSs. The contrast between these findings motivated the research described in this paper which determines which one of object and object relational database management systems is better in terms of performance for fundamental database operations such as Insert, Update, Lookup and Delete. This paper presents the results of a fair comparison of the performance of ODBMSs and ORDBMSs by means of an object oriented application and it takes the object's complexity into account.

Section 2 describes related work. In Section 3, we describe the performance criteria for this work and justify why benchmarks are not used. Section 4 presents the environment of the case study, the results of our evaluations and an analysis of the results. In Section 5, we briefly summarize the main contributions of this paper and identify the need for further research in this area.

2   Related Work

Over the last two decades, when ODBMSs were still rather new, there were a variety of studies to assess the performance of this kind of DBMS. For example, [9] compared the performance of various commercial ODBMSs. More recently, [11] compared the performance of ODBMSs and Object Relational Mapping (ORM) tools.

In the study by Van zyl et al. [11], Db4o represents the ODBMS and Hibernate represents the ORM tool. Both of these are popular open source products. Hibernate is an ORM tool that stores and retrieves in-memory objects to and from a RDBMS. Hibernate can be used with any RDBMS but in their research it was used with Postgres for persisting objects. The OO7 benchmark was used to compare the speed of execution of a suite of typical persistent-related operations in both candidates. For good documentation of OO7 benchmark, see [4]. Van zyl et al. [11] decided to use Java objects for their research study because they believed that "most of the large persistence mechanism providers provide persistence for Java objects". As a result of this decision, they had to re-implement OO7 in Java because the OO7 benchmark had been developed in C++ for Versant. Db4o can be run as an embedded DBMS, as a local server in the same virtual machine or as a remote server; for their research Db4o was run as an embedded DBMS. Both of Db4o and Hibernate were to persist the in–memory Java objects generated by the OO7 benchmark. Van zyl et al. [11] concluded that Db4o's overall performance is better than that of Hibernate. They propose that the overhead of object-relational translation causes ORM-based implementations to be consistently slower than staying in object form with an ODBMS. The study by Van zyl et al. [11] is similar to the one described in this paper in the sense that both compare the performance of Db4o with a hybrid database solution, on an artificial dataset. However our study is different to the one by Van zyl et al. [11] because they used OO7 benchmark for performance evaluation while we use an object oriented application.

Hohenstein et al. [9] performed an application-specific comparison of the three best known commercial ODBMSs. The goal of their evaluation was to create a realistic test for ODBMSs, allowing for a fair and precise comparison of performance. The researchers took as their starting point an existing warehouse application running on a relational DBMS. The application was a large software system that maintains automatic warehouses. For simplicity and to reduce the effort, they restricted the application to only one procedure, namely storing materials. The researchers also compared the ODBMSs with the original, real-world relational system; however they believed that this comparison is vague because the times for the RDBMS were measured while concurrent processes may influence locking and elapsed times. In the study by Hohenstein et al. [9] the ODBMSs remain anonymous and they are introduced as ODBMS1, 2 and 3. Each ODBMS has been tuned heavily according to its specific architecture. Their experiments measure the times for the whole application's test rather than for simple database operations. The test consists of placing 860 containers with articles in the warehouse and specific functions such as queries.

Hohenstein et al. [9] concluded that traversals of relationships are much faster in the page server ODBMSs than in related SQL queries. Since ODBMSs do update operations in the primary memory and update in the server and disk is postponed to the commit, this results in slower update operations by ODBMSs compared to RDBMS. The complex search is also very fast in ODBMSs. The study by Hohenstein et al. [9] is similar to our work in that it evaluates the performance of DBMSs by means of a concrete object-oriented application. However they use a real dataset for their experiments while we use an artificial dataset. We justify our use of an artificial dataset in Section 4.2.

3   Performance Measurement

In this work we aim to evaluate and compare the efficiency of Db4o and Informix DBMSs for performing four fundamental database operations: insert, update, look up and delete. The efficiency of these operations in any database system is a vital factor of performance. For measuring performance, we use Response time. Response time measures the performance of an individual transaction or query. Response time is typically treated as the elapsed time from the moment that a query's execution starts until the time that the execution finishes successfully.

One approach used by research studies aiming to evaluate the performance of database systems is benchmarking. A lot of standard benchmarks have been published in the literature. Benchmarks are general applications that reduce the effort required to implement and perform performance tests. For example, the OO1 benchmark [6] models a graph of interconnected nodes in which each node is related with three other nodes [5]. Other benchmarks such as HyperModel [1] and OO7 [3] model more complex schemas; they take into account inheritance hierarchies and various forms of relationships between nodes. Nevertheless, these benchmarks are compact, general and do not meet the requirements of all performance tests. In reality, applications interface database systems and use them to store and retrieve data. Also applications perform access and make additional demands of DBMSs that standard benchmarks do not cover at all; therefore performance of database systems should be evaluated by means of applications. In addition, a benchmark that meets the requirements of our research could not be found.

4   Case Study

4.1   Database Products for This Case Study

Db4o[1] is an open source pure ODBMS that enables Java and .NET developers to store and retrieve any application object; eliminating the need to predefine or maintain a separate, rigid data model. Db4o's programming can be integrated in the application code; therefore database access is largely transparent, which is one of the main objectives of ODBMSs [10]. *Informix Dynamic Server*[2] is a well-known commercial ORDBMS that completely supports the object relational specifications. Informix provides an application programming interface for C, C++, Java and .NET.

4.2   Dataset

Datasets have an important role in experimental studies which evaluate the performance of databases. Data is the core of a database system and it affects the database's performance. This means that a performance test on a specific database system with two different datasets may result in different conclusions. One of the common approaches in experimental studies is to use a dataset which is already in the public domain. For this work an online dataset that fits in the designed database could not be found. The other common approach is to create an artificial dataset by randomly generating data of the required form. This is the approach we use. Objects are populated with random data when they are instantiated.

4.3   Object Oriented Database Schema

This section describes the design of the object oriented database schema used in the experiments. Since the aim of the research is to compare the performance of two database systems which are both object oriented, three objects of varying complexity were designed. Project, Staff and Department objects represent objects with low, medium and high complexity respectively. As Fig. 1 shows, Project, Staff and Department objects consist of different attributes. For simplicity the objects have no

---

[1] Db4o 6.4 .Net 2.0.
[2] Informix Dynamic Server v11.50.

method. Project object is an object with low complexity because its attributes are of basic data types such as String, Integer and Date that have low complexity from database management point of view. The Staff object is more complex. It includes the Project attribute that is an ordered list of the projects that the employee took part in. Each of the elements in this list is a Project object. Also it includes the address attribute which is a user defined data type. Address consists of four attributes of type String which hold the employee's address.

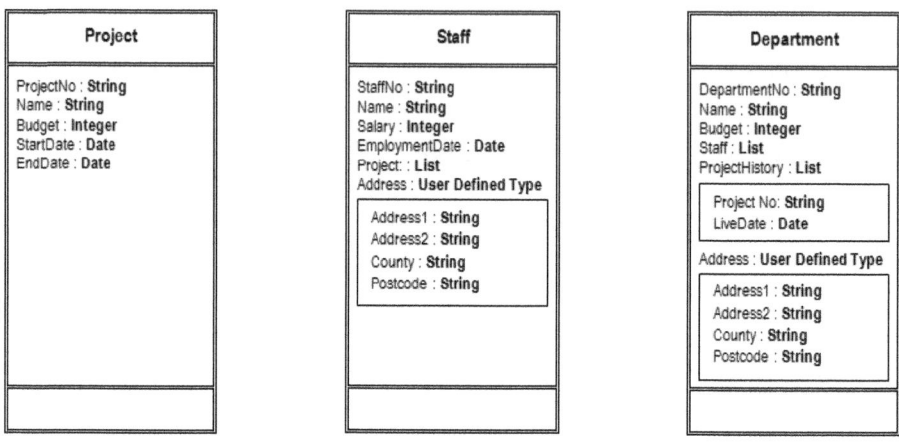

Fig. 1. The schema of Project, Staff and Department objects

The Department object includes the Staff attribute which is an ordered list of Staff who work for the department. Each element in this list is a Staff object. Another attribute of Department object is the ProjectHistory. This attribute is an ordered list of a user defined data type that holds the previous projects and their live date. The Department object also includes the Address attribute which is a user defined data type that holds the Department's address. Therefore, Department object is considered as an object with high complexity.

4.4   Object Oriented Test Application

The Object Oriented Test Application (OOTA) is a .NET object oriented application that has been developed to perform the performance tests against both Db4o and Informix DBMSs. OOTA implements the Project, Staff and Department objects which represent the objects with low, medium and high complexity respectively. OOTA also implements four test functions for each object to perform the performance tests against the database systems for the object. Each test function performs a specific performance test against the DBMSs.

4.5   Methodology

To perform the empirical experiments, the object oriented database schema has been implemented with both Db4o and Informix DBMSs. OOTA was developed to interface both Db4o and Informix DBMSs and performs the performance tests against them. OOTA performs the performance tests through test functions. OOTA obtains the response time by measuring the time before the functions' call and after the functions' execution. All experiments have been repeated five times and the mean of response times is reported in the results. The standard deviation was less than 3% in every experiment.

In all empirical experiments, the performance of both Db4o and Informix databases has been evaluated for six different quantities of objects. The six different quantities are 1000, 5000, 10000, 20000, 50000 and 100000. These quantities represent a variety of small to large databases. For each experiment, each test function has been called six times against both Db4o and Informix DBMSs for the six different quantities of each object. The experiments allow a fair comparison of Db4o and Informix DBMSs because:-

- The same hardware and operating system was used in all the experiments.
- The same database model (i.e., the same objects) has been implemented with both Db4o and Informix.
- The same performance test application, (i.e., the OOTA) is used to perform the tests against both Db4o and Informix.
- The same performance tests have been performed against both Db4o and Informix.
- The mechanism for creating new objects within OOTA is the same for both Db4o and Informix.
- The object's data that OOTA generates in the object construction process is completely random and the mechanism is the same for both Db4o and Informix.
- The most optimized function's code has been developed within OOTA for both Db4o and Informix DBMSs according to the database vendors' release notes and tutorials.
- The interface creation time for Db4o and the connection time for Informix have been excluded from the response time.

4.6   Object Insertion

The aim of this experiment is to determine whether Informix or Db4o has a better performance for the insert operation. The response times for insert operations in this experiment includes the object's creation time. The results of the Object Insertion experiment for inserting different quantities of objects with low, medium and high complexity into both of Db4o and Informix DBMSs are shown in Fig. 2.

As Fig. 2 shows, for objects with low complexity, although both database systems' response times are very close until 5,000 objects, Db4o performed the insert operations in less time compared to Informix throughout the experiment. The more objects in the insert operation, the bigger the difference between their response times. Another point is that Informix has the same performance during the experiment but Db4o's performance is slightly variable and is best when inserting 5000 to 10000 objects.

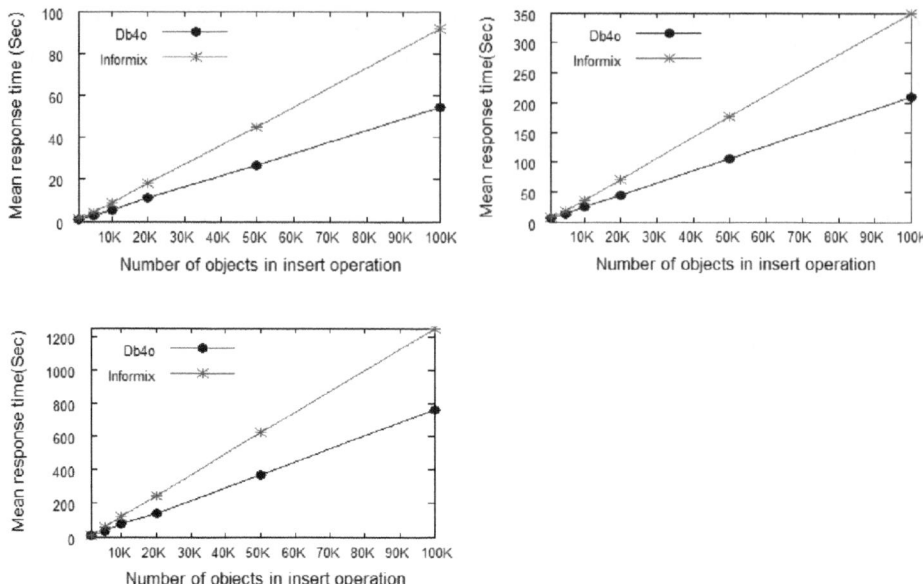

Fig. 2. Results of inserting objects with low (top left), medium (top right) and high (bottom left) complexity

According to results for object with medium complexity, Db4o's performance is better throughout the experiment. The performance of Informix is nearly the same as Db4o for inserting less than 5000 objects but after this point the Informix's performance decreases. Db4o has a constant performance for inserting more than 10000 objects. Surprisingly, Informix's performance is not the same during the experiment for all the number of objects; it performed better for quantities between 1,000 and 5,000.

Db4o has inserted the high complexity object in less time than Informix for every quantity. Similar to the medium complexity experiment, Db4o's performance is constant for inserting more than 10,000 objects. The Informix's performance is worse than that of Db4o and it is constant throughout the experiment.

4.7   Object Modification

The aim of this experiment is to determine whether Informix or Db4o has a better performance for the update operation. In each update operation one object is modified. The results of the Object Modification experiment for updating objects with low, medium and high complexity with both Db4o and Informix DBMSs while they hold different quantities of these objects are shown in Fig. 3.

According to Fig. 3, the performance of Informix is far better than that of Db4o for updating objects with low complexity. With the exception of 5000 to 10000 objects, the response times of both Db4o and Informix increase as the number of objects in the databases increases. Informix's performance is more consistent compared to Db4o during the experiment.

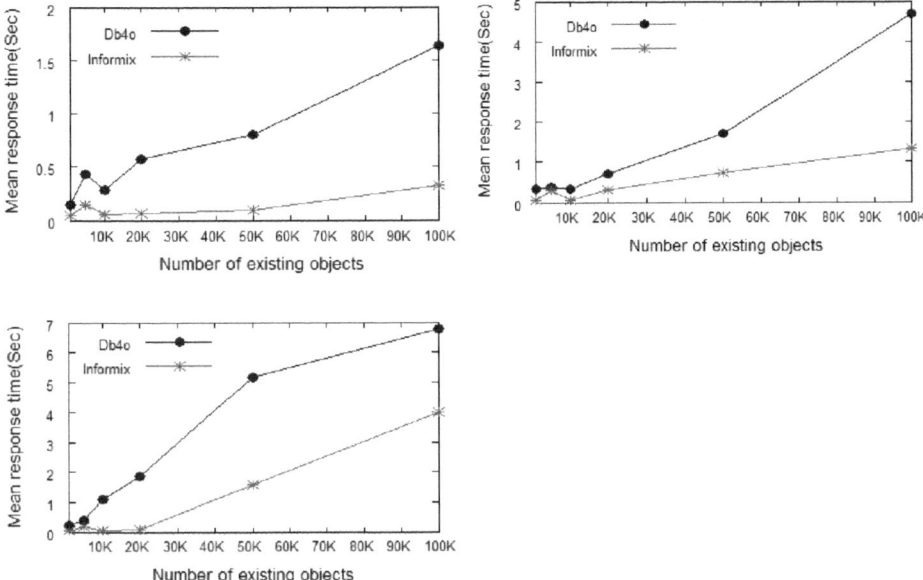

Fig. 3. Results of updating objects with low (top left), medium (top right) and high (bottom left) complexity

As Fig. 3 shows, Informix's response time is less than that of Db4o for updating objects with medium complexity. Informix has a better performance while less than 5,000 objects exist. The two DBMSs have nearly the same performance while 5,000 objects exist but, after this point, again the Informix has a better performance. Informix's performance is consistent while more than 20,000 objects exist. After 50,000 objects, the difference between their performances becomes considerable.

The results for objects with high complexity shows that Informix performs the update operation faster than Db4o because the response time of Informix is less than Db4o's throughout the experiment. The response times are very close while less than 5,000 objects exist in the databases. After this point, the difference between their performances becomes considerable.

4.8 Object Lookup

The aim of this experiment is to determine whether Informix or Db4o has a better performance for the lookup operation. In this experiment just one project object was looked up as a result of the look up query. For Staff and Department objects when different quantities of these objects exist in the database, different number of these objects were looked up but the number of returned objects for Db4o and Informix is nearly the same. The results of the Object Lookup experiment for objects with low, medium and high complexity with both Db4o and Informix DBMSs while they hold different quantities of these objects are shown in Fig. 4.

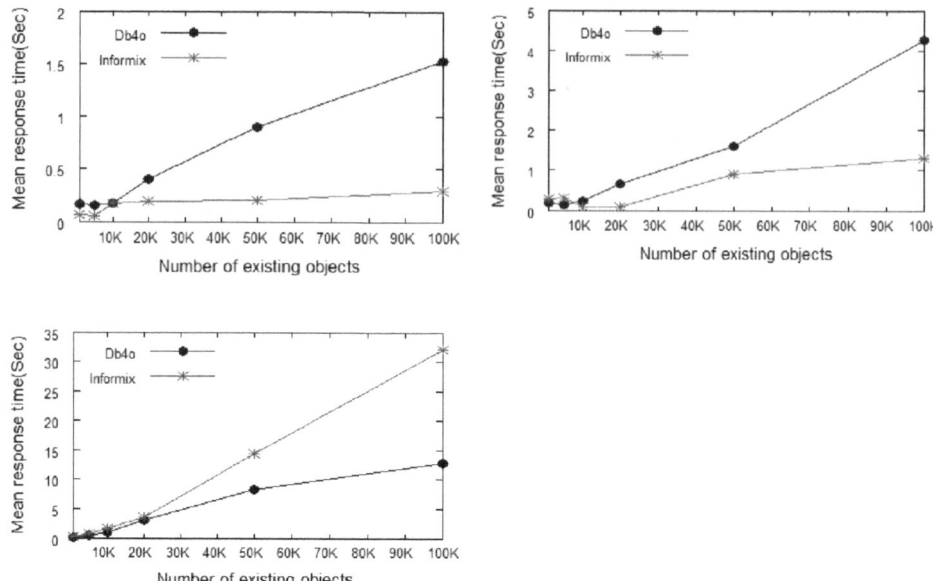

Fig. 4. Results of looking up objects with low (top left), medium (top right) and high (bottom left) complexity

As the results for object with low complexity show, the response time of Informix is less than that of Db4o while less than 10,000 objects exist in the DBMSs. The two DBMSs have the same performance at 10,000. For the rest of the experiment, increasing the number of objects increases Db4o's response time significantly. As Fig. 4 shows, the Informix's performance is more consistent than that of Db4o in looking up object with low complexity.

The results for object with medium complexity show that Db4o's response time is less than that of Informix while less than 8,000 objects exist in the databases. As the number of objects increases, Db4o's response time increases. After 8,000 objects Db4o's performance is worse than Informix's. Informix's performance is the best while between 10,000 and 20,000 objects exist. The results show that the performance of Informix is better than Db4o for looking up object with medium complexity.

As Fig. 4 shows, Db4o's response times are less than those of Informix for looking up objects with high complexity. There is only a tiny difference between the response times of the two DBMSs while less than 20,000 objects exist. For the rest of experiment, as the number of objects increases, the performance of Db4o becomes better compared to Informix. Overall, the results show that the Db4o is better than Informix for looking up object with high complexity.

4.9   Object Deletion

The aim of this experiment is to determine whether Informix or Db4o has a better performance for the delete operation. In this experiment one project object has been deleted as result of delete operation. For Staff and Department objects when different quantities of these objects exist in the database, different number of objects has been deleted but the number of deleted objects for Db4o and Informix is nearly the same. The results of the Object Deletion experiment for objects with low, medium and high complexity with both Db4o and Informix DBMSs while they hold different quantities of these objects are shown in Fig. 5.

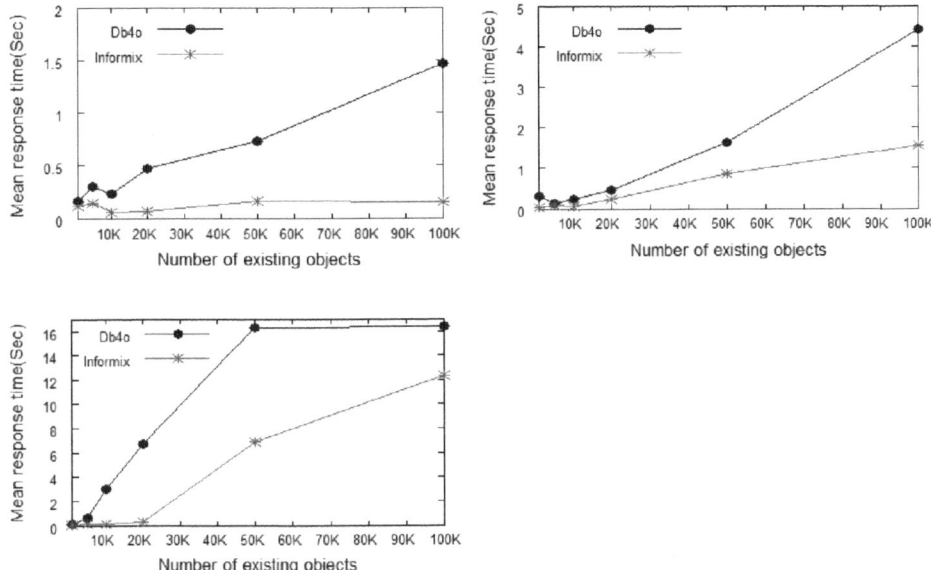

Fig. 5. Results of deleting objects with low (top left), medium (top right) and high (bottom left) complexity

As Fig. 5 shows, Informix's response time for deleting an object with low complexity is less than that of Db4o. Both DBMSs have similar response times up to 10,000 objects. After this point, the difference in their performance increases as the number of objects increases. Informix's performance is more constant compared to Db4o's for delete operation on objects with low complexity.

The results for medium complexity (see Fig. 5 top right) show that the performance of Informix is better than that of Db4o. Db4o's response time for deleting an object while 5,000 objects exist is less than when 1,000 objects exist. Db4o's response time starts increasing when more than 5,000 objects exist but the corresponding number of objects for Informix is 10,000.

As Fig. 5 shows, throughout the experiment, Informix's response time is less than that of Db4o for deleting objects with high complexity. Informix's response time is very low while less than 20,000 objects exist but after this point its response time increases considerably. Although Db4o's response time is low while less than 5,000 objects exist, its response time increases after this point until 50,000 objects; after which point its response time remains the same for the rest of the experiment.

The results of all empirical experiments are summarized in Table 1. For each experiment it shows which DBMS is better in terms of performance according to the complexity of object. For example, it shows that Db4o has better performance for inserting objects with low complexity; Informix is better in terms of performance for updating objects with medium complexity and so on.

Table 1. Summary of the empirical experiments' results

Empirical experiment	Object complexity		
	Low	Medium	High
Object Insertion	Db4o	Db4o	Db4o
Object Modification	Informix	Informix	Informix
Object lookup	Informix	Informix	Db4o
Object Deletion	Informix	Informix	Informix

According to Table 1, Informix has better performance for modifying, looking up and deleting objects with low complexity. Db4o is just better than Informix in terms of performance for inserting this kind of object. The results for fundamental database operations on objects with medium complexity are the same as objects with low complexity. For objects with high complexity, the results are different; Db4o has a better performance than that of Informix for inserting and looking up objects with high complexity while Informix has a better performance for modifying and deleting this kind of objects.

5   Conclusions and Future Work

The findings from this work suggest that the complexity of the object in use affects the performance of object and object relational DBMSs. The performance of the object relational DBMS is better than the object DBMS for fundamental database operations with the exception of insert operations for objects with low and medium complexity. Increasing the level of object's complexity affects the performance of object relational DBMS. For objects with high complexity, in addition to insert operation, the object DBMS has better performance for the look up operation compared to the object relational DBMS.

The findings suggest that system developers should consider the following factors when selecting a DBMS for persisting objects: 1) The complexity of the object in use; 2) The database operations that the system will perform most frequently. For example, if a system uses objects that are mainly highly complex and it performs a lot of look up operations then this research suggests that an ODBMS is more efficient than ORDBMS as a mechanism for persisting objects.

Due to limited time, this work focused on the performance of object and object relational DBMSs for fundamental database operations such as Insert, Update, look up and Delete. The following could be the subject to further studies.

First of all, the performance analysis of ODBMSs and ORDBMSs for fundamental database operations on objects that have behaviour (methods). In reality objects have behaviour and adding methods to objects may impact the performance of DBMSs. Also the performance analysis on Binary Large OBjects (BLOBs) and Character Large OBjects (CLOBs) could be evaluated and compared for these two database technologies. With the rise in popularity of image, audio and multimedia databases, further research is required to determine which one of ODBMSs and ORDBMSs have better performance for database operations on these kinds of objects.

Secondly, in addition to the fundamental database operations, the performance of object and object relational DBMSs for complex queries involving two or more objects could be evaluated and compared. Today's systems are more complex than before and further research is required to determine which one of ODBMSs and ORDBMSs have better performance for complex queries.

Finally, other object and object relational database systems could be taken into account in the comparison. Evaluating the performance of other database products, would make the results more precise and realistic.

References

1. Anderson, T.L., Berre, A.J., Mallison, M., Porter, H.H., Schneider, B.: The HyperModel Benchmark. In: Bancilhon, F., Zhang, J., Thanos, C. (eds.) EDBT 1990. LNCS, vol. 416, pp. 317–331. Springer, Heidelberg (1990)
2. Brown, P.: Introduction to Object-Relational Database Development. Prentice Hall, USA (2001)
3. Carey, D.J., DeWitt, D., Naughton, J.F.: The OO7 Benchmark. In: Proceeding of the ACM SIGMOD Int. Conf. on Management of Data, Washington DC, pp. 12–21 (1993)
4. Carey, M.J., Dewitt, D.J., Naughton, J.F.: The OO7 Benchmark. CS Tech Report, University of Wisconsin-Madison (April 1993b)
5. Carey, M.J., Dewitt, D.J., Naughton, J.F.: A Status Report on the OO7 OODBMS Benchmarking Effort. In: Proceedings of the Ninth Annual Conf. on Object-Oriented Programming Systems, Language, and Applications, pp. 414–426. ACM Press, New York (1994)
6. Cattell, R.G.G., Skeen, J.: Object Operations Benchmark. ACM Transactions on Database Systems 17(1), 1–31 (1992)
7. Chaudhri, A.B., McCann, J.A., Osmon, P.: A Performance Study of Object Database Management Systems. Theory and Practice of Object Systems 5(4), 263–279 (1999)
8. Gorla, N.: An Object-Oriented Database Design for Improved Performance. Journal of Data & Knowledge Engineering 37, 117–138 (2001)
9. Hohenstein, U., Volkmar, P., Rainer, H.: Evaluating the Performance of Object-Oriented Database Systems by Means of a Concrete Application. Theory and Practice of Object Systems 5(4), 249–261 (1999)
10. Ritchie, C. (ed.): Database Principles and Design. Cengage Learning EMEA, London (2008)
11. Van Zyl, P., Kourie, D.G., Boake, A.: Comparing the Performance of Object Databases and ORM tools. In: Proceeding of South African Institute for Computer Scientists and Information Technologists, pp. 1–11 (2006)

An Efficient Approach to Mine Rare Association Rules Using Maximum Items' Support Constraints

R. Uday Kiran and Polepalli Krishna Reddy

Center for Data Engineering,
International Institute of Information Technology-Hyderabad,
Hyderabad, Andhra Pradesh, India - 500032
uday_rage@research.iiit.ac.in, pkreddy@iiit.ac.in

Abstract. Rare association rule is an association rule consisting of rare items. It is difficult to mine rare association rules with a single minimum support (*minsup*) constraint because low *minsup* can result in generating too many rules (or frequent patterns) in which some of them are uninteresting. In the literature, "maximum constraint model," which uses multiple *minsup* constraints has been proposed and extended to Apriori approach for mining frequent patterns. Even though this model is efficient, the Apriori-like approach raises performance problems. With this motivation, we propose an FP-growth-like approach for this model. This FP-growth-like approach utilizes the prior knowledge provided by the user at the time of input and discovers frequent patterns with a single scan on the transactional dataset. Experimental results on both synthetic and real-world datasets show that the proposed approach is efficient.

Keywords: rare association rules, frequent patterns, multiple minimum supports, maximum items' support constraints.

1 Introduction

Association rules are an important class of regularities that exist in a dataset. Since the introduction of association rules in [1], mining the association rules has been extensively studied in the literature [2, 3]. The basic model of association rules is as follows:

Let $I = \{i_1, i_2, ..., i_n\}$ be a set of items. Let $T = \{t_1, t_2 \cdots, t_m\}$ be a set of transactions (dataset), where each transaction t_j, $1 \leq j \leq m$, is a set of items such that $t_j \subseteq I$. The size of T is m. A pattern (or an itemset) $X = \{i_1, i_2, \cdots, i_k\}$, $1 \leq k \leq n$, is a set of items such that $X \subseteq I$. Pattern containing k number of items is called as k-pattern and the level of this pattern is k. The support of X, $S(X) = \frac{f(X)}{m}$, where $f(X)$ is the frequency of pattern X in T. An association rule is an implication of the form, $A \Rightarrow B$, where $A \subset I, B \subset I$ and $A \cap B = \emptyset$. The confidence of a rule $A \Rightarrow B$, $C(A \Rightarrow B) = \frac{S(A \cup B)}{S(A)}$. A rule $A \Rightarrow B$ is **strong** if its support and confidence are greater than or equal to user-specified minimum support (*minsup*) and minimum confidence (*minconf*) respectively. Pattern $A \cup B$ (or $\{A, B\}$) is a frequent pattern if $S(A, B) \geq minsup$.

Example 1. Let our running example be the transaction dataset shown in Figure 1(a). The set of items, I = {Bread, Jam, Ball, Bat, Bed, Pillow, Pen}. The dataset contains

L.M. MacKinnon (Ed.): BNCOD 2010, LNCS 6121, pp. 84–95, 2012.

10 transactions, therefore, $m = 10$. The set of items {Bread, Jam} is a pattern. It occurs in four transactions. Hence, its support i.e., $S(Bread, Jam) = \frac{f(Bread, Jam)}{m} = \frac{4}{10} = 0.4$ (in support count it is 4). An association rule from this pattern, say $Jam \Rightarrow Bread$, will have $confidence$ i.e., $C(Jam \Rightarrow Bread) = \frac{S(Bread, Jam)}{S(Jam)} = \frac{0.4}{0.4} = 1$. If $minsup = 0.4$ and $minconf = 0.75$, the pattern {Bread, Jam} is a frequent pattern and the rule $Jam \Rightarrow Bread$ is a strong rule. Throughout this paper, we discuss examples in support counts.

Tid	Items
1	Bread, Jam
2	Bread, Ball, Pen, Bat
3	Ball, Bed, Pillow
4	Bread, Jam
5	Ball, Bed, Pillow
6	Bread, Ball, Bat
7	Bread, Jam
8	Ball, Bat
9	Bread, Jam
10	Ball, Bat

(a)

Pattern	F	I	II
Bread	6	Y	Y
Ball	6	Y	Y
Jam	4	Y	Y
Bat	4	Y	Y
Pillow	2	Y	Y
Bed	2	Y	Y
Bread, Jam	4	Y	Y
Bread, Ball	2	Y	N
Bread, Bat	2	Y	N
Ball, Bat	4	Y	Y

Pattern	F	I	II
Ball, Pillow	2	Y	N
Ball, Bed	2	Y	N
Bed, Pillow	2	Y	Y
Bread, Ball, Bat	2	Y	N
Ball, Bed, Pillow	2	Y	N

(b)

Fig. 1. Running Example. (a) Transactional dataset and (b) Patterns having support count (or support) greater than or equal to 2. The column titled 'F' represents the support count (frequency) of the pattern. The columns titled I and II corresponds to frequent patterns generated in "single *minsup* framework" and *maximum constraint model*. The terms 'Y' and 'N' in these columns correspond to frequent patterns generated and have not generated in the respective approaches.

Minsup corresponds to minimal number of transactions in which a pattern should appear in a transaction dataset. Using only a single *minsup* to discover frequent patterns, frequent pattern mining techniques like Apriori [1] and FP-growth [4] implicitly assume that all items within a dataset have uniform or similar frequencies. This is seldom not the case in most of the real-world applications. In many applications, some items appear frequently in the data, while others appear relatively infrequent or rare. In such datasets, using a single *minsup* constraint to mine frequent patterns consisting of both frequent and rare items raises the dilemma, called *rare item problem* [5]. This problem is as follows.

1. If *minsup* is set very high, we miss the frequent patterns consisting of rare items because rare items fail to satisfy high *minsup*.
2. In order to find frequent patterns consisting of both frequent and rare items, *minsup* should be set very low. However, this may cause combinatorial explosion, producing too many frequent patterns, because those frequent items will be associated with one another in all possible ways and many of them are meaningless or uninteresting to the user.

Example 2. For mining frequent patterns, let us consider the transactional dataset shown in Figure 1(a). At high *minsup*, say *minsup* = 4, we miss the frequent patterns consisting of the rare items i.e., Bed and Pillow. To generate frequent patterns consisting of these rare items, let us specify low *minsup*, say *minsup* = 2. The frequent patterns discovered at this *minsup* are shown in the third column of Figure 1(b). It can be observed that along with the interesting patterns, uninteresting patterns {Bread, Ball}, {Bread, Bat}, {Ball, Pillow}, {Ball, Bed}, {Bread, Ball, Bat} and {Ball, Bed, Pillow} have also generated as frequent patterns. The patterns {Bread, Ball}, {Bread, Bat} and {Bread, Ball, Bat} are uninteresting because they consist of frequent items (Bread, Ball and Bat) occurring together in very less number of transactions. The patterns {Ball, Pillow}, {Ball, Bed} and {Ball, Bed, Pillow} are also uninteresting because they contain highly frequent item (Ball) occurring along with rare items (Bed and Pillow) in very less number of transactions.

To address the "rare item problem," efforts have been made in the literature to find frequent patterns using "multiple minimum support framework" [5, 7–13]. In this framework, different models have been proposed to satisfy various user and application requirements. *Maximum constraint model* [7] is one among them. In this model, each item is specified with a support constraint, called *minimum item support (MIS)*. Next, *minsup* of a pattern is represented with the maximal *MIS* value among all its items. Thus, each pattern can satisfy a different *minsup* depending upon the items within it. For this model, an Apriori-like approach based on granular computation of bit strings was proposed for mining frequent patterns. Describing granular computation technique is beyond the scope of this paper. More information on granular computation technique is available in [6].

Example 3. Continuing with Example 2, let *MIS* values for the items Bread, Ball, Pen, Jam, Bat, Pillow and Bed be 4, 4, 3, 3, 3, 2 and 2 respectively. The frequent patterns discovered by using *maximum constraint model* are shown in the fourth column of Figure 1(b). It can be observed that the uninteresting frequent patterns which have generated at *minsup* = 2 in Example 2 have been pruned in this model as they have failed to satisfy their respective *minsups*.

The *maximum constraint model* can efficiently find rare association rules. However, due to the Apriori-like approach, mining frequent patterns using this model raises performance problems. They are generating huge number of candidate patterns and multiple scans on a transactional dataset.

In this paper, we propose an FP-growth-like approach for mining frequent patterns using *maximum constraint model*. We call the proposed approach as Maximum Constraint based Conditional Frequent Pattern-growth (MCCFP-growth). The proposed MCCFP-growth utilizes the prior knowledge (items' *MIS* values) provided by the user at the time of input and discovers frequent patterns with a single scan on the transactional database. Experimental results show that the proposed approach is efficient.

The rest of the paper is organized as follows. Section 2 summarizes the efforts made to discover rare association rules (or frequent patterns) in transactional datasets. In Section 3, we present the proposed approach for mining rare association rules. Experimental results are presented in Section 4. Section 5 concludes with future research directions.

2   Related Work

It is difficult to mine rare association rules because single *minsup* based frequent pattern mining approaches like Apriori [1] and FP-growth [4] suffer from "rare item problem." That is, at high *minsup*, the frequent patterns consisting of rare items will be missed, and at low *minsup*, the number of frequent patterns explode. In the literature, efforts are being made to discover frequent patterns using "multiple *minsup* framework" [5, 7–13]. In this framework, different models have been proposed to satisfy various user and application requirements. Broadly, they are: (*i*) *minimum constraint model* [5, 8, 10, 11] (*ii*) *maximum constraint model* [7] and (*iii*) other models [9, 13].

2.1   Minimum Constraint Model

This model was proposed in [5]. In this model, each item is specified with a support constraint, called *minimum item support* (*MIS*). Next, *minsup* of a pattern is represented with the minimal *MIS* value among all its items. Thus, each pattern can satisfy a different *minsup* value depending upon the items within it.

The frequent patterns mined using this framework do not satisfy *downward closure property*, instead they satisfy *sorted closure property* [5]. According to *sorted closure property*, "all non-empty subsets of a frequent pattern need not be frequent, only the subsets consisting of the item having lowest *MIS* value within it should be frequent." Hence, independent to the detailed implementation technique, Apriori-like [5, 10] or FP-growth-like [8, 11, 12] approaches which are based on this model have to consider both frequent and infrequent patterns for generating further or higher order frequent patterns. The *sorted closure property* was elaborately discussed in [5].

2.2   Maximum Constraint Model

In the *minimum constraint model*, for a pattern to be frequent, it must satisfy only the lowest *MIS* value among all its items. Hence, a pattern can be frequent even though it fails to satisfy the *MIS* values of all other items within it. But, in certain scenarios, when a user specifies *MIS* value for an item, it can mean that any pattern involving the respective item should not have support less than its *MIS* value to be interesting.

Example 4. In the transactional dataset shown in Figure 1(a), if the user specifies *MIS* value for Bread as 4, it can mean that any pattern involving the item Bread to be interesting, it should have support greater than or equal to than 4.

With this motivation, another model, called *maximum constraint model* has been proposed in [7]. In this model, given the items' *MIS* values, a pattern is frequent if it satisfies the *MIS* values of all the items within it. In other words, a pattern is frequent, if it satisfies the maximal *MIS* value among all its items.

This model also efficiently prunes the uninteresting patterns while mining rare association rules. But, the issue is that there exists only an Apriori-like approach for this model. Hence, mining frequent patterns using this model leads to performance problems. Also, we cannot extend the existing *minimum constraint model* based FP-growth-like approaches to *maximum constraint model* because frequent patterns mined using this model follow *downward closure property*.

With this motivation, we propose an FP-growth-like (or pattern-growth) approach that uses this model for finding frequent patterns.

2.3 Other Models

An approach has been suggested to mine association rules by considering only infrequent items i.e., items having support less than the *minsup* [9]. However, this approach fails to discover associations between frequent and rare items.

In [13], an Apriori-like approach which tries to use a different *minsup* at each level of iteration has been discussed. This model still suffers from "rare item problem" because it uses a single *minsup* constraint at each iteration. In addition, this approach being an Apriori-like approach suffers from the performance problems like generating huge number of candidate patterns and multiple scans on the dataset.

In the next section, we present the proposed FP-growth-like approach which uses *maximum constraint model* for finding frequent patterns.

3   Maximum Constraint Based Conditional Frequent Pattern-Growth (MCCFP-Growth)

The MCCFP-growth accepts transactional dataset *Tran* and items' *MIS* values as input parameters. Using the items' *MIS* values as prior knowledge, the MCCFP-growth approach discovers frequent patterns with a single scan on the transactional dataset. The MCCFP-growth involves three steps. They are: (*i*) Construction of a tree, called *MIS*-tree with every item in the transactional dataset (*ii*) Deriving *compact MIS-tree* by pruning out those items from the *MIS*-tree that cannot generate any frequent pattern and (*iii*) Mining the *compact MIS-tree* using *conditional pattern bases* to discover complete set of frequent patterns.

Structure of *MIS*-tree: The *MIS*-tree consists of two components: *MIS*-list and prefix-tree. The *MIS*-list is a list having three fields - item name (*item*), frequency (*S*) and minimum item support (*MIS*). The structure of the prefix-tree in *MIS*-tree is same as that in FP-tree [4]. However, the difference is that items in the prefix-tree of FP-tree are arranged in sorted descending order of their support values, whereas items in the prefix-tree of *MIS*-tree are arranged in sorted descending order of their *MIS* values. To facilitate tree-traversal, node-links are maintained in the *MIS*-tree as in FP-tree.

Using the transactional dataset shown in Figure 1(a), we illustrate the mining of frequent patterns in the proposed approach. Let *MIS* values for the items Bread, Ball, Pen, Jam, Bat, Pillow and Bed be 4, 4, 3, 3, 3, 2 and 2 respectively.

Construction of *MIS*-tree: Given the items' *MIS* values, sort the items in descending order of their *MIS* values. Let this sorted list of items be *L*. Thus, $L = \{Bread, Ball, Pen, Jam, Bat, Pillow, Bed\}$. In *L* order, insert each item into the *MIS*-list with $f = 0$ and *MIS* equivalent to their respective *MIS* value. In the prefix-tree, create a root node and label it as "null". The *MIS*-tree created before scanning the transactional dataset is shown in Figure 2(a).

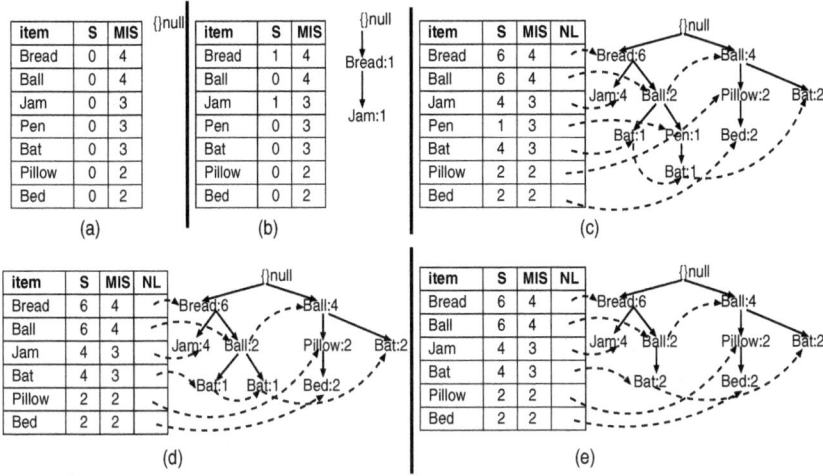

Fig. 2. Construction of compact *MIS*-tree. (a) *MIS*-tree before scanning the transactional dataset (b) *MIS*-tree after scanning first transaction (c) *MIS*-tree after scanning every transaction (d) *MIS*-tree after pruning item 'Pen' (e) compact *MIS*-tree derived after tree-merging operation.

Next, the first transaction "1 : *Bread,Jam*" containing two items in the transactional dataset is scanned in *L* order i.e., {*Bread,Jam*}, and their frequencies are updated by 1 in the *MIS*-list. For this transaction, in *L* order, a branch is created in the prefix-tree as in FP-growth. The updated *MIS*-tree after scanning first transaction is shown in Figure 2(b). Similarly, every transaction is scanned and *MIS*-tree is updated. The updated *MIS*-tree after scanning every transaction is shown in Figure 2(c). For tree traversal, node-links are maintained as in FP-tree. The algorithm for constructing the *MIS*-tree is show in Algorithm 1.

Deriving *Compact MIS-tree*: The *MIS*-tree is constructed with every item in the transactional dataset. Due to *downward closure property*, items which have support less than their respective *MIS* values cannot generate any frequent pattern (apriori property [1]). Therefore, such items can be pruned from the *MIS*-tree so that it is compact.

In the constructed *MIS*-tree, the item Pen has frequency less than it's respective *MIS* value. So this item is removed from the *MIS*-list. Also all nodes of item Pen are removed from the prefix-tree by connecting the child nodes of a pruned node to its parent node. As there exists no other item in the *MIS*-list which has frequency less than its *MIS* value, the pruning operation ends. The resultant *MIS*-tree after pruning item Pen is shown in Figure 2(d).

After tree-pruning operation, it can be observed in the resultant *MIS*-tree that a node can have many child nodes with a same item. Therefore, tree-merging operation is performed to merge such child nodes of a parent node into a common node. The common node will have the frequency which is equivalent to the summation of the frequencies of merged child nodes. The resultant tree is shown in Figure 2(e). We call this tree as *compact MIS-tree*. The algorithm for generating compact *MIS*-tree is shown in Algorithm 2.

Algorithm 1. MIS-tree(Tran:transaction dataset, I: itemset containing n items, MIS: minimum item support values for n items)

1: Sort the items in descending order of their MIS values. Let this order of items be L.
2: Let MIS-list be a list to stores details of each item along with their frequencies and MIS values.
3: **for** each item $i_j \in L$ **do**
4:     Insert i_j into MIS-list with $f = 0$ and $MIS = MIS(i_j)$.
5: **end for**
6: Create a root of a MIS-tree, T and label it as "null".
7: **for** each transaction t in $Tran$ **do**
8:     Sort the items in t in L order.
9:     **for** each item i_j in t **do**
10:         In the MIS-list, update the f value of the respective item by 1.
11:     **end for**
12:     Let the sorted items in t be $[p|P]$, where p is the first item and P is the remaining list. Call insert_tree($[p|P]$,T). (This function is same as that in FP-tree. Hence, we are not discussing this function.)
13: **end for**

Mining Frequent Patterns from *Compact MIS-tree*. Mining of frequent patterns from the *compact MIS-tree* is same as the mining of frequent patterns from the FP-tree. However, the difference is that MIS value of the prefix-item (or pattern) in the *conditional pattern base* of a suffix pattern is used as *minsup*. As the mining of frequent patterns in compact MIS-tree is almost same as that in FP-tree, we are not describing the algorithm for mining frequent patterns.

Before discussing the mining of frequent patterns from the *compact MIS-tree*, we discuss the following lemma.

Lemma 1. *Let α be a pattern in* compact *MIS*-tree. *Let B be α conditional pattern base, and β be an item in B. Let $S_B(\beta)$ be the support of β in the B. Let $MIS(\beta)$ be the minimum item support of β. If α is frequent and $S_B(\beta) \geq MIS(\beta)$ then the pattern $< \alpha, \beta >$ is also a frequent pattern.*

Proof. According to the definition of conditional pattern base and MIS-tree, each subset in B occurs under the condition of the occurrence of α in the transactional database. If an item β appears in B n times, it appearers with α in n times. As the definition of MIS-tree, we know that the $MIS(\beta)$ will be greater than or equal to the MIS of the items in its suffix-path i.e., $MIS(\beta) \geq minsup(\alpha)$. Therefore, if $S_B(\beta) \geq MIS(\beta)$ then $< \alpha, \beta > \geq MIS(\beta)$ and is therefore a frequent pattern.

Based on the Lemma 1, mining of *compact MIS-tree* is as follows. Start from each frequent length-1 pattern (as an initial suffix pattern), construct its conditional pattern base (a "subdatabase," which consists of the set of prefix paths in the compact MIS-tree co-occurring with the suffix pattern), then construct its *conditional MIS-tree* (using Lemma 1), and perform mining recursively on such a tree. The pattern growth is achieved by the concatenation of the suffix pattern with the frequent patterns generated from a conditional MIS-tree.

Algorithm 2. compact-*MIS*-tree(*MIS*-tree)

```
1: Let Tree is the prefix-tree is MIS-tree.
2: for each item i_j in MIS-list of MIS-tree do
3:    if f(i_j) < MIS(i_j) then
4:       Delete the item from the MIS-list with item = i_j.
5:       /* tree pruning operation */
6:       for each node in the node-link of i_j in Tree do
7:          if the node is a leaf then
8:             remove the node directly;
9:          else
10:            remove the node and then its parent node is linked to its child node(s).
11:         end if
12:      end for
13:   end if
14:   /* tree merging operation */
15:   for each item i_j in the compact MIS-list do
16:      if there are child nodes with the same item name then
17:         merge these nodes and set the count as the summation of these nodes' counts;
18:      end if
19:   end for
20: end for
```

Continuing with the example, for the constructed *compact MIS-tree* shown in Figure 2(e), mining of frequent patterns is shown in Table 1. Briefly, we explain the mining procedure for finding frequent patterns using the frequent 1-pattern Bed. Similar' procedure can be adopted for finding frequent patterns using other frequent 1-patterns. Bread occurs in one branch of *compact MIS-tree* of Figure 1(c). The path formed is ⟨Ball, Pillow, Bed: 2⟩. Choosing Bed as suffix, its corresponding prefix path is ⟨Ball, Pillow: 2⟩, will form its conditional pattern base. Its *conditional MIS-tree* contains only a single path, ⟨Pillow: 2⟩; Ball is not included because its support in this conditional pattern base is less than its respective *MIS* value. The single path generates the frequent pattern {Pillow, Bed: 2}. Similar procedure is followed for remaining items in the *MIS*-list of compact *MIS*-tree. The complete set of frequent patterns generated are shown in the fourth column of Figure 1(b).

After generating frequent patterns, the approach discussed in [1] can be used to discover rare association rules.

3.1 Relation between the Frequent Patterns Generated in Different Models

Let F be the set of the frequent patterns generated when $minsup = x\%$. Let $MinF$ be the set of frequent patterns generated in *minimum constraint model*, when items' *MIS* values are specified such that no items' *MIS* value is less than $x\%$. For the same items' *MIS* values, let $MaxF$ be the set of frequent patterns generated in *maximum constraint model*. The relationship between these frequent patterns is $MaxF \subseteq MinF \subseteq F$.

Table 1. Mining frequent patterns using conditional pattern bases

item	conditional pattern bases	conditional MIS-tree	frequent patterns
Bed	{Pillow, Ball:2}	⟨Pillow:2⟩	{Pillow, Bed:2}
Pillow	{Ball:2}	-	-
Bat	{Bread, Ball, Pen:2} {Ball:2}	⟨Ball: 4⟩	{Ball, Bat:4}
Jam	{Bread:4}	⟨Bread:4⟩	{Bread, Jam:4}
Ball	{Bread: 2}	-	-

3.2   Differences between FP-Growth and MCCFP-Growth Approaches

Even though MCCFP-growth is an FP-growth-like approach, it differs from FP-growth as follows. (*i*) FP-growth uses only a single *minsup* to discover complete set of frequent patterns. MCCFP-growth uses multiple *minsups* to discover complete set of frequent patterns. (*ii*) To discover frequent patterns, FP-growth requires two scans on the dataset. But, MCCFP-growth requires only a single scan on the dataset. It is because MCCFP-growth constructs tree by utilizing the prior knowledge (items' *MIS* values) provided by the user before its execution. (*iii*) The FP-growth constructs a tree, called FP-tree with support descending order of items. However, the MCCFP-growth do not construct a tree in support descending order of items. Instead, MCCFP-growth constructs tree in *MIS* descending order of items. As the MCCFP-growth need not have to construct tree in support descending order of items, it requires relatively more memory; however, it is still efficient because it avoids the combinatorial explosion of candidate generation and multiple scans on a transactional dataset. (*iv*) In FP-growth, tree is constructed with only frequent items in a transaction dataset. In MCCFP-growth, initial tree is constructed with every item in a transaction dataset. However, in the next stage, all infrequent items are pruned from the initial tree because they cannot generate any frequent pattern.

4   Experimental Results

In this section, we present the results pertaining three experiments. In the first experiment, we analyze the *MIS*-tree and compact *MIS*-tree sizes on various (synthetic and real-world, sparse and dense) datasets. In the second experiment, we compare the runtime of the proposed approach against Apriori-like approach [7]. In the third experiment, we present the results pertaining to the number of frequent patterns generated in single *minsup* framework, *minimum constraint model* and *maximum constraint model*. All programs are written in C++ and run with Windows XP on a 2.66 GHz machine with 2GB memory. The runtime specifies the total execution time.

For experimental purposes, we have chosen two kinds of datasets: (*i*) synthetic dataset (T10I4D100K) and (*ii*) real-world datasets (retail [14] and chess). T10I4D100k is a large sparse dataset with 100,000 transactions and 870 distinct items. The retail dataset [14] is also a large sparse dataset with 88,162 transactions and 16,470 items. The chess dataset is a dense dataset containing 3,196 transactions and 75 distinct items. For calculating *MIS* values for the items, we have chosen the method discussed in [5].

$$MIS(i_j) = M(i_j) \quad \quad if \ M(i_j) > LS \quad \quad \quad (1)$$
$$= LS \quad \quad Else$$
$$M(i_j) = \beta \times f(i_j)$$

where, $f(i)$ is the actual frequency (or the support) of item i_j in the data. *LS* is the user-specified lowest *minimum item support* allowed. $\beta \in [0,1]$ is a parameter that controls how the *MIS* values for items should be related to their frequencies.

For both kinds of datasets, we have set $LS = 0.1\%$ and varied β by calculating $\beta = \frac{1}{a}$, with *a* varying from 1 to 20.

4.1 Experiment 1

The size of *MIS*-tree generated in T10I4D100K, Chess and Retail datasets are 15.01 MB, 0.81 MB and 14.99 MB. The runtime taken for generating the *MIS*-tree in these datasets is 15, 8, 16 seconds respectively.

In Table 2, we present the compact *MIS*-tree sizes derived for these three datasets when items' *MIS* values are specified with $a = 2$ and by varying *LS* values. Note that the value of *a* do not effect the size of compact *MIS*-tree. It is because compact *MIS*-tree is constructed by involving only frequent 1-patterns. From the results it can be observed that the size of compact *MIS*-tree decreases with increase in *LS* value. The reason is that with the increase in *LS* value, there is a decrease in number of frequent items.

Table 2. Compact *MIS*-tree sizes *(MB)* at different *LS* values

LS	T10I4D100K	Chess	Retail
0.01%	14.99	0.81	13.75
0.05%	14.97	0.81	11.49
0.10%	14.91	0.81	9.1

4.2 Experiment 2

In this experiment, we compare the runtime performance of the proposed approach against the Apriori-like approach that was discussed in [7].

Both Figure 3 (a) and Figure 3 (b) shows the runtime taken by the Apriori-like and MCCFP-growth approaches at different *a* values. From these figures, the following observations can be made: (*i*) Increase in *a* has increased the runtime for both of these approaches. This is due to increase in number of frequent patterns with increase in *a*. (*ii*) The proposed approach requires less runtime as compared with Apriori-like because Apriori-like approach has utilized more runtime in generating candidate patterns (or itemsets). (*iii*) It can be observed that at smaller *a* values, runtime of the proposed approach is almost same as Apriori-like approach. It is because very few number of frequent patterns have generated. However, as the *a* increases, the runtime of Apriori-like approach is more than the proposed approach because Apriori-like approach utilizes runtime for generating candidate patterns.

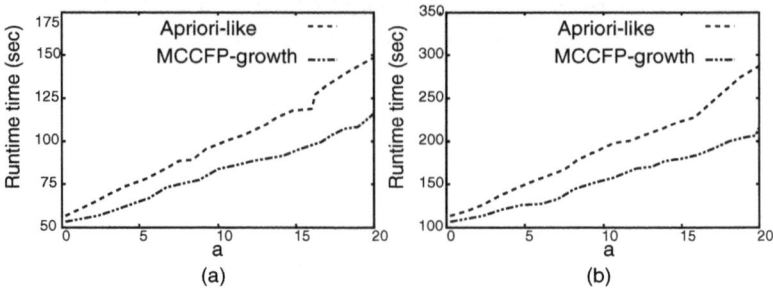

Fig. 3. Comparison of runtime. (a) Synthetic dataset and (b) Real-world dataset.

4.3 Experiment 3

Both Figure 4 (a) and Figure 4 (b) shows the number of frequent patterns generated with single *minsup* framework (*minsup* = 0.1%), *minimum constraint model* (MinCM) and *maximum constraint model* (MaxCM) in T10I4D100k and Retail datasets respectively. From these figures, it can be observed that the *maximum constraint model* has significantly reduced the number of frequent patterns when *a* is not too large. When *a* becomes larger, the number of frequent patterns found by this method gets closer to that found by the single *minsup* method (Apriori). The reason is that when *a* becomes larger, more and more items' *MIS* values reach *LS*. These experimental results were not presented in [7].

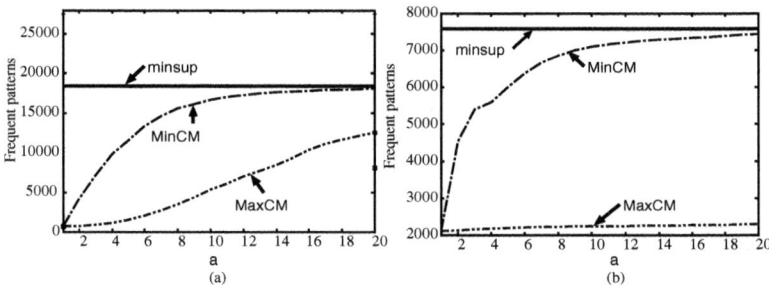

Fig. 4. Number of frequent patterns generated at different *MIS* values. (a) T10I4D100k dataset and (b) Retail dataset.

Due to page limitations, we are not presenting the experimental results on Chess dataset. However, similar observations can be drawn.

5   Conclusions and Future Work

Maximum constraint model is an efficient model to discover rare association rules. However, due to the existence of only an Apriori-like approach, mining rare association rules (or frequent patterns) using this model raises performance problems. In this paper, we proposed an efficient FP-growth-like approach, called MCCFP-growth. The effectiveness of the MCCFP-growth is shown by conducting experiments on both synthetic and real-world datasets.

As a part of future work, we are going to analyze the behavior of various interesting measures on mining rare association rules.

References

1. Agrawal, R., Imielinski, T., Swami, A.: Mining association rules between sets of items in large databases. In: ACM SIGMOD International Conference on Management of Data, vol. 22, pp. 207–216. ACM Press, Washington DC (1993)
2. Hipp, J., Guntzer, U., Nakhaeizadeh, G.: Algorithms for Association Rule Mining - A General Survey and Comparision. ACM Special Interest Group on Knowledge Discovery and Data Mining 2(1), 58–64 (2000)
3. Melli, G., Osmar, R.Z., Kitts, B.: Introduction to the Special Issue on Successful Real-World Data Mining Applications. SIGKDD Explorations 8(1), 1–2 (2006)
4. Jiawei, H., Jian, P., Yiwen, Y., Runying, M.: Mining Frequent Patterns without Candidate Generation: A Frequent-Pattern Tree Approach. In: ACM SIGMOD Workshop on Research Issues in Data Mining and Knowledge Discovery, pp. 53–87 (2004)
5. Liu, B., Hsu, W., Ma, Y.: Mining Association Rules with Multiple Minimum Supports. In: ACM Special Interest Group on Knowledge Discovery and Data Mining Explorations, pp. 337–341 (1999)
6. Lin, T.Y.: Data Mining and Machine Oriented Modeling: A Granular Computing Approach. Journal of Applied Intelligence 13(2), 113–124 (2000)
7. Lee, Y., Hong, T., Lin, W.: Mining Association Rules with Multiple Minimum Supports using Maximum Constraints. International Journal of Approximate Reasoning (2005)
8. Hu, Y.-H., Chen, Y.-L.: Mining Association Rules with Multiple Minimum Supports: A New Algorithm and a Support Tuning Mechanism. Decision Support Systems 42(1), 1–24 (2006)
9. Zhou, L., Yau, S.: Association Rule and Quantitative Association Rule Mining among Infrequent Items. In: 8th International Workshop on Multimedia Data Mining, pp. 156–167 (2007)
10. Uday Kiran, R., Krishna Reddy, P.: An Improved Multiple Minimum Support Based Approach to Mine Rare Association Rules. In: IEEE Symposium on Computational Intelligence and Data Mining, pp. 340–347 (2009)
11. Uday Kiran, R., Krishna Reddy, P.: An Improved Frequent Pattern-growth Approach To Discover Rare Association rules. In: International Conference on Knowledge Discovery and Information Retrieval (2009)
12. Uday Kiran, R., Krishna Reddy, P.: Mining Rare Association Rules in the Datasets with Widely Varying Items' Frequencies. In: Kitagawa, H., Ishikawa, Y., Li, Q., Watanabe, C. (eds.) DASFAA 2010. LNCS, vol. 5981, pp. 49–62. Springer, Heidelberg (2010)
13. Kanimonzhi Selvi, C.S., Tamilarasi, A.: Mining Association rules with Dynamic and Collective Support Thresholds. International Journal on Open Problems Computational Mathematics 2(3), 427–438 (2009)
14. Brijs, T., Swinnen, G., Vanhoof, K., Wets, G.: The use of association rules for product assortment decisions - a case study. In: Knowledge Discovery and Data Mining (1999)

Defining Spatio-Temporal Granularities for Raster Data

Gabriele Pozzani[1] and Esteban Zimányi[2]

[1] Dept. of Computer Science, University of Verona, Italy
`gabriele.pozzani@univr.it`
[2] Dept. of Computer & Decision Engineering (CoDE), Université Libre de Bruxelles, Belgium
`ezimanyi@ulb.ac.be`

Abstract. The notion of granularity is used in several areas of computing. In temporal databases, granularity relates to the fact that the time frame associated to an event of interest (e.g., an accident) can be envisaged at several levels of detail (e.g., hour, day, month, etc.). Similarly, granularity in data warehousing is the level of detail at which facts (e.g., sales) are captured in dimensions (e.g., product, store, and day). However, there is no commonly-agreed definition of spatial or spatio-temporal granularities. Sometimes, the term spatial granularity is confounded with multiple resolutions. Further, the few proposals about them are mainly focused on the vector data model. In this paper, we define spatial and spatio-temporal granularities for raster data models. In our framework, relations and operations between spatial and spatio-temporal granularities are also defined.

1 Introduction

In the database research field the concept of *temporal granularity* is a well-known notion used to temporally qualify and aggregate classical information. Different temporal granularities in a lattice represent different qualification levels. For example, we can say that a car accident has happened in January 1st, 2010, or, considering a coarser temporal granularity (i.e., coarser temporal level of detail), in January, 2010. Transposing the same idea to the spatial context, we obtain the notion of *spatial granularity*. Intuitively, a spatial granularity may represent any partition of a space domain (e.g., $\mathbb{R}^2$) in disjoint regions (e.g., African nations), called *granules*. This concept is not meant to represent the same object in different ways at different levels of detail, as happen in the multi-representation approach [11], but to study and aggregate objects at different levels. For example, the position of a car accident is always represented by a pair of coordinates but we can consider it at several levels, e.g., municipality, region, and country.

The idea to model spatial and temporal granularities in the same way is confirmed observing spatio-temporal applications. For example, as it has been noted in [7], in spatio-temporal data warehouses, every fact (e.g., a sale) is characterized by a temporal granularity (e.g., day) and/or a spatial granularity (e.g., store) and then the different spatial and temporal hierarchies are used to aggregate the same fact at other granularities (e.g., month, year for the temporal dimension, province, country for the spatial dimension). Thus, spatial and temporal granularities need to be modeled homogeneously.

Spatial information can be represented in two different, but related, ways using *raster* and *vector* data models. A raster map consists of a grid (or matrix) of cells, each one

L.M. MacKinnon (Ed.): BNCOD 2010, LNCS 6121, pp. 96–107, 2012.

storing a value. Each cell represents an area whose size changes depending from the resolution of the map. Cells are arranged in rows and columns where rows represent the x-axis of a Cartesian plane and the columns the y-axis [11]. Stored values can represent continuous data such as altitude or temperature, or categorical data such as soil type or land-use class. On the other hand, the vector approach uses geometries such as points, lines, or polygons to represent objects [11]. For example, a hotel can be represented as a point, a road can be represented as a combination of lines, and a province as one or several polygons. Vector features can be made to respect spatial integrity through the application of topology rules such as polygons not being allowed to overlap.

The choice between raster and vector data depends on the application field. In general, raster data are more suited to environmental applications, involving continuous spaces, while vector data are more suited to human activity [11]. Raster data allow easier and more efficient implementations of some spatial analysis techniques, e.g., quantitative and overlay analysis. Moreover, raster data are compatible with remote sensing.

In [1], a definition of spatial and spatio-temporal granularity suitable for spatial data represented in a vector model has been presented. In this proposal, we face the problem to define similar notions based on raster data. Thus, we define spatial and spatio-temporal granularities on raster maps and extends these frameworks defining also relationships and operations over them.

The rest of the paper is organized as follows. In the next section we briefly report main related work. In Sect. 3 we outline the proposal [1] about spatial and spatio-temporal granularities based on a vector data model. In Sects. 4 and 5 we present our proposal, respectively, of a framework for spatial and spatio-temporal granularities based on a raster data model. Finally, in Sect. 6 we conclude and outline some future work.

2 Related Work

In this section we discuss proposals in literature about formalisations of spatial and spatio-temporal granularities.

In [4], Erwig et al. define a spatial partition as a function from a space point set (e.g., $\mathbb{R}^2$) to a set of labels and define several operations needed to modify and create them. Moreover, they demonstrate that the set of all partitions is closed with respect to these operations. A granule is then defined as the set of points having the same label.

In [8], McKenney and Schneider extend [4] showing how to represent a partition using a graph whose nodes represent intersection points between regions and whose edges represent the boundaries of the regions. Moreover, they associate labels no longer with points but with spatial regions identified by cycles in the graph.

In [13], Wang and Liu define a spatial granularity as a mapping from an index set to a spatial domain, similarly to the approach used in the temporal context. Their granules represent nonoverlapping regions and are totally ordered using a generic index set isomorphic to $\mathbb{N}$, that they do not discuss further. They also define the finer-than relationship between granularities following the temporal one.

The same approach has been used by Camossi et al. [2]. They give an object-oriented formalization of granularities by extending the ODMG (Object Data Management

Group) model [3]. They define new datatypes to represent temporal and spatial information. They also define two spatial operators that allow one to convert information from a finer (respectively, coarser) granularity to a coaser (respectively, finer) one.

Considering spatio-temporal granularities, Wang and Liu [13] define a spatio-temporal granularity as a pair composed of a temporal and a spatial granularity. Formally, if SG is a spatial granularity and TG a temporal granularity then $STG = SG \otimes TG$ is a spatio-temporal granularity. $STG(i,j)$ represents a spatio-temporal granule composed of the ith spatial granule of SG and the jth temporal granule of TG. This means that at instants belonging to $TG(j)$ the spatial granule $SG(i)$ is valid (i.e., exists).

A different approach consists to attach valid time to spatial granularities. Thus, a spatio-temporal granularity is defined as a partial function that associates a spatial granularity to those temporal granules representing instants during which it is valid. This approach has been used by Camossi et al. [2] and Belussi et al. [1].

Considering raster spatial maps, Tomlin et al. introduce in [12] the map algebra, a language defining operations for handling map layers. In this model, a raster map is represented as a matrix in which each cell contains a value representing a survey. This model has been extended to the spatio-temporal case by Mennis et al. [9]. They extend the usual two-dimensional space adding time as third dimension. They represent spatio-temporal maps as mappings from a three-dimensional matrix to a set of labels. Using this model, they extend also the map algebra functions.

3   Frameworks for Vector-Based Granularities

In this section we briefly recall the notions, based on vector data, of spatial (Sect. 3.1) and spatio-temporal (Sect. 3.2) granularities proposed in [1].

3.1   Spatial Granularities

A spatial granularity represents a partition of a space domain in regions, called *granules*. Each granule may have holes and may be composed of several disjoint areas. Each granule is an indivisible entity useful to spatially qualify classical information.

In [1] spatial granularities are defined by using a two-level model. The lower level represents the spatial domain, which contains geometrical information and in which vector data representing granules are defined. The higher level is an index structure used to access and manage granules. In order to represent in the same structure the granules and the relationships between them, multidigraphs are used as index sets. A multidigraph is a labelled directed graph with multiple labelled edges. This two-level structure of a spatial granularity is exemplified in Fig. 1.

In the multidigraph each node represents a spatial granule and it is mapped to its vector geometrical representation. On the other hand, edges represent relations between granules (e.g., direction- and distance-based relations). Each edge is labelled with the name of the relation it represents. The association of edge labels with the mathematical definition of relations they represent is maintained by an ad-hoc mapping.

The framework for spatial granularity may be completed defining relations and operations over spatial granularities. *Relations* between granularities allow one to compare

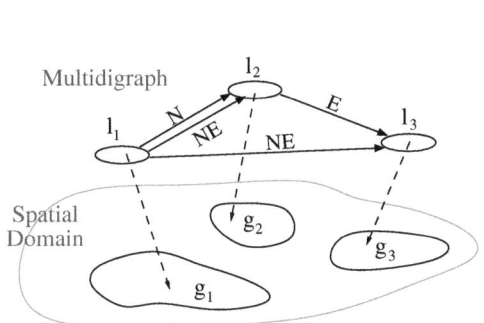

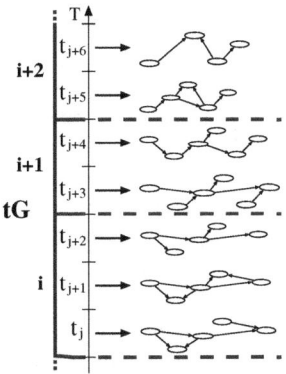

Fig. 1. Structure of a vector-based spatial granularity

Fig. 2. Structure of a vector-based spatio-temporal granularity

granules belonging to different granularities. This feature is useful for aggregating data already aggregated with a granularity G by using a different granularity H. The following relations between spatial granularities have been defined:

- **GroupsInto**(G, H): each granule of H is equal to the union of a set of granules of G, e.g., provinces group into regions;
- **FinerThan**(G, H): each granule of G is contained in one granule of H, e.g., university campuses are contained in municipalities;
- **Subgranularity**(G, H): for each granule of G, there exists a granule in H with the same spatial extent, e.g., European nations are a subgranularity of all nations;
- **Partition**(G, H): G groups into and is finer than H, e.g., countries partition continents;
- **CoveredBy**(G, H): the image of G (i.e., the union of the spatial extent of its granules) is contained in the image of H, e.g., national parks are covered by provinces, but they are not finer than, since a park can be shared by two provinces;
- **Disjoint**(G, H): images of G and H are disjoint, e.g., national parks and municipal parks are disjoint;
- **Overlap**(G, H): images of G and H overlap, e.g., national parks and lakes overlap each other.

Further, *operations* over spatial granularities have been proposed. They may be used to create new granularities from already defined ones. For example, if we have a granularity representing provinces, we may create automatically a granularity representing regions by grouping appropriately granules of provinces. In other cases, we may want to create a new granularity selecting only granules of a given granularity satisfying a given constraint.

Considering application-driven requests and users' requirements, the following operations over spatial granularities, where G and H are input granularities, have been defined:

- **Grouping** creates a new granularity grouping granules of G accordingly to a given partition. For example, a new granularity partitioning a city in three granules representing rich, middle class, and poor quarters can be obtained grouping together quarters accordingly to a user-defined partition based on population wealth;

- **Combine** groups together granules of G included in one granule of H, e.g., European parks can be grouped together with respect the nation they belong to;
- **Subset** selects only granules of G belonging to a given set, e.g., from the European nations select only those that do not touch any sea;
- **SelectInside** selects only granules of G that are contained in a granule of H, e.g., we can select only those national parks belonging to a single province;
- **SelectContain** selects only granules of G that contain at least one granule of H, e.g., given a granularity representing nuclear plants, we can select only those nations having at least one plant;
- **SelectIntersect** selects only granules of G that intersect at least one granule of H, e.g., from provinces we can obtain only those overlapping national parks;
- **Union** creates a new granularity containing all granules of G and H (eventually deleting from the granules of H the extents already contained in G), e.g., we can obtain all parks by joining national, regional, and municipal parks;
- **Intersect** creates a new granularity containing only granules representing intersections of one granule of G with one of H, e.g., we can refine national parks dividing them with respect to provinces;
- **Difference** creates a new granularity obtained from G by deleting those areas covered also by some granules of H, e.g., we can obtain only terrestrial extent of provinces by deleting from them the lakes.

3.2   Spatio-Temporal Granularities

Spatio-temporal granularities represent the changes over time of a spatial granularity (see Fig. 2). A spatio-temporal granularity has two components. The former is a temporal granularity, tG, that aggregates time points, while the latter is a mapping (called *spatial evolution*) that associates to each time point t the spatial granularity valid on it.

Relations and operations have been defined for spatio-temporal granularities. In both cases, the spatial definitions have been extended to the spatio-temporal context by adding a time domain. Considering relationships, spatio-temporal relations add to the spatial ones two temporal quantifications, one at the granule level and another at the time point level. Quantifications allow to control when spatial relationships must be valid during the spatial evolution in order to satisfy a spatio-temporal relation. This extension allows one to represent concepts such as "spatial relation R is always valid" or "for each time granule there exists a time point in which spatial relation S is valid". For example, we can state that regions always partition countries.

A similar extension has been defined for spatio-temporal operations. Spatio-temporal operations apply the original spatial operations to each spatial granularity recorded in a given spatio-temporal granularity. Spatio-temporal operations allow one to compute, for example, grouping, union, and selection by containment over spatio-temporal granularities. For example, we can calculate the granularity representing, instant by instant, African countries intersecting areas where cholera cases have been surveyed.

4   Raster-Based Spatial Granularities

In this section, we define a notion of spatial granularity for the raster data model. More-over, based on this notion, we redefine relationships and operations already defined for vector-based spatial granularities.

In the *raster* model, maps are represented by partitioning the space domain in equal-sized square areas (see Fig. 3). The size of areas depends on the resolution (i.e., the accuracy needed) of the map, it may range from centimeters to kilometers. Inside each area, the physical characteristic of interest is measured and its average value is associated to the area. Areas can be uniquely and totally numbered starting from a specific point, the origin of the raster map. Usually, areas are numbered defining a Cartesian coordinate system: in this way each area corresponds to a unique pair of integers. Thus, a raster map can be represented by a matrix whose components are called *cells*. Knowing the position in the space domain of the origin of the map and its resolution (i.e., the size of areas), it is possible to know what area corresponds to each cell. Hereafter, we suppose that all maps have the same coordinates system and resolution. Each cell stores the value of the corresponding area. In this paper we do not consider the construction of raster maps, but only the mapping associating to each cell the corresponding label.

A spatial granularity for raster maps represents the partitioning of cells, and then of areas in the space domain, accordingly to their associated values, called *labels*. Hence, we formally define a spatial granularity σ as a total function from two-dimensional coordinates in $\mathbb{Z}^2$ to a label set L, $\sigma : \mathbb{Z}^2 \to L$. In this way, given a cell $c \in \mathbb{Z}^2$, $\sigma(c)$ represents the label associated to c. The same model has been used also by Erwig et al. [4]. Note that the label set can be of any type, e.g., integer numbers, pairs, or strings. To ensure that σ is a total function, we assume that each label set L contains the special label $\perp$ (called *undefined*) and that cells whose areas are not covered by σ are all labeled with $\perp$. We define the image of a spatial granularity as the set of all cells with a non-undefined label, i.e., $\mathbf{Image}(\sigma) = \{c \in \mathbb{Z}^2 \mid \sigma(c) \neq \perp\}$.

Granules composing a granularity are the sets of all cells with the same label. Since each cell belongs to exactly one granule and areas corresponding to cells are disjoint by construction, granules are therefore disjoint without imposing any further constraint. Given a granularity σ, the granule with label $l \in L$, denoted with $\gamma_\sigma(l)$, is then represented by all cells labelled with l, $\gamma_\sigma(l) = \{c \in \mathbb{Z}^2 \mid \sigma(c) = l\}$. Moreover, given a cell $c \in \mathbb{Z}^2$, we denote with $\gamma_\sigma(c) = \gamma_\sigma(\sigma(c))$ the granule to which c belongs. We define the set of all granules composing σ as $\Gamma_\sigma = \{g \in \mathcal{P}(\mathbb{Z}^2) \mid g = \gamma_\sigma(l) \wedge l \in \mathbf{range}(\sigma)\}$ where $\mathbf{range}(\sigma)$ is the set of all labels actually used in σ.

Fig. 4 depicts an example of raster spatial granularity representing land usage. For the sake of simplicity, we represented each label with a different color, explained beside. In this example, the granularity is made up of three granules representing areas covered by commercial, recreational, and residential buildings.

Note that the above definition of spatial granularity is also suitable for representing granularities that are regular subdivisions of the space, as in the example depicted in Fig. 5. For example, knowing that cells (squares with thiner borders) represent square areas in the space domain whose size is 10×10 meters, we would like to make granules (squares with thicker borders) representing sets of cells whose total extent in the space domain is 20×20 meters. In this case, cells are grouped together in bigger squares.

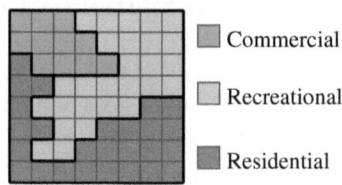

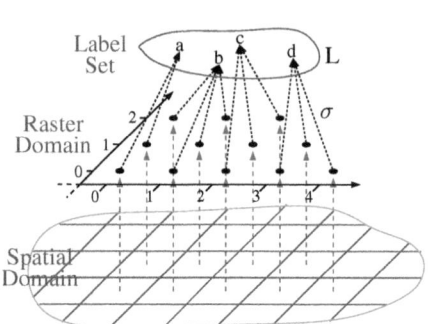

Fig. 4. Example of a raster spatial granularity

10	10	11	11	14	14	15	15
10	10	11	11	14	14	15	15
8	8	9	9	12	12	13	13
8	8	9	9	12	12	13	13
2	2	3	3	6	6	7	7
2	2	3	3	6	6	7	7
0	0	1	1	4	4	5	5
0	0	1	1	4	4	5	5

Fig. 3. Structure of a raster spatial granularity   **Fig. 5.** A raster regular spatial granularity

The number of cells, on the x- and y-axis, to be grouped together depends on the ratio between the granule size (20×20) and the map resolution (10×10), in this case it is two. To each group (i.e., granule) must be associated a different label. Labels can be calculated, for example, by using space-filling curves, e.g., Z-order (exemplified in the figure).

Given two spatial granularities σ_1 and σ_2, we define next *relations* between them, whose meaning is equivalent to that of relations between vector-based spatial granularities given in Sect. 3.1.

- The **GroupsInto** relation requires that each granule in σ_2 is equal to the union of a set of granules in σ_1.
  $$\mathbf{GroupsInto}(\sigma_1, \sigma_2) \triangleq \forall g \in \Gamma_{\sigma_2}.\exists G \subseteq \Gamma_{\sigma_1}.g = \bigcup_{h \in G} h.$$
- The **FinerThan** relation requires that each granule in σ_1 is contained in a granule of σ_2:
  $$\mathbf{FinerThan}(\sigma_1, \sigma_2) \triangleq \forall g_1 \in \Gamma_{\sigma_1}.\exists g_2 \in \Gamma_{\sigma_2}.g_1 \subseteq g_2.$$
- The **Partition** relation corresponds to imposing both the **GroupsInto** and the **FinerThan** relations:
  $$\mathbf{Partition}(\sigma_1, \sigma_2) \triangleq \mathbf{GroupsInto}(\sigma_1, \sigma_2) \wedge \mathbf{FinerThan}(\sigma_1, \sigma_2).$$
- The **Subgranularity** relation requires that each granule in σ_1 has a correspondent equal granule in σ_2:
  $$\mathbf{Subgranularity}(\sigma_1, \sigma_2) \triangleq \forall g_1 \in \Gamma_{\sigma_1}.\exists g_2 \in \Gamma_{\sigma_2}.g_1 = g_2.$$
- The **CoveredBy** relation requires that the image of σ_1 is covered (i.e., is a subset) of that of σ_2:
  $$\mathbf{CoveredBy}(\sigma_1, \sigma_2) \triangleq \mathbf{Image}(\sigma_1) \subseteq \mathbf{Image}(\sigma_2).$$
- The **Disjoint** relation imposes that the images of σ_1 and σ_2 be disjoint:
  $$\mathbf{Disjoint}(\sigma_1, \sigma_2) \triangleq \mathbf{Image}(\sigma_1) \cap \mathbf{Image}(\sigma_2) = \emptyset.$$
- Finally, the **Overlap** relation requires that the images of σ_1 and σ_2 have a non-empty intersection:
  $$\mathbf{Overlap}(\sigma_1, \sigma_2) \triangleq \mathbf{Image}(\sigma_1) \cap \mathbf{Image}(\sigma_2) \neq \emptyset.$$

We can also redefine the operations given for vector-based spatial granularities. In the following definitions we assume that $\sigma : \mathbb{Z}^2 \to L$, $\sigma_1 : \mathbb{Z}^2 \to L_1$, and $\sigma_2 : \mathbb{Z}^2 \to L_2$ are raster-based spatial granularities. The meaning of each operation is the same as we explained in the previous section about vector-based spatial granularities.

- The **Grouping** operation creates σ' in which granules of σ are grouped together with respect to a partition of its labels. Formally, if $P = \{Q_1, \ldots, Q_n\}$ is a partition on the label set L such that $\bigcup_{i=1}^{n} Q_i = L \smallsetminus \{\bot\}$, then **Grouping**$(\sigma, P)$ is defined as the mapping $\sigma' = \mathbb{Z}^2 \to \mathcal{P}(L)$ such that:
$$\forall c \in \mathbb{Z}^2 . \sigma'(c) = Q_i \text{ iff } \sigma(c) \in Q_i.$$

- The **Combine** operation groups together the granules of a given granularity σ_2 to form a new granule. Conversely to **Grouping**, in this case the groups are given by the partition of the space defined by the granularity σ_1. All granules of σ_2 completely contained in a granule of σ_1 are grouped together, and they receive the label of the granule in σ_1. Formally, $\sigma' = \mathbf{Combine}(\sigma_1, \sigma_2) : \mathbb{Z}^2 \to L_1$ is such that
$$\forall c \in \mathbb{Z}^2 . \sigma'(c) = \begin{cases} \sigma_1(c) & \text{if } \gamma_{\sigma_2}(c) \subseteq \gamma_{\sigma_1}(c) \wedge \sigma_2(c) \neq \bot \\ \bot & \text{otherwise.} \end{cases}$$

- The **Subset** operation returns a new granularity σ_1 in which only cells having their label in a given label set I are maintained, while the other ones are set to $\bot$. Formally, if $I \subseteq L$ then $\sigma' = \mathbf{Subset}(\sigma, I) : \mathbb{Z}^2 \to I$ is defined as
$$\forall c \in \mathbb{Z}^2 . \sigma'(c) = \begin{cases} \sigma(c) & \text{if } \sigma(c) \in I \\ \bot & \text{otherwise.} \end{cases}$$

- The **SelectContain** operation sets to $\bot$ all cells of σ_1 whose granules do not contain at least one granule of σ_2. Formally, $\sigma' = \mathbf{SelectContain}(\sigma_1, \sigma_2) : \mathbb{Z}^2 \to L_1$ is defined such that
$$\forall c \in \mathbb{Z}^2 . \sigma'(c) = \begin{cases} \sigma_1(c) & \text{if } \exists l_2 \in L_2 \smallsetminus \{\bot\} . \gamma_{\sigma_2}(l_2) \subseteq \gamma_{\sigma_1}(c) \\ \bot & \text{otherwise.} \end{cases}$$

- The **SelectInside** operation keeps only those granules of σ_1 that are contained (i.e., inside) in a granule of σ_2. Formally, $\sigma' = \mathbf{SelectInside}(\sigma_1, \sigma_2) : \mathbb{Z}^2 \to L_1$ is such that
$$\forall c \in \mathbb{Z}^2 . \sigma'(c) = \begin{cases} \sigma_1(c) & \text{if } \gamma_{\sigma_1}(c) \subseteq \gamma_{\sigma_2}(c) \wedge \sigma_2(c) \neq \bot \\ \bot & \text{otherwise.} \end{cases}$$

- The **SelectIntersect** operation keeps only those granules of σ_1 that intersect at least one granule of σ_2. Formally, $\sigma' = \mathbf{SelectIntersect}(\sigma_1, \sigma_2) : \mathbb{Z}^2 \to L_1$ is defined as:
$$\forall c \in \mathbb{Z}^2 . \sigma'(c) = \begin{cases} \sigma_1(c) & \text{if } \exists l_2 \in L_2 \smallsetminus \{\bot\} . \gamma_{\sigma_2}(l_2) \cap \gamma_{\sigma_1}(c) \neq \emptyset \\ \bot & \text{otherwise.} \end{cases}$$

- The **Union** operation calculates the union of two granularities σ_1 and σ_2 by taking all granules of σ_1 and also those parts of the granules of σ_2 that do not intersect any granule of σ_1. Formally, $\sigma' = \mathbf{Union}(\sigma_1, \sigma_2) : \mathbb{Z}^2 \to L_1 \cup L_2$ is defined as the mapping such that:
$$\forall c \in \mathbb{Z}^2 . \sigma'(c) = \begin{cases} \sigma_1(c) & \text{if } \sigma_1(c) \neq \bot \\ \sigma_2(c) & \text{otherwise.} \end{cases}$$

- We can define two versions of the intersection of two granularities, that we call inner intersection and outer intersection. The first one considers only cells that have an associated label in both parameter granularities. It is defined as $\sigma' = \mathbf{InnerIntersect}(\sigma_1, \sigma_2) : \mathbb{Z}^2 \to L_1 \times L_2$ such that

$$\forall c \in \mathbb{Z}^2.\sigma'(c) = \begin{cases} \langle \sigma_1(c), \sigma_2(c) \rangle & \text{if } \sigma_1(c) \neq \bot \wedge \sigma_2(c) \neq \bot \\ \bot & \text{otherwise.} \end{cases}$$

The second one considers also cells that have not an associated label in one of the two parameter granularities, i.e., $\sigma' = \mathbf{OuterIntersect}(\sigma_1, \sigma_2) : \mathbb{Z}^2 \to L_1 \times L_2$ is such that

$$\forall c \in \mathbb{Z}^2.\sigma'(c) = \begin{cases} \bot & \text{if } \sigma_1(c) = \bot \wedge \sigma_2(c) = \bot \\ \langle \sigma_1(c), \sigma_2(c) \rangle & \text{otherwise.} \end{cases}$$

– The **Difference** operation keeps the label of only those cells of σ_1 that are undefined in σ_2. Formally, $\sigma' = \mathbf{Difference}(\sigma_1, \sigma_2) : \mathbb{Z}^2 \to L_1$ is such that:

$$\forall c \in \mathbb{Z}^2.\sigma'(c) = \begin{cases} \sigma_1(c) & \text{if } \sigma_2(c) = \bot \\ \bot & \text{otherwise.} \end{cases}$$

We can also adapt to our definition of spatial granularity the **Relabel** operation proposed by Erwig and Schneider [4]. This operation allows to modify the labels of a granularity. To do that, it uses a total function r that associates to each label of the given granularity a new label. Then, if I is a label set and $r : L \to I$ is a relabelling total function, $\sigma' = \mathbf{Relabel}(\sigma, r) : \mathbb{Z}^2 \to I$ is defined such that $\forall c \in \mathbb{Z}^2.\sigma'(c) = r(\sigma(c))$.

We note that the **Grouping** and **Subset** operations can be expressed by using the **Relabel** operation. Given a partition $P = \{Q_1, \dots, Q_n\}$ of the label set of σ (say L), we can define the relabelling function $r_P : L \to \mathcal{P}(L)$ such that, for each label $l \in L$, $r_P(l) = Q_i$ if and only if $l \in Q_i$. Then, $\mathbf{Grouping}(\sigma, P) \equiv \mathbf{Relabel}(\sigma, r_P)$.

On the other hand, given a subset I of the label set of σ (say L) we can define the relabelling function $r_I : L \to I$ such that, for each label $l \in L$, $r_I(l) = l$ if $l \in I$, and $r_I(l) = \bot$ otherwise. Then, $\mathbf{Subset}(\sigma, I) \equiv \mathbf{Relabel}(\sigma, r_I)$.

5   Raster-Based Spatio-Temporal Granularities

Following the same approach used for vector-based spatio-temporal granularities, we now extend the notion of granularity for raster maps to the spatio-temporal case. This approach has been used also by Frank [5] for representing time series of spatial layers.

We denote with Σ_L the set of all raster spatial granularities over the label set L. Hence, a raster-based evolution over L, that represents the evolution over time of a raster-based spatial granularity, is defined as a total function $\epsilon : \mathbb{Z} \to \Sigma_L$ that associates to each time point the spatial granularity that is valid on it. We denote with $\sigma_\bot$ the spatial granularity that associates to each point in $\mathbb{Z}^2$ the value $\bot$. Thus, in order to ensure that an evolution is a total mapping, we impose that, whenever no spatial granularity is valid at one time point, the evolution associates $\sigma_\bot$ to this time instant. The spatial granularity valid at time t is $\epsilon(t)$. The spatial granule with label l at time t is denoted with $\gamma_{\epsilon(t)}(l)$.

We define a raster-based spatio-temporal granularity τ over a label set L as a pair $\langle tG, \epsilon \rangle$ composed of a temporal granularity tG [10] and a raster-based evolution ϵ over L. The temporal granularity tG associates to each index i of an index set I (e.g., $\mathbb{Z}$) the set of all time points belonging to the time granule identified by i. In this way, it aggregates time points and the spatial granularities valid on them. The spatio-temporal

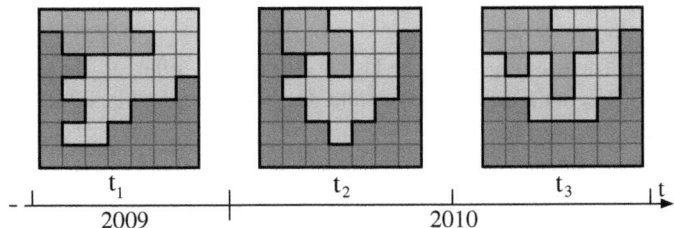

Fig. 6. An example of raster-based spatio-temporal granularity

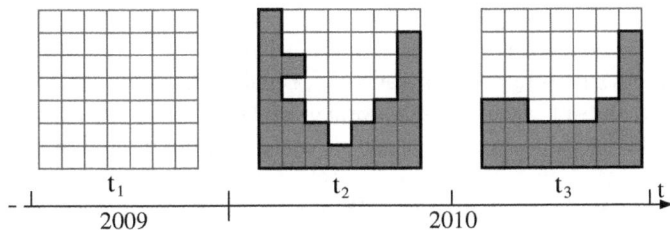

Fig. 7. The $\tau(2010, \texttt{Residential})$ spatio-temporal granule

granule $\tau(i, l)$ represents the evolution during time granule i of the spatial granule l. We call $\mathcal{T}_L$ the set of all raster spatio-temporal granularities over the label set L.

Fig. 6 depicts the spatio-temporal granularity $\langle\texttt{Years}, \texttt{LandUsage}\rangle$. To each time point t_i (aggregated with respect to the temporal granularity $\texttt{Years}$) is associated the spatial granularity valid on it. In Fig. 7 the spatio-temporal granule representing residential cells during the time granule 2010 is depicted.

We now define relations between raster spatio-temporal granularities. The basic idea defining relationships between two spatio-temporal granularities is to compare, instant by instant, the spatial granularities they store. In spatio-temporal granularities, time is arranged in two levels, granule and time point level. We introduce at both these levels a temporal quantification operator, *All* ($\forall$) or *Exists* ($\exists$). These quantifications, prefixed to the spatial relation R, specify when R must be verified in order that the spatio-temporal relation holds. For example, given two spatio-temporal granularities $\tau_1 = \langle tG_1, \epsilon_1\rangle$ and $\tau_2 = \langle tG_2, \epsilon_2\rangle$, the spatio-temporal relation $\forall\exists R(\tau_1, \tau_2)$ corresponds to impose that

$$\forall i \in I.\exists t \in tG_1(i).R(\epsilon_1(t), \epsilon_2(t)),$$

i.e., in each time granule of tG_1 there exists an instant on which R holds. Similar definitions can be given for the other three possible combinations of the two time quantification operators (i.e., $\forall\forall$, $\exists\exists$, $\exists\forall$). For example, the spatio-temporal relationship $\forall\forall\textbf{FinerThan}(\texttt{stCultures}, \texttt{stSoilType})$ checks whether, at every time point of each time granule, the cultures types are finer than the soil types.

Operations over spatial granularities can be similarly extended in order to achieve a definition over spatio-temporal granularities. The main idea is to redefine them in order to accept spatio-temporal parameters and to return a spatio-temporal granularity. To do that, each spatio-temporal operation (whose name is equal to the correspondent spatial one) simply applies, instant by instant, the spatial operation to all spatial granularities evolving during it. This approach corresponds to the *lifting* of operations proposed by Güting et al. [6] for moving objects. This extension is reflected by signatures of operations. Unary (**Grouping, Subset,** and **Relabel**) and binary (all the other ones) operations over spatial granularities have the following signatures (where Par generically represents the type of non-spatial parameters requested by unary operations):

$Op_1 : \Sigma_L \times Par \to \Sigma_{L_1}$ and
$Op_2 : \Sigma_{L_1} \times \Sigma_{L_2} \to \Sigma_L,$

respectively, and they can be extended as follow:

$Op_1 : \mathcal{T}_L \times Par \to \mathcal{T}_{L_1},$
$Op_2 : \mathcal{T}_{L_1} \times \mathcal{T}_{L_2} \to \mathcal{T}_L,$
$Op_2 : \mathcal{T}_{L_1} \times \Sigma_{L_2} \to \mathcal{T}_L,$ and
$Op_2 : \Sigma_{L_1} \times \mathcal{T}_{L_2} \to \mathcal{T}_L$

in order to accept spatio-temporal parameters. Binary operations can accept two spatio-temporal parameters or one spatio-temporal granularity plus a spatial one.

Formally, the evolution resulting from a unary spatio-temporal operation Op_1, applied to $\langle tG, \epsilon \rangle$, is ϵ' such that $\forall t \in \mathbb{Z}.\epsilon'(t) = Op_1(\epsilon(t), Par)$, i.e., Op_1 is applied to each spatial granularity evoling in ϵ. While evolutions resulting from binary operations $\tau' = Op_2(\tau_1, \tau_2)$, $\tau'' = Op_2(\tau_1, \sigma)$, and $\tau''' = Op_2(\sigma, \tau_2)$ are ϵ', ϵ'', and ϵ''', respectively, such that, for each time point $t \in \mathbb{Z}$:

$\epsilon'(t) = Op_2(\epsilon_1(t), \epsilon_2(t)),$
$\epsilon''(t) = Op_2(\epsilon_1(t), \sigma),$ and
$\epsilon'''(t) = Op_2(\sigma, \epsilon_2(t)).$

Spatio-temporal operations allow one to calculate, for example, `stResidential` = **Subset**(`stLandUsage`, {`Residential`}), representing the spatio-temporal granularity in which, at each time point t, only the granule labelled with `Residential` is selected. The binary operation **SelectInterset**(`stPollution`, `stResidential`) creates the granularity representing at each time point the pollution granules intersecting residential areas. While with **SelectIntersect**(`MineralRes`, `stUnused`) we calculate the granularity representing at each time the mineral resources (that do not change over time) that intersect unused areas (that evolve over time).

Finally, it is useful to define the new **Remodulate** operation that, given a spatio-temporal granularity $\tau = \langle tG, \epsilon \rangle$ and a temporal granularity tH, creates a new spatio-temporal granularity replacing with tH the temporal granularity in τ. Formally:

$\quad$ **Remodulate**$(\tau, tH) \triangleq \langle tH, \tau.\epsilon \rangle.$

For example, from `stLandUsage` based on the temporal granularity `Months`, we can obtain the land usage based on years with **Remodulate**(`stLandUsage`, `Years`).

6 Conclusions

Temporal, spatial, and spatio-temporal granularities have proved their usefulness in several application fields. However, only notions related to temporal granularities and spatio-temporal data warehouses are well established, while definitions of spatial and spatio-temporal granularities are not commonly agreed.

In [1], a framework for spatial and spatio-temporal granularities based on a vector model has been proposed, unifying and completing previous proposals. However, to the best of our knowledge, there are no proposals for spatial and spatio-temporal granularities for raster data. In this work we proposed a framework for granularities based on raster data models. We proposed also relations and operations useful to reason about them. A spatial granularity partitions the space domain with respect to the values associated to entries in a raster map. Raster-based granularities are defined directly on raster maps, avoiding the need of a processing phase to convert them in a vector model.

A spatio-temporal granularity associates to each time point, aggregated accordingly to a time granularity, the raster-based spatial granularity valid on it. Then, relationships and operations can be extended to the spatio-temporal case just applying them, instant by instant, to all spatial granularities evolving in a spatio-temporal granularity.

As for future work we want to deeply study relationships and operations formalizing their semantics. Then, we want to develop an implementation of raster-based granularities studying how they can be represented in GIS software and in DBMSs, and their computational complexity. Moreover, we will consider how proposed vector- and raster-based granularities can be integrated in models for spatio-temporal data warehouses.

References

1. Belussi, A., Combi, C., Pozzani, G.: Formal and conceptual modeling of spatio-temporal granularities. In: Proceedings of the International Database Engineering and Applications Symposium, pp. 275–283. ACM (2009)
2. Camossi, E., Bertolotto, M., Bertino, E.: A multigranular object-oriented framework supporting spatio-temporal granularity conversions. Int. J. Geogr. Inf. Sci. 20(5), 511–534 (2006)
3. Cattell, R.G.G., Berler, D.K.B.M., Eastman, J., Jordan, D., Russell, C., Schadow, O., Stanienda, T., Velez, F. (eds.): The Object Data Standard: ODMG 3.0. Morgan Kaufmann Publishers Inc., San Francisco (2000)
4. Erwig, M., Schneider, M.: Partition and Conquer. In: Frank, A.U. (ed.) COSIT 1997. LNCS, vol. 1329, pp. 389–407. Springer, Heidelberg (1997)
5. Frank, A.U.: Map Algebra Extended with Functors for Temporal Data. In: Akoka, J., Liddle, S.W., Song, I.-Y., Bertolotto, M., Comyn-Wattiau, I., van den Heuvel, W.-J., Kolp, M., Trujillo, J., Kop, C., Mayr, H.C. (eds.) ER Workshops 2005. LNCS, vol. 3770, pp. 194–207. Springer, Heidelberg (2005)
6. Güting, R.H., Böhlen, M.H., Erwig, M., Jensen, C.S., Lorentzos, N.A., Schneider, M., Vazirgiannis, M.: A foundation for representing and querying moving objects. ACM Trans. Database Syst. 25(1), 1–42 (2000)
7. Malinowski, E., Zimányi, E.: Advanced data warehouse design: From conventional to spatial and temporal applications. Springer, Heidelberg (2008)
8. McKenney, M., Schneider, M.: Spatial Partition Graphs: A Graph Theoretic Model of Maps. In: Papadias, D., Zhang, D., Kollios, G. (eds.) SSTD 2007. LNCS, vol. 4605, pp. 167–184. Springer, Heidelberg (2007)
9. Mennis, J., Tomlin, C.D.: Cubic map algebra functions for spatio-temporal analysis. Cartogr. and Geogr. Inform. 32(1), 17–32 (2005)
10. Ning, P., Wang, X.S., Jajodia, S.: An algebraic representation of calendars. Ann. Math. Artif. Intel. 36(1-2), 5–38 (2002)
11. Shekhar, S., Xiong, H. (eds.): Encyclopedia of GIS. Springer, Heidelberg (2008)
12. Tomlin, C.D., Berry, J.K.: A mathematical structure for cartographic modeling in environmental analysis. In: Proceedings of the 39th Symposium of the American Congress on Surveying and Mapping, pp. 269–283 (1979)
13. Wang, S., Liu, D.: Spatio-temporal Database with Multi-granularities. In: Li, Q., Wang, G., Feng, L. (eds.) WAIM 2004. LNCS, vol. 3129, pp. 137–146. Springer, Heidelberg (2004)

Load Shedding in Data Stream Management Systems Using Application Semantics*

Raman Adaikkalavan

Computer and Information Sciences & Informatics
Indiana University South Bend
raman@cs.iusb.edu

Abstract. Data Stream Management Systems (DSMSs) process highly bursty
streams in real time and are used in diverse application domains. Satisfying Quality of Service (QoS) requirements and providing accurate results are critical to
the success of DSMSs and the applications that use them. In order to maintain
QoS, various approaches have been proposed in the literature, including capacity planning, scheduling, and load shedding. Existing load shedding approaches
drop tuples either randomly or based on the characteristics of data or continuous queries. On the other hand, utilizing application characteristics for dropping
tuples would increase the accuracy of the results and at the same time maintain
QoS. In this paper, we introduce load shedding schemes that are based on the application semantics. The techniques presented in this paper complement existing
load shedding approaches.

Keywords: Load Shedding, Data Stream Processing, Application Semantics.

1 Introduction

Data Stream Management Systems (DSMSs) [1–3] process continuous queries (CQs)
[3] over stream data. Quality of Service (QoS) plays a major role in data stream processing as DSMSs compute functions over data streams in realtime and in a continuous manner. QoS-related challenges include capacity planning and QoS verification,
scheduling, and load shedding and run-time optimization [1]. *Capacity planning* calculates the required resources to compute the given CQs and to satisfy their QoS requirements. When multiple CQs are executed simultaneously, the scheduling of queries
or individual operators of a query is critical to resource allocation and is handled by
various *scheduling strategies*. No matter how good a scheduling strategy is, a DSMS
may be short of resources for processing all the CQs and satisfy their QoS requirements during temporary overload periods. *Load shedding* [4–9] techniques handle this
by dropping tuples without affecting QoS or with minimal loss in accuracy.

Current load shedding [4–9] techniques are based on *data* or *system* characteristics or
both. Existing approaches monitor the system and shed load randomly or based on the
system capacity, but satisfying the QoS requirements. Load is shed from the Aurora system when the total CPU cycles required by the boxes and superboxes exceed the system

---

* This work was supported, in part by, IUSB Faculty Research Grant.

L.M. MacKinnon (Ed.): BNCOD 2010, LNCS 6121, pp. 108–112, 2012.

capacity [4]. This is carried out by dynamically inserting and removing drop operators into query plans and dropping tuples either randomly or based on the importance of the content. Das et al. [5] present various load shedding techniques for sliding window join operator. They show that dropping tuples based on their values yields better results than randomized load shedding. Load shedding for aggregate queries are discussed in [6, 7]. To the best of our knowledge, none of the current load shedding approaches exploit the application semantics for load shedding.

1.1 Motivating Example (CarADN)

In a car accident detection and notification system (Linear road benchmark [10]), each expressway in an urban area is modeled as a linear road, and is further divided into equal-length segments (e.g., 5 miles). Each registered vehicle on an expressway is equipped with a sensor and reports its location periodically (e.g., every 30 seconds). Based on this location stream data, a car accident should be detected in a (near) real-time manner. An accident is detected when two vehicles are stopped at the same position over 2 minutes (i.e., four consecutive reports). One or more continuous queries can be defined to detect accidents based on the input stream. However, it requires an efficient, meaningful, and less redundant approach to send notifications. In other words, the number of times the accident is reported should be kept to a minimum. With current systems, if it takes 20 minutes to clear the accident, then duplicate accident notifications are sent (i.e., one notification after the first 2 minutes and every 30 seconds thereafter). This causes unnecessary overhead to the data stream system. If the number of tuples entering the system exceeds the system capacity, load shedding is activated, which in turn can drop tuples and can miss some other accident detection. When the semantics of the car accident detection and notification application is exploited (i.e., do not send duplicate notification), number of notifications is reduced and number of tuples processed by the DSMS is also reduced by dropping redundant tuples. This allows the system to shed load without losing accuracy and without affecting QoS.

This is just one scenario where avoiding duplicates is critical. Other applications have other requirements like accumulating various occurrences together and computing the results based on them. In this paper, we will only look at the application scenario discussed above.

1.2 Summary

In this paper, we present a novel approach that exploits application semantics to shed load. Our approach is not a replacement for existing load shedding approaches, rather it *complements* them. Our approach also avoids unnecessary computations that are being carried out by the data stream system, as the applications that use the system do not need those computation results. Currently, when a system exceeds the capacity, tuples are shed based on the data or system characteristics. With our approach, first tuples are shed based on application semantics and when the system exceeds load even after that, regular load shedding approaches are used to maintain the QoS.

2   Load Shedding Using Application Semantics

First, we need to identify the places to shed load. Second, we need to identify whether we need new operators that can drop load based on application semantics, or modifications to existing algorithms alone is sufficient.

We will first discuss a simple query plan that involves a select, binary-join, and sliding windows. A simple query is shown below and its corresponding query plan is shown in Figure 1.

```
SELECT *
FROM    S1 [ROW 10 TUPLES], S2 [ROW 10 TUPLES]
WHERE   S1.id = S2.id
```

As shown in Figure 1, queues q1 and q2 maintain tuples from streams s1 and s2, respectively. Synopses 1 and 2 are used by the binary-join operator for computations. Queue q3 feeds the select operator and q4 stores the output of the select operator.

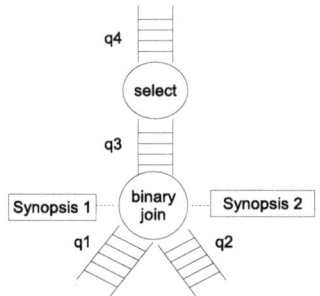

Fig. 1. A simple query plan

Consider our CarADN motivating example. The format of car location data stream (i.e., CarLocStr) is given below:

CarLocStr(timestamp, car_id, speed, exp_way, lane, dir, segment)

Let us assume that two cars C1 and C2 are sending position reports every 30 seconds (see below) and after colliding with each other. In this case, the input queue of the query operator that processes this stream will contain the following tuples until the accident is cleared. This is assuming the size of 10 tuples or 2 minutes for a sliding window.

CAR C1	CAR C2
10 : 00 : 00, C1, 0, I465, 1, N, 120	10 : 00 : 00, C2, 0, I465, 1, N, 120
10 : 00 : 30, C1, 0, I465, 1, N, 120	10 : 00 : 30, C2, 0, I465, 1, N, 120
10 : 01 : 00, C1, 0, I465, 1, N, 120	10 : 01 : 00, C2, 0, I465, 1, N, 120
10 : 01 : 30, C1, 0, I465, 1, N, 120	10 : 01 : 30, C2, 0, I465, 1, N, 120
10 : 02 : 00, C1, 0, I465, 1, N, 120	10 : 02 : 00, C2, 0, I465, 1, N, 120

For the above situation, the application needs the data stream processing system to reduce duplicate notifications. The best place to shed load in the query plan based on application semantics is in the sliding window, as it feeds to operators and is not part of the query plan. This requires no modifications to the query processor, which in turn does not alter the scheduling. Thus, the system can shed load based on the application requirements in the sliding window.

For our example, duplicates can be removed by replacing the old tuples with the new instances of the same tuple. This removal can be based on one or more attributes. For the accident notification system, we can assume that the tuple is considered a duplicate, if all the attribute values match except the timestamp. In other words, new instances of the tuple represent the occurrence of the same event. As shown in the sliding window above, old tuples from the cars can be removed when the new tuples arrive. Assume that tuple generated by C1 at 10:00:00 enters the system and is processed by the system. When a new instance arrives at 10:00:30 the sliding window can replace the old one from 10:00:00 with this new instance and mark it as processed. This is possible because all the values except the timestamp are the same. This prevents the data stream processing system from performing unnecessary computations and generating duplicate results. It also saves computation resources. Similarly, all the tuples arriving in the future can be handled. If the accident is cleared, then cars send different values for other attributes in addition to the time attribute. Since the duplication condition is not satisfied, the new tuple will not replace the old one in the sliding window.

3   Conclusions and Future Work

In this paper, we presented a novel approach for shedding load over real-time data streams. Our approach reduces unnecessary computations and complements existing load shedding approaches. Though our initial results are encouraging, we need to identify diverse load shedding modes. We will investigate the adaptation of event consumption modes or parameter contexts from the Active database (Event-Condition-Action Rules) research. In addition to the sliding windows, synopsis of operators can also be utilized for dropping tuples and needs to be explored.

References

1. Chakravarthy, S., Jiang, Q.: Stream Data Processing: A Quality of Service Perspective Modeling, Scheduling, Load Shedding, and Complex Event Processing. Advances in Database Systems, vol. 36. Springer, Heidelberg (2009)
2. Carney, D., Çetintemel, U., et al.: Monitoring streams - a new class of data management applications. In: Proc. of the VLDB (September 2002)
3. Babu, S., Widom, J.: Continuous queries over data streams. In: Proc. of the ACM SIGMOD, pp. 109–120 (September 2001)
4. Tatbul, N., Çetintemel, U., Zdonik, S., Cherniack, M., Stonebraker, M.: Load shedding in a data stream manager. In: Proc. of the VLDB, pp. 309–320 (September 2003)
5. Das, A., Gehrke, J., Riedewald, M.: Approximate join processing over data streams. In: Proc. of the ACM SIGMOD, pp. 40–51 (June 2003)

6. Babcock, B., Datar, M., Motwani, R.: Load shedding for aggregation queries over data streams. In: Proc. of the ICDE, pp. 350–361 (March 2004)
7. Tatbul, N., Zdonik, S.B.: Window-aware load shedding for aggregation queries over data streams. In: Proc. of the VLDB, pp. 799–810 (2006)
8. Tatbul, N., Çetintemel, U., Zdonik, S.B.: Staying fit: Efficient load shedding techniques for distributed stream processing. In: Proc. of the VLDB, pp. 159–170 (2007)
9. Kendai, B., Chakravarthy, S.: Load Shedding in MavStream: Analysis, Implementation, and Evaluation. In: Gray, A., Jeffery, K., Shao, J. (eds.) BNCOD 2008. LNCS, vol. 5071, pp. 100–112. Springer, Heidelberg (2008)
10. Arasu, A., et al.: Linear road: A stream data management benchmark. In: Proc. of the VLDB, pp. 480–491 (September 2004)

Test Data Provisioning for Database-Driven Applications

Klaus Haller

COMIT AG,
CH-8004 Zürich,
Switzerland
klaus.haller@comit.ch

Abstract. Most of today's business applications rely on database management systems (Database-Driven Applications or DBAPs). Testing DBAPs requires not only knowing the functions to invoke and test, the input values, and the expected results; testers also need an initial database state (DBAP test data). Popular methods for deriving database test data include generators for synthetic test data, manual test data design, and live system snapshots. In this paper we analyze the major impact factors important for commercial projects when choosing a DBAP test data provisioning method.

Keywords: Information Systems, Information System Engineering, Database-Driven Applications, Testing, Test Data.

1 Introduction

Most of today's business applications are database-driven applications (DBAPs), which rely on a database for storing and managing data. Testing a DBAP requires testing the application logic *and* its interaction with the database. A DBAP test case consists not only of input and output parameter values and the procedure to invoke and test; it also comprises an initial database state (DBAP test data). Willmor and Embury were the first to formalize DBAP test cases and, thereby, the need for DBAP test data, with their quintuple model [WE06]. Crucial research exists about how to derive DBAP test data automatically. The AGENDA prototype [CD04] might be the best-known approach, but many more exist (e.g., [DC07] and [HT06]). In this paper we take a different perspective. Although there are various test data provisioning methods, no methodology exists for guiding commercial software development projects to the method best-suited to their concrete needs. This paper fills that gap. Section 2 compiles the popular provisioning methods; Section 3 discusses our methodology and the various factors relevant when choosing a provisioning method; and Section 4 gives a detailed example for analyzing one specific factor (DBAP test data quality).

2 Provisioning Methods

Provisioning methods describe (a) how we derive DBAP test data and (b) how we load those data into the database. These are the two dimensions of our DBAP test data

L.M. MacKinnon (Ed.): BNCOD 2010, LNCS 6121, pp. 113–117, 2012.

provisioning matrix (Figure 1). Three options exist for the first dimension, i.e., for deriving DBPA test data: manual design, data generation, and live data. Manual design requires a tester to analyze the specification. He defines the test cases, which also comprise suitable DBAP test data. Data generation is based on a generator, which takes a DBAP as input and returns DBAP test data. The third option is using live data, in which case we copy data from a live system into a test environment. The second dimension–how we load the data into tables–has two options: inserting the data directly into the database tables or using the regular way via GUI (or interfaces). If we choose the regular way, the data goes through the normal validations and processing in the business logic layer before being written into the database tables.

There are six ways to combine the options for the dimensions "deriving" and "loading." The methods for four of them apply directly to commercial projects. For method *GUI Input*, a tester designs the test data, then she inputs the data manually via the GUI. She repeats the task every time a new testing environment is needed. The *Capture & Replay* method also requires a tester to design and input the test data manually via GUI the first time. Then, capture and replay tools such as Selenium capture the input process. The next time someone needs test data, the capture and replay tool replays the input. *Insert Scripts* rely on DBAP test data designed by testers, too. In contrast to the previous methods, testers write SQL statements that insert the test data directly into the database tables. *Commercial Data Generation Tools* such as the datanamic DB Data Generator analyze the database catalogue, then generate data automatically and write it directly into the database tables.[1] *DB Snapshots* rely on tools such as Oracle Datapump. They read the live data from all DBAP's database tables, store them, and load them into a DBAP test environment when needed.

	Manual Design	**Data Generation**	**Live Data**
Regular (GUI/Interface)	GUI Input, Capture & Replay	No out-of-the-box solution	No out-of-the-box solution
DB direct	Insert Scripts	Commercial Data Generation Tools	DB Snapshots

Fig. 1. DBAP Test Data Provisioning Matrix

3   The Methodology and Influence Factors

When project managers choose a provisioning method, three criteria are relevant: initial set-up costs, maintenance costs, and quality. Quality addresses the DBAP test data quality, but also the resulting test quality. A project manager has to evaluate the three criteria for all provisioning methods in our DBAP test data matrix, before he can make an informed decision. The evaluation and the decision form Steps 2 and 3 of our

---

[1] We listed some promising research prototypes in Section 1. They take the DBAP's application code into account, too; however, these ideas cannot be used in commercial settings yet.

methodology (Figure 2). They both are based on an analysis of the underlying influence factors from Step 1. Two groups of factors exist: context factors and DBAP test factors.

DBAP-specific factors address the specifics of a DBAP:

- The *compliance level* reflects the needed test data quality (the following section addresses this factor in more detail).
- *Path distribution* looks at (i) how many execution paths exist and (ii) how likely it is that tests based on random test data cover all those paths.
- Certain tests, such as performance tests, need many data. The factor *test data quantity* covers this aspect.
- *GUI/Interface firmness* and *data model firmness* address the fact that, if a DBAP changes, the test data also have to. Relevant factors are the change frequency of the presentation layer and the change frequency of database table changes.

Context factors do not depend on the DBAP itself, but on the application area and the organization of the software development company and the customer.

- *Privacy* is important in certain areas such as banking or hospitals. No one risks that data leaves such an institution because of leaks in the testing process.
- *Test data responsibility* addresses the know-how of the persons responsible for the test data. Power users, for example, have very good domain knowledge; test engineers have in-depth testing methodology know-how.
- *Set-up effort* and *maintenance effort* reflect the amount of effort needed to set up or maintain test data for actual and subsequent projects.
- *Environmental complexity* reflects the fact that DBAPs coupled with many other systems pose needs different from those of stand-alone systems.

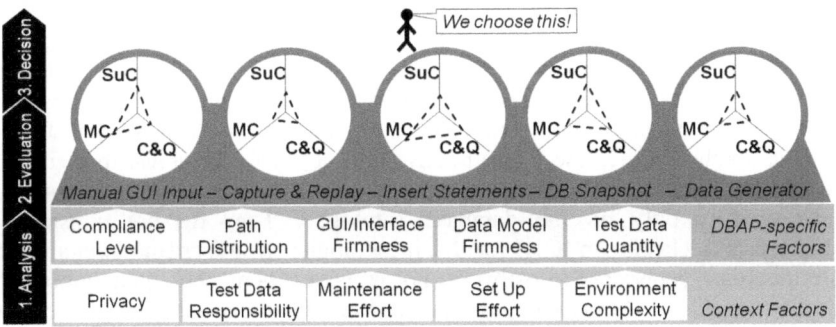

SuC: Initial Costs, MC: Maintenance Costs, C&Q: Coverage and Quality

Fig. 2. DBAP Test Data Provisioning Methodology

4   Test Data Quality: The Compliance Level Factor

Our methodology requires analyzing the DBAP-specific factors and the context factors to identify the best method for a given project. This section illustrates the process for analyzing one factor, the test data compliance level [Ha09]. Test data

Compliance Level	Characteristics	GUI Input	Capture & Replay	Insert Statements	Data Generator	DB Snapshot
Path Compliance	Intended execution path taken	✓	✓	✓	?	✓*)
Application Compliance	Application logic considered, no false positives	?	?	?	?	✓*)
Schema Compliance	Schema constraints considered, all rows loaded			?	(✓)	
Type Compliance	Attribute types correct				✓	

Fig. 3. Compliance Levels - ✓ guaranteed, ? possible, *) regarding version in use

compliance levels are a notion of quality They enable quality comparisons of test data. The lowest compliance level is *type compliance* (Figure 3). It guarantees that the attribute types of the tables are considered. It ensures that, e.g., only dates, and not strings or numbers, are inserted into date columns. The second level is *schema compliance*, which considers all constraints, such as primary-foreign-key relationships, NOT NULL, etc. Thus, all test data that we try to insert into our DBAP's database tables can be loaded. The third level is *application compliance*. It ensures that our test data could also result from "normal" processing. If the validation in the presentation layer rejects balance sheets when assets and liabilities are not equal, our test data must not have such rows, even if no database constraints enforce that assets and liabilities are equal. Testers benefit from application compliance because it eliminates the risk of false positives as a result of bad test data. The best compliance level is *path compliance*. If we want to test a DBAP's behavior for balance sheet sums of more than one billion, we need such a balance sheet sum in our test data. Path compliance guarantees that our DBAP test data fits our test case.

When testers design DBAP test data for their test cases (methods *GUI Input, Capture & Replay,* and *Insert Statements*), the test data is path-compliant. Even if testers make mistakes during design or input, the input via GUI ensures at least application compliance for the methods *GUI Input* and *Capture & Replay*. The *Insert Statements* method writes the data directly into the database tables; thus, in case of mistakes, the data is only schema-compliant after the load. Commercial *Data Generators* rely only on the database catalogue. They do not consider, e.g., validations and checks in GUI or business logic. If a schema contains check constraints, data generators (mostly) do not consider them; thus, generators achieve only type compliance. If there are no check constraints, the test data might be schema-compliant. By chance (in other words, if our data model is simple), our data might be better than type-compliant, i.e., application-compliant or path-compliant. *DB snapshots* contain data that result from using a DBAP. Such data is application-compliant and covers all practical relevant execution paths. However, the data is only test data for the DBAP version currently in use, not the version under development.

***

In this paper we address DBAP test data, which is crucial when developing commercial software. This paper is the first to present a methodology that guides projects systematically to the DBAP test data provisioning method that best suits their specific needs.

Acknowledgements. The author would like to thank Michael Mlivoncic for the valuable discussions.

References

[CD04] Chays, D.: An AGENDA for testing relational database applications. Software Testing, Verification & Reliability (STVR) 14(1) (2004)

[DC07] Dai, Z., Chen, M.-H.: Automatic Test Generation for Database-Driven Applications. In: SEKE 2007, Boston, MA, July 9-11 (2007)

[Ha09] Haller, K.: White-Box Testing for Database-driven Applications: A Requirements Analysis. In: DBTest 2009, Providence, RI, June 29 (2009)

[HT06] Houkjær, K., Torp, K., Wind, R.: Simple and realistic data generation. In: VLDB 2006, Seoul, Korea, September 12-15 (2006)

[WE06] Willmor, D., Embury, S.: An Intensional Approach to the Specification of Test Cases for Database Systems. In: ICSE 2006, Shanghai, China, May 20-28 (2006)

Enabling Decision Tree Classification in Database Systems through Pre-computation

Nafees Ur Rehman and Marc H. Scholl

University of Konstanz, Box D 188,
78457 Konstanz, Germany
{Nafees.Rehman,Marc.Scholl}@Uni-Konstanz.de

Abstract. Integration of data mining in database systems is an open topic of research. The DBMS's power of dealing with lots of data and maintaining data integrity adds to the motivation of integrating it with data mining. We propose a method to integrate decision tree classification to do the required pre-computations and store it in database objects for later use. These pre-computed values get updated with the introduction of new data or change in the existing data for classification. Decision tree classification can readily make use of these pre-computed values to build classification models. Our approach is based on the column database to use it effectively for feature oriented calculations. This comparatively improves performance if classification is deemed to be performed on a high dimensional data.

Keywords: Data Mining, Decision Tree Classification, Database Systems.

1   Introduction

The tight coupling of data mining with database systems is an interesting challenge. The first study about integrating data analysis methods into DBMSs came with the development of data warehousing and On-Line Analysis Processing (OLAP) in particular [1]. Most DBMS vendors included data mining features into their products[2,3,4]. The motivation to integrate data mining with databases comes from the facts that these both fields are data oriented. Data mining is itself a merged field of various domains to analyze mostly large volumes of data and find useful patterns in it. While database systems store, manipulate and retrieve tons of data efficiently. DM lacks the scalability feature to be able to deal with volumes of data. It then depends on feature selection [5] or sampling [6] to reduce the size of the data in order to perform in- memory data mining. On the other hand, database management system is meant to handle large volume of data and maintain data integrity. Bringing the best of the both worlds together would help data analysts to perform complex analysis with least concern for scalability of data mining and integrity of the data.

2   Pre-computations

Databases and Data Warehouses are natural repositories to store data for different purposes. These data are processed using a variety of ways. One common approach is

L.M. MacKinnon (Ed.): BNCOD 2010, LNCS 6121, pp. 118–121, 2012.

to query data using SQL statements. Complex queries can take considerable time. One method to answer queries efficiently is to use pre-compute data and *materialize* it in an object, called Materialized View. Materialized views are query results that have been stored in advance so long-running calculations are not necessary when SQL statements are actually executed. From a physical design point of view, materialized views resemble tables or partitioned tables and behave like indexes [7]. This improves performance of the queries significantly.

Our idea of pre-computations for data mining is partially based on this concept of materialized views. As data mining is not a one shot activity but rather an iterative and interactive process. Data mining can be thought of set of various algorithms. Each algorithm operates on a data set by performing various computations over it. Decision tree classification algorithms are re-cursive in its operation. To build a decision tree model, at each step of the algorithm, all features (attributes) are evaluated to choose the best feature as a root node. We consider the ID3 algorithm to show how various values can be pre-computed for it.

ID3 algorithm takes in a set of categorical variables and evaluates each variable to find the best split variable using the *information gain* method. This process is then repeated recursively until all variables are tested and/or all instances are classified according to a given output variable. The evaluation of each variable involves performing a series of calculations from counting instances to calculating entropy and information gain. This operation can become costlier when numbers of variables are more. And this is the motivation for our method of pre-computations. All these mentioned calculations can be performed in advance and can be stored in a materialized view. And later, can be exploited by the algorithm without re-computations.

As soon as a decision tree model is declared and the number of classes is known, Entropy and Information gain can be calculated and stored. And when the algorithm is actually run, it can make use of these values. This saves time and makes the algorithm work efficiently.

3   Storage of Pre-computations for DTC

In order to store potentially pre-computable values that would later be fed to DTC program, there can be two simple ways to do it. One way is to have a separate storage structure for each of the table that contains observations for the training of the decision tree. Figure 1 depicts this method where for each base table there is one associated dependent MV to hold these pre-computed values. This method is simpler but it will require having the same number of MV as the number of base tables. That would contribute to the maintenance efforts in a negative way.

But as new data is pumped into the base tables, only corresponding MVs would be updated to reflect the change in the source data. The second approach is to have a central database-wide table to hold potentially pre-computable values for all base tables. Figure 2 represents this approach. This single table approach would reduce the maintenance efforts.

Base_tbl_1

ObsNo	Form	Parenting		Class
1	1	usual		Rec
2	2	Great		Ntr
3	1	Prêt		Ntr
---	---	---		---

DPMCtbl_1

CNo	FieldID	CalcType	Value
1	Form	E	0.45
2	Parent	E	0.32

Base_tbl_2

ObsNo	Outlook	Temp		Class
1	cloudy	High		1
2	sunny	Low		0
3	over	Med		0
---	---	---		---

DPMCtbl_2

CNo	FieldID	Calc_Type	Value
1	Outlook	E	0.693
2	Outlook	E	0.247

Base_tbl_n

ObsNo	F1	F2		Class
1	A	X		Y
2	B	Y		N
3	C	Z		N
---	---	---		---

DPMCtbl_n

CNo	FieldID	CalcType	Value
1	---	---	---
2	---	---	---

Fig. 1. Representation of pre-computation structures: One MV for one each table containing observations for DTC training

CNo	TableID	FieldID	C_Type	Value
1	PlayGOLF	PlayGOLF	Entropy	0.940
2	PlayGOLF	Outlook	Entropy	0.693
3	PlayGOLF	Outlook	Gain	0.247

Database

Fig. 2. Representation of pre-computation structures: A database-wide table for all datasets containing observations for training DTCs

4   Storage of DM Results into an Appropriate Storage Structure

Data Mining is a complex set of operations and takes a lot of efforts and resources to perform it. The output of almost each phase of DM is input to another phase. The time taken for processing at each phase can vary from microseconds to hours depending upon the size of the data, machine and type of tasks. Results of each phase and of the whole DM process can be stored in the existing DB/DWH structures to provide for efficient retrieval at a later stage.

There can be two ways to store trees. One is to use a separate table for each tree that is constructed. This may take more space on the disk and will result in more maintenance efforts as not all trees will be useful. Trees not useful will be discarded. The other method is to use a database-wide table to store all trees that are constructed. Each node of each tree will be inserted as a record in this table along with information about the node's level number, the SplitVar (attribute in database vocabulary), Split_Value, Operator, Parent Node, Version and TableID to keep track of the table for which the tree is constructed.

5   Summary and Conclusion

In this paper we proposed a method of integrating Decision Tree Classifiers in Database Systems. The integration aims to figure out pre-computable values required for the construction DTCs and store these values in MV or in a central database-wide table. These values can then be fed to the ID 3 algorithm allowing not only for integration but also to make it efficient. All computations requires for to choose the root node, are already performed. The algorithm will carry out its process further at the sub-tree levels. Furthermore, storage of the DTCs is also proposed which allows for interactive and iterative data mining model construction.

References

1. Codd, E., Codd, S., Salley, C.: Providing OLAP (on-line analytical processing) to user-analysts: An IT mandate. Technical report, EF Codd and Associates (1993)
2. IBM. DB2 intelligent miner scoring (2001),
   http://www4.ibm.com/software/data/iminer/scoring
3. Oracle, Oracle 9i data mining. White Paper (2001)
4. Soni, S., Tang, Z., Yang, J.: Performance Study of Microsoft Data-Mining Algorithms. Microsoft White Paper pages (October 2000)
5. Liu, H., Motoda, H.: Feature Selection for Knowledge Discovery and Data Mining, p. 214 (1998)
6. Chauchat, J., Rakotomalala, R.: A new sampling strategy for building decision trees from large databases (2000)
7. Oracle, Oracle 9i Data Warehousing Guide (2002)

Flexible Range Semantic Annotations
Based on RDFa

José Luis Navarro-Galindo and José Samos Jiménez

Department of Computer Languages and Systems, Universidad de Granada
C/ Periodista Daniel Sucedo Aranda s/n, 18071 Granada (Spain)
{jlnavar,jsamos}@ugr.es

Abstract. In this paper, a new flexible range markup technique for Web documents is presented as an alternative to XPointer technology, based on the RDFa standard. The principal objective is to define semantic annotations that support the evolution of annotated Web documents more effectively than XPointer. The term 'Flexible Range' indicates that annotations can be defined over different ranges of text within a Web page and multimedia objects within it, independently of its HTML tags.

Keywords: RDFa, semantic annotation, metadata, semantic web.

1   Introduction

The emergence in 2001 of the Semantic Web concept marked an important stage in the Web's evolution. As stated in [1] it was "an extension of the current Web in which information is given well-defined meaning, better enabling computers and people to work in cooperation." This proposition has not yet been realized, and although many efforts have been made in this direction much remains to be done.

One of the main issues to be resolved in order to progress towards the Semantic Web is how to convert existing and new Web content that can be understood by humans into semantically-enriched content that can be understood by machines.

The semantic markup of Web documents is the first step towards adapting Web content to the Semantic Web. Providing the information elements that currently make up the Web with a well-defined meaning would, among other things, improve its contextual search capabilities, increase interoperability between systems in 'collaborative' contexts and, when combined with Web services, ultimately compose applications automatically based on published Web services [2] [3]. However, most Web content remains unstructured because of the difficulty and cost of markup.

The main contribution of this paper is to present the flexible range markup technique on Web documents for the creation of semantic annotations. The paper begins with an introduction to markup methods. Then undertakes a detailed study of this technique, demonstrating its advantages over XPointer technology. Finally, the paper ends with conclusions and bibliography.

L.M. MacKinnon (Ed.): BNCOD 2010, LNCS 6121, pp. 122–126, 2012.

2   Markup Methods

This is a very important issue when carrying out semantic annotations, as it is necessary to delimit the range of text on which the annotation is performed.

XPointer [4] is a robust technology when used as a method for locating the text component to which an annotation refers, but presents problems when changes are made to a document on which there are annotations. When a document is edited there are typically additions, deletions and/or alterations to the order of paragraphs within it, a fact which causes the anchor points defined in XPointer for annotations to be lost. This means that the markup process has to be done each time a document is modified.

A *Range* is an arbitrary part of a HTML document, defined by boundary points denoting the beginning and the end. DOM Range technology [5] allows a Range object to be created from the text selection made by the user from the Web browser.

3   Flexible Range Definition

Flexible Range Technique uses the capacity of DOM Range technology to delimit text ranges on which annotations are to be made, coupled with RDFa language [6] which allows embedded annotations to be made within the Web document that is annotated, thus addressing the problems presented by XPointer.

This section explains the text fragment delimitation and identification technique for simple texts, and subsequently for more complex ones.

3.1   Simple Delimitation and Identification

When working with an HTML document from a Web browser and making a text selection such as the one below in Example 1.A with a grey background, the aim of the text selection is to define the text fragment on which the annotation is to be performed.

\<p>Lorem ipsum dolor sit amet, consectetur adipiscing elit.\</p>
 \
 	
 \<ul>
      \<li>Duis orci tellus, **dignissim ac laoreet sit** amet, porttitor et purus. \</li>
 \</ul>   **A**
	\<p>Lorem ipsum dolor sit amet, consectetur adipiscing elit.\</p>
	 \
	
	 \<ul>
	      \<li>Duis orci tellus, **\<span id=”748”>**
	      dignissim ac laoreet sit \</span> amet,
	      porttitor et purus. \</li> **B**
	 \</ul>

Example 1. A) Text selection HTML code B) Text selection delimitation and identification

In Example 1.A, the process of assigning a unique identifier to the selected text fragment is easier this time because of the functionality that Range objects offer. First a Range object is created with which to delimit the text fragment to be annotated.

Then an HTML SPAN element is created to which an identifier is attached, along with other attributes (RDFa) deemed appropriate. To complete the process the primitive 'Surround content' of Range object is applied which allows the range created with the SPAN element that identifies the text fragment to be surrounded. The result can be seen in Example 1.B.

Once the text fragment to be annotated is identified, the annotation process in RDFa standard language is easy.

3.2   Multi-tag Delimitation and Identification

In Example 2.A can be seen how the delimited text selection with a grey background crosses over various HTML tag boundaries. This fact causes a problem when trying to delimitate with a unique identifier.

If following a process similar to that described above and creating Range object that defines the text selection, and then creating an HTML SPAN element to which the identifier "654" is attached, and finally applying the Range object primitive 'surround a content', one arrives at the source code in Example 2.B. This is an invalid solution because identifiers must be unique and in this case they are duplicated.

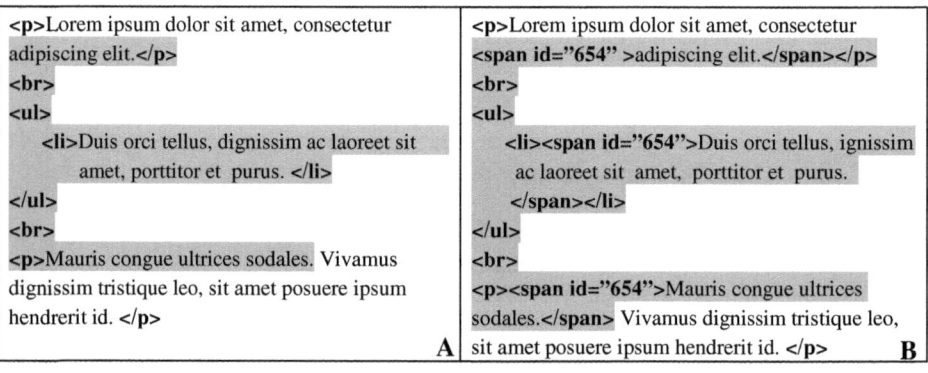

Example 2. A) HTML code for multi-tag text selection **B**) Invalid multi-tag delimitation

The adopted solution, when defining the flexible range semantic annotation technique, is assigned a global identifier that references the whole text selection, and local identifiers are used for the fragments that form the different HTML elements that appear in the text selection. This is a definition of a whole and its parts.

Example 3.A illustrates what unique identification of the fragments that make up the user's selection of text would be like. In this case it is indeed a valid unique identification. Note that there is no global identifier (654) of the annotation being undertaken; this work is carried out below in RDFa.

<p>Lorem ipsum dolor sit amet, consectetur **<span id="654-1" >adipiscing elit.</span></p>** **
** **<ul>**   **<li><span id="654-2">Duis orci tellus,** ignissim   ac laoreet sit amet, porttitor et purus.   **</span></li>** **</ul>** **
** **<p><span id="654-3">**Mauris congue ultrices sodales.**</span>** Vivamus dignissim tristique leo, sit amet posuere ipsum hendrerit id. **</p>** **A**	<span id="654" **about**="http://w3.ex.org/p.htm#654" **rel**="rdf:Seq"> <span **rel**="rdf:li" **resource**="http://w3.ex.org/p.htm#654-1"/> <span **rel**="rdf:li" **resource**="http://w3.ex.org/p.htm#654-2"/> <span **rel**="rdf:li" **resource**="http://w3.ex.org/p.htm#654-3/> </span> **B**

Example 3. A) Valid multi-tag selection delimitation **B)** RDFa fragment definition

Example 3.B illustrates how fragment definition in RDFa language is performed by employing the container element RDF Seq, used to define an ordered list of values. In particular it has been used to describe the fragments that make up the annotation.

4   Conclusions and Future Work

This paper has studied in detail the semantic annotation technique based on the definition of flexible ranges using RDFa language. The advantages of this technique over other markup techniques have been justified and are summarised below:

- Enables consistent evolution of Web documents that have semantic annotations defined by this technique.
- Avoids the "Deep Web" problem: Enables search engines indexers can access to semantic information stored in documents that use this technique of annotation.
- Makes possible the dual storage of semantic annotations defined in a document, both on the server-side and embedded in the document that is marked. In a document with embedded semantic annotations in RDFa language, it is easy to obtain these annotations expressed in a way that is equivalent to RDF language, by means of an RDFa processor.

Nowadays, we have just developed FLERSA (Flexible Range Semantic Annotation), a tool for manual annotation of Web content that illustrates the markup technique studied in this paper. The tool is available at the Web address **http://www. scms.es/joomla**. It has a test user (username and password: demo) from which to make annotations to documents hosted on the site.

As regards future work, the FLERSA tool can be understood as a base module from which to compose more complex and functional semantic systems. Work will continue along these lines, with the aim of achieving automation of the annotation process and conversion of the infrastructure of Web Portals/CMS into its semantic equivalent, thus extending the benefits of the Semantic Web.

References

1. Berners-Lee, T., Hendler, J., Lassila, O.: Semantic Web. Scientific American (2001)
2. Sheth, A., Bertram, C., et al.: Managing Semantic Content for the Web. IEEE Internet Computing 6(4), 80–87 (2002)
3. Tse-Ming, T., Han-Kuan, Y., et al.: Ontology-Mediated Integration of Intranet Web Services. Computer Magazine 36(10), 63–71 (2003)
4. DeRose, S., Maler, E., Daniel Jr, R.: XML Pointer Language (XPointer) Version 1.0 (February 2001), http://www.w3.org/TR/xptr/
5. Kesselman, J., Robie, J., Champion, M., Sharpe, P., Apparao, V., Wood, L.: Document object model (dom) level 2 traversal and range specification, Technical report, W3C (2000), http://www.w3.org/TR/2000/REC-DOM-Level-2-Traversal-Range-20001113/
6. Adida, B., And Birbeck, M.: RDFa primer: Bridging the human and data Webs. W3C Working Group Note (October 2008), http://www.w3.org/TR/xhtml-rdfa-primer/

Issues of Flash-Aware Buffer Management for Database Systems

Yi Ou and Theo Härder

University of Kaiserslautern, Germany
{ou,haerder}@cs.uni-kl.de

Abstract. Classical buffer replacement policies, e.g., LRU, are suboptimal for database systems having flash disks for persistence, because they are not *aware* of the distinguished characteristics of those storage devices. We discuss the basic principles of flash-aware algorithms and issues related to transaction management. An efficient flash-aware algorithm, CFDC, is presented and compared to several previous proposals.

1   Introduction

Flash disks are considered an important alternative to magnetic disks. Therefore, we focus here on the problem of buffer management for DBMSs having only flash disks as secondary storage. Many efforts are made to systematically benchmark the performance of flash disks [1,2]. The most important conclusions of these benchmarks are:

- For sequential read-or-write workloads, flash disks often achieve a performance comparable to high-end magnetic disks.
- For random workloads, the performance asymmetry of flash disks and their difference to magnetic disks is significant: random reads are typically two orders of magnitude faster than those on magnetic disks, while random writes on flash disks are often even slower than those on magnetic disks.
- Interestingly, due to the employment of device caches and other optimizations in the FTL (flash translation layer), page-level writes with strong spatial locality can be served by flash disks more efficiently than write requests without locality.

In particular, many benchmarks show that flash disks can handle random writes with larger *request sizes* more efficiently. For example, the bandwidth of random writes using units of 128 KB is more than an order of magnitude higher than writing at units of 8 KB. In fact, a write request of, say 128 KB, is internally mapped to 64 *sequential* writes of 2-KB flash pages inside a flash block. Note that sequential access is an extreme case of high spatial locality.

2   Basic Principles

Historically, the fact "whether a page is read only or modified" is an important criterion for the replacement decision. To guarantee data consistency, a modified

L.M. MacKinnon (Ed.): BNCOD 2010, LNCS 6121, pp. 127–130, 2012.

buffer page (also called dirty page) has to be written back to disk (called *physical write* or *page flush*), before the memory area can be reused. Hence, if the re-placement victim is dirty, the process or thread requesting an empty buffer frame must wait until page flush completion—potentially a performance bottleneck.

This criterion is now much more important in our context, because, for flash disks, the average cost of a page write (including block erasure) may be two orders of magnitude higher than that of a page read. At a point in time running a given workload, if a clean page p has to be re-read n times and a dirty page q has to be re-modified m times ($n \sim m$), it is better for the buffer manager to replace p in favor of q, because the cost of n flash reads is much lower than the benefit of serving m write requests directly in the buffer.

Yet, the total cost of page flushing is not linear to the number of page flushes. As introduced in Sect. 1, write patterns strongly impact the efficiency of flash writing; hence, they have to be addressed as well.

Even with flash disks, maintaining a high hit ratio—the primary goal of con-ventional buffer algorithms—is still important, because the bandwidth of main memory is at least an order of magnitude higher than the interface bandwidth of storage devices. Based on the flash disk characteristics, we summarize the basic principles of flash-aware buffer management as follows:

P1. Minimize the number of physical writes, esp. the random writes.
P2. Address write patterns to improve write efficiency.
P3. Keep a relatively high hit ratio.

3   The CFDC Algorithm

The CFDC (clean-first dirty-clustered) algorithm [3] manages the buffer in two regions: the *working region* W for keeping *hot* pages that are frequently and recently revisited, and the *priority region* P responsible for optimizing replace-ment costs by assigning varying priorities to page clusters. A cluster is a set of pages located in proximity, i.e., whose page numbers are close to each other. Though page numbers are logical addresses, because of the space allocation in most DBMSs and file systems, the pages in the same cluster have a high proba-bility of being physically neighbored, too.

A parameter λ, called *priority window*, determines the size ratio of P relative to the total buffer. Therefore, if the buffer has B pages, then P contains λ pages and the remaining $(1 - \lambda) \cdot B$ pages are managed in W. Note, W does not have to be bound to a specific replacement policy. Various conventional replacement policies can be used to maintain high hit ratios in W and, therefore, prevent hot pages from entering P. The two-region scheme makes it easy to integrate CFDC with conventional replacement policies in existing systems.

Page movement is illustrated in Fig. 1. If a page in P is hit, the page is moved (promoted) to W, at the same time, a page $min(W)$ is determined by W's victim selection policy and demoted to P. If the page hit is in W, the base algorithm of W should adjust its data and structures accordingly. For example, if LRU is the base algorithm, it should move the page that was hit to the MRU end of its

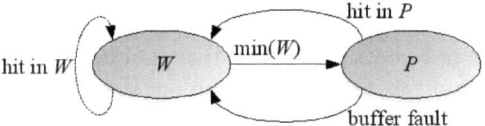

Fig. 1. Page movement

list structure. In case of a buffer fault, the victim is always first selected from P. Only when all pages in P are fixed, we select the victim from W. Considering recency, the newly fetched page is first promoted to W.

From P, the least-recently-used clean page is first selected as victim. If there is no such page available, the pages from the lowest-priority cluster are considered as victims. The priority of clusters is defined by a priority function [3] which considers both recency and access patterns (sequential or random).

In principle, recovery demands needed to guarantee ACID behavior for transaction processing [4] may interfere with the optimization objectives P1 – P3. To achieve write avoidance and clustered writes to the maximum possible extent, the buffer manager should not be burdened with conflicting write/update propagation requirements. Fortunately, our CFDC approach implies a NoForce/Steal policy for the logging&recovery component providing maximum degrees of freedom [4]. NoForce means that pages modified by a transaction do not have to be forced to disk at its commit, but only the redo logs. Steal means modified pages can be replaced and its content can be written to disk even when the modifying transaction has not yet committed, provided that the undo logs are written in advance (observing the WAL principle (write ahead log)). Furthermore, log data is buffered and sequentially written—the preferred output operation for flash disks. With these options together, the buffer manager has a great flexibility in its replacement decision, because the latter is decoupled from transaction management. In particular, the replacement of a specific dirty page can be delayed to save physical writes or even advanced, if necessary, to improve the overall write efficiency. Hence, it comes as no surprise that NoForce/Steal is the standard solution for DBMSs.

In practice, page flushes are normally decoupled from the victim replacement process as well—most of them are performed by background threads. Obviously, these threads can benefit from CFDC's dirty queue, where the dirty pages are already collected and clustered.

4   Discussion

Several buffer management algorithms have been proposed for flash-based systems. CFLRU [5] is a flash-aware replacement policy for operating systems based on LRU. It addresses the asymmetry of flash I/O by evicting clean pages first, thus allowing dirty pages to stay in the buffer for a longer period. LRUWSR [6] uses the same policy to save physical writes, but the algorithm is based on a combination of LRU and Second Chance [7]. The clean-first policy can also be utilized in hybrid systems, where flash and magnetic disks coexist [8]. However, hybrid systems are not the focus of our discussion.

REF [9] is a flash-aware replacement policy based on LRU. Victim pages are only selected from the so-called *victim blocks*, which are blocks with the largest numbers of pages. From the *set* of victim blocks, pages are evicted in LRU order. This way, REF ensures that during a certain period of time, the pages evicted are all accommodated by a small number of log blocks, thus improving the efficiency of the log-block-based FTL.

In case of a crash, the clean-first policies including CFDC, CFLRU, and LRUWSR, which hold more dirty pages in the buffer, require potentially more redo operations. However, it does not necessarily lead to longer recovery times due to the superior read performance on flash. Because flash disks handle sequential writes efficiently, we did not discuss the cost of logging due to its sequential nature. It is common practice to do logging on a separate high-performance device to ensure that it is not the performance bottleneck.

CFLRU and LRUWSR do not address the problem of write patterns, while REF does not distinguish between the clean and dirty states of pages. To the best of our knowledge, CFDC is the only flash-aware algorithm that applies all three basic principles P1 to P3 introduced in Sect. 1. According to our experiments (see poster), CFDC significantly outperformed the competitor algorithms in all settings.

References

1. Gray, J., Fitzgerald, B.: Flash disk opportunity for server applications. ACM Queue 6(4), 18–23 (2008)
2. Bouganim, L., Jónsson, B.T., Bonnet, P.: uFLIP: Understanding flash IO patterns. In: CIDR (2009)
3. Ou, Y., Härder, T., Jin, P.: CFDC: a flash-aware replacement policy for database buffer management. In: DaMoN, pp. 15–20. ACM, Providence (2009)
4. Härder, T., Reuter, A.: Principles of transaction-oriented database recovery. ACM Computing Surveys 15(4), 287–317 (1983)
5. Park, S., Jung, D., et al.: CFLRU: a replacement algorithm for flash memory. In: CASES, pp. 234–241 (2006)
6. Jung, H., Shim, H., et al.: LRU-WSR: integration of LRU and writes sequence reordering for flash memory. Trans. on Cons. Electr. 54(3), 1215–1223 (2008)
7. Tanenbaum, A.S.: Operating Systems, Design and Impl. Prentice-Hall (1987)
8. Koltsidas, I., Viglas, S.D.: Flashing up the storage layer. VLDB Endow. Arch. 1, 514–525 (2008)
9. Seo, D., Shin, D.: Recently-evicted-first buffer replacement policy for flash storage devices. Trans. on Cons. Electr. 54(3), 1228–1235 (2008)

A Quality Framework for Data Integration

Jianing Wang

Department of Computer Science and Information Systems,
Birkbeck College, University of London, London WC1E 7HX
jianing@dcs.bbk.ac.uk

Abstract. Data Integration (DI) aims to combine heterogeneous distributed information and provide integrated interfaces for accessing such information. DI is a complex process and its quality may be difficult to assess. This paper aims to determine and improve DI quality by presenting an ontology-based quality framework focusing on the users' requirements, extended with quality criteria and factors defined specifically in the DI context.

1 Introduction

In the heterogeneous DI context, distributed information conforming to different data models can be accessed through an integrated schema using mappings between this schema and the data sources (note this is virtual DI, which is the focus of this paper). A typical DI setting, involving a Global Schema (GS), the Local Schemas (LSs) and Mappings (M) between the GS and the LSs, is commonly considered in DI research. Much research has focused on solving the heterogeneity issues involved in the DI process, including data model, schematic and semantic heterogeneities [1]. In practice, other factors also have impact on the design of an integrated resource (by 'integrated resource' we mean here the data sources, global schemas, mappings and other metadata). Examples of such factors include the user requirements, domain knowledge of the end-users and data integrators, query capabilities of the available data sources, incomplete information etc. Although many DI tools have been designed to assist integrators in DI tasks such as similarity matching and mapping generation (semi-)automatically, DI design is still a complex and error-prone process [2] and the quality of the integrated resources generated is also difficult to determine and control.

In the current DI domain, there lacks a systematic study of the quality assessment problem, although work has been undertaken on developing and evaluating individual DI quality criteria. Two categories of quality criteria and methods have been proposed, termed *data-oriented* and *schema/mapping oriented*. In the data-oriented methods, researchers adopt quality criteria from general data quality research, such as completeness, consistency, accuracy and timeliness. Measurement methods for such characteristics are proposed in [3]. In the schema/mapping-oriented methods, DI quality is considered as the quality of the GS and LSs in [4], with criteria such as schema completeness, GS minimality and datatype consistency. Mappings are crucial in data integration and much research has focused on the problems of mapping generation and query answering in DI settings with respect to the precision, consistency and completeness of information [5]. Mapping minimality is studied in [6] with the concept of core mappings, from which other mappings can be derived.

However, despite the work in studying individual DI quality criteria, tradeoffs between these criteria have not been investigated formally. The exception is recent research in [7] into using ontology techniques to represent quality models designed for e-Science projects. An advantage of such an ontology approach is that an integrated and consistent quality view based on formal quality representation can be generated using ontology reasoning techniques. This paper takes a similar approach of representing the quality framework using an ontology. However, in our quality framework, user requirements with respect to DI quality are directly supported and associated with elements available in the DI resources, e.g., data, metadata, mappings. DI-related quality criteria are also proposed in this paper.

2   DI Quality Framework

Our quality framework (illustrated in Figure 1) is composed of four major parts, termed ITEM, METRIC, QUALITY CRITERIA and USER.

ITEM contains the representations of knowledge extractable from the elements comprising a DI setting. By 'elements' we mean the fundamental units of a DI setting, including *Data Item*, *Schema Construct*, *Mapping* and *Assertion*. Assertions are defined by integrators so as to express domain-specific knowledge relating to a DI setting. Links exist between these sub-concepts, represented as the 'link' ontology property, to represent how the extent of one concept relates to that of another.

In the **METRIC** part, different measurement methods (metrics) are represented by the *Metric* concept. Each metric is defined over the extent of the Item concept in the ITEM part. The measurement results are stored as the extent of the *Value* concept associated with the Metric concept.

QUALITY CRITERIA contains the ontological representation of the quality hierarchy as defined by the data integrator for a particular DI setting. This hierarchy is built from two concepts, *Criterion* and *Factor*, and the relationships between them namely, 'is-a' and 'isAssociatedWith'. Each quality criterion can be associated with several quality factors, and each quality factor can be associated with one or more quality metrics in the METRIC part. The quality criteria we focus on in this paper are completeness, consistency, accuracy, minimality and performance.

USER contains the *User* concept and allows different representations of users' requirements on DI quality. Different categories of user requirements can be related by using the 'isAssociatedWith' property. Each User concept is composed of quality criteria, quality factors and the relationships between them. If the extent of the concepts in the QUALITY CRITERIA and METRIC parts are satisfactory for the users, then the user requirements can be regarded as being satisfied by the DI setting.

We currently express this quality framework in the OWL-Lite ontology language (http://www.w3.org/TR/owl-guide/) which is sufficient for representing the inclusion and implication constraints considered so far. However, OWL-Lite is not sufficiently expressive for representing broader constraints, such as conditional functional dependencies, conditional inclusion dependencies, many to many relationships, etc. Hence, the OWL-DL ontology language will be adopted in our future work.

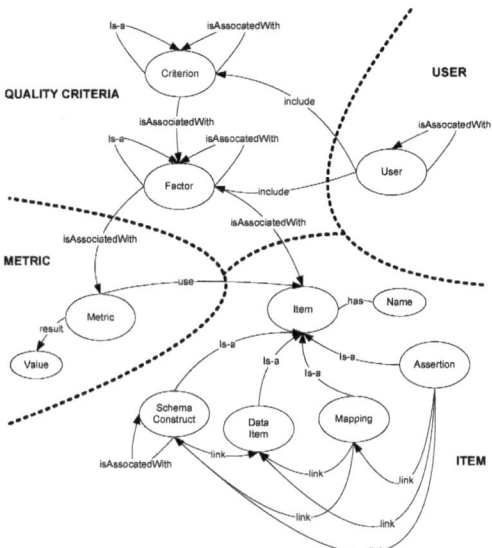

Fig. 1. DI Quality Framework

3   Quality Criteria

In our DI quality work so far, we have considered five major quality criteria: *completeness, consistency, accuracy, minimality* and *performance.* Each of them can be associated with one or more quality factors, which could be quantified by different quality metrics. We briefly discuss these next and refer the reader to [8] for details:

- The *completeness* criterion considers the degree of coverage of information in a DI setting. It is categorised into three sub-concepts: *schema completeness, mapping completeness* and *query completeness.* Our notion of '*coverage*' is a measure of the number of real-world entities reflected in different aspects of the DI setting, taking into account both the representation of real-world entities at the schema level as well as the existence of instances of those entities extractable from the corresponding data sources.
- The *consistency* criterion considers the degree of satisfaction of the semantics of a DI setting. Such semantics may be expressed at three levels: modelling, metadata and data. The consistency criterion can be categorised into three sub-criteria: *schema consistency, mapping consistency* and *query consistency.*
- The *accuracy* criterion considers the degree of precision of information represented in a DI setting. By '*precision of information*' we mean its scope, conformance to constraints and granularity. This criterion is also categorised into *schema, mapping* and *query* accuracy sub-criteria.

- The *minimality* criterion considers the degree of redundancies existing in a DI setting. By '*redundancy*' we mean overlapping information represented in data and schemas, and unnecessary transformations occurring in mappings. Minimality is categorised into *data*, *schema* and *mapping* minimality sub-criteria.
- The *performance* criterion considers the cost of query processing in a DI setting. The cost of query processing is affected by the capability of the DI tool's global query processor and the data sources' local query processors. The capability of the global query processor determines how user queries are reformulated, optimised and evaluated.

4   Summary and Conclusions

In this paper, we have proposed a DI quality framework which is represented as an ontology. Our quality framework formalises the tradeoffs between quality criteria and factors, and enables ontology reasoning to be applied in order to generate an integrated and consistent quality view of the DI setting. This framework is also capable of expressing different users' requirements on DI quality. Detailed discussion of DI quality criteria and factors is given in [8], where we also describe an architecture that embeds quality assurance capabilities throughout the DI life-cycle. This architecture includes a pre-existing schema and ontology matching tool (COMA++), a pre-existing data integration tool (AutoMed) and the new Quality Measurement tool that we are developing.

References

1. Bouzeghoub, M., Lenzerini, M.: Introduction to the Special Issue on Data Extraction, Cleaning, and Reconciliation. Inf. Syst. 26, 535–536 (2001)
2. Halevy, A., Rajaraman, A., Ordille, J.: Data Integration: The Teenage Years. In: VLDB 2006, pp. 9–16 (2006)
3. Ballou, D.P., Chengalur-Smith, I.N., Wang, R.Y.: Sample-Based Quality Estimation of Query Results in Relational Database Environments. IEEE Trans. on Knowl. and Data Eng., 639–650 (2006)
4. Batista, M., Salgado, A.C.: Information Quality Measurement in Data Integration Schemas. In: 5th DQB Int. Workshop on Quality in Databases, pp. 61–72 (2007)
5. Cabibbo, L.: On Keys, Foreign Keys and Nullable Attributes in Relational Mapping Systems. In: EDBT 2009, pp. 263–274 (2009)
6. Fagin, R., Kolaitis, P.G., Popa, L.: Data Exchange: Getting to the Core. ACM Trans. Database Syst. 30, 174–210 (2005)
7. Preece, A., Jin, B., Pignotti, E., Missier, P., Embury, S., Stead, D., Brown, A.: Managing Information Quality in e-Science Using Semantic Web Technology. In: Sure, Y., Domingue, J. (eds.) ESWC 2006. LNCS, vol. 4011, pp. 472–486. Springer, Heidelberg (2006)
8. Wang, J.: Quality Assessment in Data Integration, Birkbeck DCSIS Technical Report (April 2010), http://www.dcs.bbk.ac.uk//research/techreps/2010/

Uses of Peer Assessment in Database Teaching and Learning

James Paterson[1], John N. Wilson[2], and Petra Leimich[3]

[1] School of Engineering and Computing, Glasgow Caledonian University,
Glasgow, G4 0BA, UK
James.Paterson@gcu.ac.uk
[2] Department of Computer and Information Sciences, University of Strathclyde,
Glasgow, G1 1XQ, UK
john.wilson@cis.strath.ac.uk
[3] School of Computing and Engineering Systems, University of Abertay Dundee,
Dundee, DD1 1HG, UK
p.leimich@abertay.ac.uk

Abstract. This discussion paper introduces three very different methods and contexts for the use of peer assessment in introductory database classes, each of which is supported by different learning software tools. In the first case study, at Glasgow Caledonian University, Contributing Student Pedagogy is used, where students contribute to the learning of others through the collaborative creation of a bank of self-assessment questions. This is supported by the Peerwise software tool. Secondly, at the University of Strathclyde, students undertake formative assessment of others in providing feedback on an initial element of a larger coursework assessment. A number of virtual learning environments (VLEs) are capable of supporting this method through customisable discussion fora. Finally, at the University of Abertay Dundee, peer and self assessment are used in a group project to adjust the group grade for individual students. This is effected through the use of the WebPA software tool.

1 Introduction

Peer assessment by students of other students' work, both formative and summative, has many potential benefits to learning for all concerned. It develops the ability to evaluate and make judgements, and in doing so students gain insights into their own learning. The results of evaluation by peers can also provide a valuable source of feedback. This paper describes a variety of approaches to peer assessment and feedback, and the software tools which support them, which have been used within introductory database classes.

2 A Contributing Student Pedagogy in an Introductory Database Class

A Contributing Student Pedagogy (CSP) is an approach in which students contribute to the learning of others, and value the contribution of others [7]. One

L.M. MacKinnon (Ed.): BNCOD 2010, LNCS 6121, pp. 135–146, 2012.

example of a software tool which provides support for the implementation of a CSP is PeerWise [4]. PeerWise provides a means to create an online repository of multiple choice questions (MCQs) in which students themselves write the questions. Students can then answer questions which have been contributed by others, and they have the opportunity to evaluate those contributions. The authors of PeerWise assert that asking students to write MCQs, and to provide appropriate explanations, gives a richer and deeper learning experience than simply answering practice questions which have been provided by staff [3]. The possibility that questions may be poorly thought out, or that the provided answers may be wrong, gives students an opportunity to develop skills in critical evaluation. The PeerWise system is in use in a number of institutions throughout the world. The relationship of its use to exam performance and the topic coverage represented in the students' contributions in introductory programming courses has been studied [3,5]. Recently, PeerWise has been used in an introductory database course at Glasgow Caledonian University. This section of the paper reports on the experience and on the topic coverage represented in the student contributions within that course.

2.1   Implementation

The module, Introduction to Database Development, was delivered over a short (6 week) timescale as part of a set of short introductory modules within a first year course which is common to all computing programmes. The main assessment instrument is a hand-in assignment, but there is also an online MCQ test. To encourage participation in PeerWise, a component of the overall module mark (10%) was awarded on the basis of that participation. Participation was required to be completed within weeks 2 to 5 of the module. To attain full credit, students were required to contribute at least 5 questions and answer 10 questions contributed by others. Students were made aware that they were not being assessed on the quality of their questions or the correctness of their answers. For each question, students were required to provide a question stem and a set of up to five answers, and also to indicate which answer they consider to be correct. They could optionally provide an explanation of their answer. On answering a question, a student can see the question author's choice of correct answer, and also the distribution of answers previously given for that question. It is entirely possible that the indicated correct answer may not in fact be correct, and the weight of opinion expressed in other students' answers may reflect this. The student can then optionally rate the question on a scale of 0 to 5 and provide a text comment. Factors which students may take into account in rating questions may include, for example, the correctness of the given answer and the quality of the explanation.

   A total of 105 students contributed questions, which essentially is all the students who engaged with the module. Of these, only 4 contributed less than the required 5 questions. The highest number of questions contributed by any student was 10. The majority of students contributed exactly 5 questions. The total number of questions submitted was 545, and the average number of responses to each question was 2.8. Most students answered 10 questions, or a few more than that. However, 15 students answered double the required amount of questions or more, and the highest number answered by any student was 45.

2.2   Evaluation

Evaluation of the CSP approach has focused initially on two aspects. Question quality is likely to be an indicator of depth of learning. Writing a question which is challenging, and to provide good explanations for correct and incorrect choices of response requires a good understanding, as does recognizing a good question when providing ratings. Topic coverage gives a collective view of the students' viewpoint on the course material and the relative importance of each topic.

Question quality. Denny et al. [6] have applied a metric to measure objectively the quality of student-created questions in their courses. This has not been done yet in the initial analysis described here which focuses on the student ratings. The average rating of questions which were rated by more than 10 respondents (a figure chosen to provide a reasonable 'body of opinion') was 3.3. It is interesting to consider what students consider to be a 'good' question. For example, there was relatively little difference in average rating between a question which was a simple true/false question (True or False: SQL can be used to create a database?) and a more sophisticated question which requires a set of four SQL statements to be examined to identify the one which would correctly produce a specified result. It seems likely that experienced instructors would rate the questions significantly differently from the students. However, it is evident that students give low ratings to questions which they consider to have errors, for example where the stated correct answer is not correct, or where more than one answer could be correct. The provision of an explanation along with a question appears to have little influence on the rating. From the questions with more than 10 ratings, the average rating for questions with explanations was 3.3 compared to 3.1 for those without. In fact, less than 25% of the questions included explanations. It should be noted that no guidance was given to students on what constitutes a 'good' question. Given that the aim of the exercise is to enrich the learning experience, not to simply create a bank of practice questions, the quality of the questions is not the main concern. However, it seems likely that providing some discussion of question types and quality could be beneficial in encouraging students to devise questions which require deep understanding and to provide explanations.

Topic coverage. Denny et al. [4] studied the coverage of topics within student-created MCQs in an introductory programming course. They concluded that the coverage was broad, included all major topics and showed a distribution similar to that in assessments set by instructors. They also noted that a significant number of questions touched on 2 or more topics. A preliminary analysis along similar lines has been done here with the database questions. One of the decisions

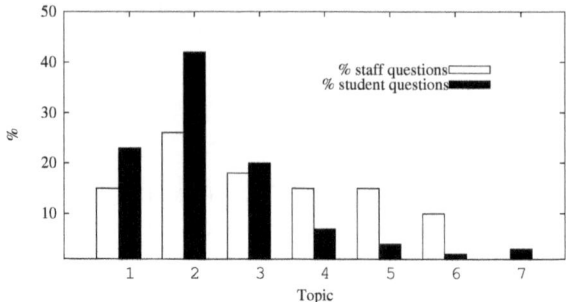

Fig. 1. Topic coverage of student and staff questions. Numbers on horizontal axis refer to course material chapters, the content of which is indicated in the text.

which has to be made in this analysis is the granularity with which topics are defined. Denny et al. used coursebook chapters as topic descriptors, and noted in support of this decision that these topics matched well to those identified in an international study of introductory programming courses involving 200 teachers at University level [12]. We have used a similar classification according to the course structure. The course materials were organised into 6 chapters:

1. Introduction to database systems, nomenclature and data models
2. Database design and relationships
3. SQL SELECT and aggregates
4. Normalisation
5. Indexes, SQL JOIN, INSERT, DELETE, UPDATE
6. Building database applications.

This is a preliminary classification, and is not necessarily ideal. In particular, there are in some cases several identifiable topics within a particular chapter. On the other hand, the structure is used by staff to guide the setting of MCQ assessments, and is familiar to students.

Figure 1 shows the distribution among these topics of students-contributed questions compared to that of staff-created assessment questions. Topic 7 is included to cover topics which are not explicitly included in the course but which students may have included on topics discovered through independent reading. Figure 1 shows that all major topics have indeed been covered. The distributions of student and staff questions are quite different. Although both show a bias towards topic 2 (database design and relationships), the bias is more marked in student questions, while coverage of topics which are delivered later in the module is very limited. It was also noted that questions were in almost all cases focused on isolated topics, with no real integration of topics within a single question. Interestingly, the latter comment also applies to the staff questions. There may be several reasons behind these results. The timescale of the exercise was quite different from that described by Denny et al. These questions were contributed within the teaching time on a short module, rather than over a period including exam revision time after teaching, which may explain a bias towards topics taught early in the course. Students essentially had 4 weeks to contribute questions on topic 2, and less than 2 weeks for topic 5. The nature of the topics covered in a database course may lend themselves differently to creating questions than the topics in a programming course. Further work is required on topic categorisation within database courses, and on the use of PeerWise in courses with different structures and timescales.

2.3   Conclusion

The PeerWise system has been used in an introductory database course to support the creation by students of a bank of MCQs. Preliminary work has been done in analysing the contributions to investigate students' perceptions of question quality and their preference for topics on which to devise questions. For the latter, there is some evidence of differences from the picture observed in programming courses, but further study is required to clarify this. Further study is also required to evaluate the contribution to the students' learning experience.

3   Peer-Based Feedback

The issue of feedback is consistently highlighted in the context of student opinions of their experiences in higher education. Typically universities and colleges have moved to encourage quick and constructive feedback from lecturers to their students. There is however still an issue of the need to provide intermediate feedback on students' ongoing work and it is here especially that peer-based feedback can make a particularly useful contribution. As well as helping the recipient of the feedback, students also benefit by viewing the work of their colleagues from a critical perspective. Students find that peer review based assessment encourages reflective thinking and self-improvement at the expense of additional time demands. While there are issues over the integrity of this process, simple, holistic feedback on review material submitted provides sufficient student benefit to make this approach worthwhile [10]. It is further recognised that peer based review can make a large contribution to building scholarly communities [1] as well as leading to significant improvements in the quality of student work [13].

Arranging that these benefits are available in the setting of large class cohorts is a major problem that was addressed by the Open University in the context of its introductory programming class by using a proprietary virtual learning environment. The approach developed requires four discrete stages:

1. Registration
2. First posting - bulletin boards are write only
3. Follow up posting - bulletin boards are read/write
4. Work completion - bulletin boards are read only.

The stages govern the permissions on the board and this fits with the work to be carried out by the student. In stage 2, students are expected to post a part of their initial solution. In stage 3, they are expected to review the work of another student and write some helpful comments. In stage 4, they complete their own work using the insight gained during stage 3 both from their own interaction and by viewing the interactions of their peers. This approach is particularly suited to complex problems where there are a number of ways of addressing the issues involved. Entity-relationship modelling presents a very apposite domain for this kind of interaction. It is a social process where the designer can learn a lot from iterations in the solution space. This is enhanced by discussing the problem with others and considering alternative and sometimes incorrect viewpoints.

This study was carried out on an introductory Databases class for second level students. The class ran in a single semester and provided 10 credits. The cohort included 107 students, most of whom were registered on a BSc Honours degree in Computer Science. Students were presented with a scenario based on a hospital, which could be represented in twelve entities and eleven relationships with assorted degree and optionality. By this stage in the module, the concept of supertype/subtype entities had been introduced and there was a clear opportunity to use such a formalism in the employment hierarchy contained within the scenario. Some many-to-many relationships typically emerged during the analysis and there existed the potential for a recursive relationship to represent supervision. In all, the problem represented a variety of challenges to students and had a number of elements that were not straightforward to represent. The overall problem could generate a number of correct solutions.

A number of common software platforms are capable of supporting the previously described posting sequence. These can be categorized as virtual learning environments (VLE) or generic software that can be tailored to incorporate the necessary capabilities. The Blackboard[1] VLE provides a typical example of the former category. It supports a discussion board idiom that includes the basic functionality that is needed to control asynchronous group interaction. The system allows the instructor to manipulate fora and allocate users in particular groups to access these fora. The bulletin board supports text as well as paste-in images and attachments. Control of permissions is mainly to define post anonymity, removal and tagging of posts, thread creation and moderation. Moodle supports a similar group-based forum concept. This implementation controls the visibility of forum contents to users from outside the forum. It restricts students to posting to one thread but permits reply postings to be made to multiple threads. Moodle[2] allows pictures to be inserted directly into postings. Turnitin[3] has also been extended to provide equivalent functionality.

WebBBS[4] presents a typical example of the range of systems available in the second category of software platforms. It can be tailored to support the required permission pattern to structure peer-based feedback in an appropriate way. The

---

[1] http://www.blackboard.com/

[2] http://moodle.org

[3] http://www.submit.ac.uk/static_jisc/ac_uk_index.html

[4] http://awsd.com/scripts/webbbs/

*** Welcome ***	John Wilson	Mon, 19 Oct 2009, 6:29 p.m.
phase2_DBClasswork_200988029	student1	Thu, 22 Oct 2009, 11:30 a.m.
Re: phase2_DBClasswork_200988029	student2	Mon, 26 Oct 2009, 10:54 a.m.
Re: phase2_DBClasswork_200988029	student1	Tue, 27 Oct 2009, 2:20 p.m.
Nurses Model	student2	Fri, 23 Oct 2009, 2:59 p.m.
Re: Nurses Model	student3	Wed, 28 Oct 2009, 12:43 p.m.
CW1 Phase 2 Post	student3	Fri, 23 Oct 2009, 4:08 p.m.
CW1 Partial Solution	student5	Fri, 23 Oct 2009, 4:09 p.m.
Re: CW1 Partial Solution	student5	Tue, 27 Oct 2009, 2:54 p.m.
Re: CW1 Partial Solution	student4	Wed, 28 Oct 2009, 3:43 p.m.
Patient Solution	student4	Fri, 23 Oct 2009, 4:55 p.m.
Re: Patient Solution	student1	Sun, 25 Oct 2009, 6:04 p.m.
Re: Patient Solution	student4	Tue, 27 Oct 2009, 11:08 p.m.
Re: Patient Solution	student1	Wed, 28 Oct 2009, 3:46 p.m.
*** End of Phase 2 ***	John Wilson	Sun, 25 Oct 2009, 4:58 p.m.
*** End of Phase 3 ***	John Wilson	Wed, 28 Oct 2009, 6:05 p.m.

Fig. 2. Typical pattern of postings in one bulletin board group

interface is very simple with postings being categorised into threads. Images can be included by writing html tags into the test of the posting.

WebBBS was chosen for the forum structure because of its simplicity and adaptability. Control of the posting sequence was implemented as part of the WebBBS Perl script. Students were allocated to groups of four or five and provided with instructions on the overall objectives of the process, the details of how to make postings and the various deadlines. Figure 2 illustrates the typical sequence of interactions between users of the system. A good posting will include a description of a difficult part of the problem and comments such as:

> In the above diagram I have produced the relationship treat between patient and doctor. But in the scenario it says that a patient is assigned to a consultant. What I am unsure of is whether my diagram should be changed so that the relationship is between patient and consultant

A poorer solution would simply list all the entities and relationships in the scenario without an attempt to draw out the difficult elements.

3.1 Conclusion

This approach to organizing peer review has been found to be very effective in motivating student involvement in assessed coursework well in advance of the final deadline. The imposition of intermediate deadlines ensures that work is carried out in a more even manner than is typically the case with a single deadline. Most students take part in the process and make contributions during both the posting phases. The overall quality of the postings is variable, with some students misinterpreting the instructions and posting their complete solution or making only a very terse contribution. Similarly response postings vary considerably in quality. Students are instructed that the tone of the response postings is to be constructively critical and this always maintained. The postings are not anonymous and this may produce a constraint on the material that is posted. Whilst WebBBS provides a useful platform for this kind on interaction, the approach to posting images can present technical challenges to students at this level.

4   Peer Assessment in the Allocation of Grades for Group Projects

The introductory database module at Abertay is taken in semester 2 of the first year by students from a number of computing-related courses. The class contact comprises a one hour lecture and two 1.5-hour labs per week per student, over 12 weeks. Group projects are used as the major assessment. These have been successful in enhancing and sustaining students' interest in the subject matter, and working closely with peers generally helps students undertake more active enquiry, contributing to the group effort. Also, reserving part of the weekly lab sessions for project work enables a close dialogue between the students and lecturer. The final group product is graded, and forms the majority of the module grade. As with group projects in general, students are concerned that grades should be fair, i.e. vary depending on the contributions made by individuals. This is mirrored by staff concerns that students should not pass the module purely on the strength of others. Group presentations, where students are graded individually, contribute to this but are insufficient as the weighting is fairly low compared to the product itself. Therefore the grading of the product (the group's database application and associated documentation) also required a way of individually adjusting grades. Initially, an attendance-based method was used. Students were allowed to miss two of the weekly in-lab group meetings without penalty, to account for unavoidable illnesses etc. However, the grades of students who missed more than two meetings were reduced by one number grade (on a 20 point scale where 20 represents A+, 9 represents D-, 0 non-submission) per meeting missed. This method was found to address the issue of contribution, but to have some major drawbacks: firstly, it relies on the lecturer maintaining accurate attendance records at all times, secondly, and more importantly, it also penalised students who made their contribution to the group work mainly outside of class, while not penalising students who contributed little despite attending class. Finally, this method had no student input, which is now regarded as good practice in assessment and evaluation (see, e.g. [11]). In an attempt to improve the process, and to avoid the drawbacks described above, peer assessment as part of the grading process was first introduced last year.

4.1   Implementation

In researching the experiences of others, several themes emerged. Several authors have described problems where students were required to discuss and agree their grades publicly within the group. For example, Cogdell et al [2] reported that students "did not like giving low marks to colleagues face to face. Consequently non-contributors would get the same marks as everyone else and the rest of the group would feel resentful. Alternatively the group would mark a member down and this person would complain vociferously." Other authors agree that peer assessment should be performed in private; for example, Lejk and Wyvill [9] found that students were more discriminating in their peer assessment when it is performed secretly. Lejk and Wyvill [9], among others, also emphasise the importance of including self-assessment in the process, in order to avoid over-generous students effectively penalising themselves. Kennedy [8] presents another, similar scenario, and found that there was little overall variation introduced in the grades through the peer assessment process, and that many students expressed reluctance to judge their peers. On the other hand, Kennedy observed that other students were keen to discriminate, and that this could lead to dysfunctional groups, with uneven distributions of tasks in the group right from the beginning of a project, when domineering students ensured they undertook the most demanding and credit bearing tasks. Kennedy questions the reliability and validity of the process also because of observed wide inconsistencies in students' judgment of each other. In Kennedy's scenario, self assessment was not incorporated, and whether the peer assessment was public or confidential is not stated.

Based on the literature, it was decided that the peer assessment used should be confidential, and include self-assessment. WebPA [14,15], open source software developed for this setting by the University of Loughborough, was used to facilitate the process and minimise any administrative burden. The students in each group were asked to rate every group member in five distinct areas, based on those suggested by WebPA [14]:

1. Co-Operation: This covers attendance at meetings, contribution to meetings, carrying out of designated tasks, dealing with problems,. helping others in the group.
2. Communication: This covers effectiveness in meetings, clarity of work submitted to the group, negotiation with the group, communication between meetings and providing feedback about the contributions made by others in the group.
3. Enthusiasm: This covers motivation, creativity and initiative during the project, including finding out about methods beyond the taught materials.
4. Organisation: This covers skills in self-organisation and the ability to organise others. It also covers planning, setting targets, establishing ground rules and keeping to deadlines.
5. Contribution: This covers the overall effort put in by an individual during the Semester.

For each area, a rating scale of 0-5 was used:

Score 0 : no help at all
Score 1 : quite poor
Score 2 : not as good as most of the group
Score 3 : about average for this group
Score 4 : better than most of the group
Score 5 : really excellent.

The WebPA software allows staff to review individual results and also aggregates the scores into a final grade. Staff also select the weight of the peer assessment component, in this case 50%. An example of the WebPA output for a single project group, is shown in Figure 3. The final grades are on the Abertay grading

Results for: Student A	A	B	C	D	E
1. CO-OPERATION	4	5	4	3	3
2. COMMUNICATION	4	3	5	2	1
3. ENTHUSIASM	4	4	4	3	3
4. ORGANISATION	3	3	3	2	2
5. CONTRIBUTION	4	5	4	1	2

Results for: Student B	A	B	C	D	E
1. CO-OPERATION	5	4	5	3	2
2. COMMUNICATION	5	4	5	1	1
3. ENTHUSIASM	5	5	5	3	3
4. ORGANISATION	4	4	4	4	1
5. CONTRIBUTION	5	5	5	5	5

Results for: Student C	A	B	C	D	E
1. CO-OPERATION	4	5	3	3	0
2. COMMUNICATION	4	4	4	2	0
3. ENTHUSIASM	4	4	3	3	0
4. ORGANISATION	3	5	3	2	2
5. CONTRIBUTION	4	5	3	1	0

Results for: Student D	A	B	C	D	E
1. CO-OPERATION	0	0	1	3	2
2. COMMUNICATION	0	0	2	3	1
3. ENTHUSIASM	0	0	1	3	2
4. ORGANISATION	0	0	0	3	2
5. CONTRIBUTION	1	0	1	3	3

Results for: Student E	A	B	C	D	E
1. CO-OPERATION	2	1	3	3	2
2. COMMUNICATIO	1	1	4	4	2
3. ENTHUSIASM	2	2	4	3	4
4. ORGANISATION	0	1	3	4	2
5. CONTRIBUTION	2	2	4	5	4

Overall group mark		80%	B16
Name	Web-PA score	Final Grade	
Student A	1.16	86.52	B17
Student B	1.4	95.99	A19
Student C	0.98	79.06	B16
Student D	0.5	60.11	C12
Student E	0.96	78.32	B16

Fig. 3. Sample WebPA output for one project group

scale (where A20 is the best possible; D9 the lowest pass mark). The group mark, B16, was converted to a percentage and then the individual grades converted back to the Abertay scale.

4.2   Evaluation

Once installed by Information Services, WebPA was easy to set up. This requires a number of steps, uploading module and student information (using templates provided), creating the assessment with relevant dates and a marking form, assigning the students to groups. WebPA allows for the use of single sign-on. In the second year of operation however, unforeseen problems were encountered in that most students could not log in and received no error message either. Eventually, the problem was fixed by Information Services. It turned out that authentication relied on the students' email address, rather than their user name, and due to very recent migration of the student email provider, email addresses did not all follow a single pattern. Despite these teething problems, which resulted in a two-week delay and countless unsuccessful attempts, students were keen to participate. However, it was decided not to apply the 100% non-submission penalty for students who had clearly participated in the project and earlier plans to seek formal feedback on the process from students this session were abandoned.

Once the students had left their peer and self assessments, group grades were entered into WebPA and its algorithms applied to calculate individual grades. The results, and detailed ratings, were inspected closely by the lecturer. As expected from the observations of group work in labs, several patterns of group outcomes emerged. In some groups, there was very little (or even no) variance, resulting in all students being awarded the group grade. In other groups, there were large differences, resulting in a wide differentiation of individual grades.

As in the example of Figure 3 above, the five different categories were used effectively, and different scores given. This indicates that students took care in arriving at their assessments. Many added thoughtful and reflective comments to their scores. This helped reconcile the very occasional wide differences between the scores given to one individual by the group members. The written comments were also useful in the few cases where the ratings were very different from the lecturer's personal impression formed during classes. Where necessary, academic judgment and performance in other module elements were used to arrive at a final grade. There was no evidence of students "ganging up" on a group member, or of students trying to improve their grade through giving themselves a very high score.

Informal feedback was received from several students by email. This showed that students found the software easy to use. One student was initially concerned:

> Can I just confirm that my ratings for the other group members will not be displayed for all to see? I just feel that this will cause problems as already there have been accusations of 'Back stabbing' between group members, it's crazy I know.

Following assurance that individual ratings were confidential, the student commented:

> It worked fine and was very easy to use! I think all group work modules should have this at the end, it's excellent.

4.3   Conclusion

While a full evaluation is yet to be carried out, initial experiences with this method based on two instances of operation are positive. The system has now been used with two cohorts, each with about 20 groups and 80 to 100 students. Not a single complaint has been received about the system's use or the resulting grade, indicating that students do find the system fair.

5   Overall Conclusion

The three very different examples introduced in this paper illustrate the potential for the use of peer assessment and feedback in introductory database classes in a wide variety of contexts and illustrate a range of software tools which are available to facilitate these processes. The approaches and tools used have been shown to be applicable in the teaching and learning of databases and have succeeded in engaging students in peer activity. Further work is required to evaluate the impact on learning and to identify activities and topics within database classes which may benefit from these approaches. As an aside, while the use of these tools is not specific to databases, or any other subject for that matter, they may have one additional use which is unique within our discipline: one thing they all have in common is that they each make use of a database and they could be nice examples of case studies which demonstrate the real-world importance of databases!

146   J. Paterson, J.N. Wilson, and P. Leimich

Acknowledgments. This paper arose from discussion at the Database Diciplinary Commons meetings organised by Prof Sally Fincher.

PeerWise was created at and is hosted by the University of Auckland, New Zealand, and the use of this facility is greatly appreciated. Thanks especially to Paul Denny for his support and advice.

References

1. Chang, C., Chen, G., Li, L.: Constructing a community of practice to improve coursework activity. Computers & Education 50(1), 235–247 (2008)
2. Cogdell, B., Brown, A., Campbell, A.: Peer-assessment of group work in a large class - development of a staff and student friendly system (2004),
ftp://www.bioscience.heacademy.ac.uk/TeachingGuides/fulltext.pdf
3. Denny, P., Hamer, J., Luxton-Reilly, A., Purchase, H.: PeerWise: students sharing their multiple choice questions. In: Proc. 4th International Workshop on Computing Education Research, pp. 51–58 (2008)
4. Denny, P., Luxton-Reilly, A., Hamer, J.: The PeerWise system of student contributed assessment questions. In: Proc. 10th Conference on Australasian Computing Education, pp. 69–74 (2008)
5. Denny, P., Luxton-Reilly, A., Hamer, J., Purchase, H.: Coverage of course topics in a student generated MCQ repository. In: Proc. 14th Annual ACM SIGCSE Conference on Innovation and Technology in Computer Science Education, pp. 11–15 (2009)
6. Denny, P., Luxton-Reilly, A., Simon, B.: Quality of student contributed questions using PeerWise. In: Proc. 11th Australasian Computing Education Conference, pp. 45–53 (2009)
7. Hamer, J.: Some experiences with the contributing student approach. In: Proc. 11th Annual SIGCSE Conference on Innovation and Technology in Computer Science Education, pp. 68–72 (2006)
8. Kennedy, G.J.: Peer-assessment in group projects: is it worth it? In: Proc. 7th Australasian Computing Education Conference, pp. 59–65 (2005)
9. Lejk, M., Wyvill, M.: The effect of the inclusion of self assessment with peer assessment of contributions to a group project. Assessment and Evaluation in Higher Education 26(6), 551–561 (2001)
10. Lin, S., Liu, E., Yuan, S.: Web-based peer assessment: feedback for students with various thinking-styles. J. Computer Assisted Learning 17(4), 420–432 (2001)
11. Nicol, D., Macfarlane-Dick, D.: Formative assessment and self-regulated learning. Studies in Higher Education 31(2), 199–218 (2006)
12. Schulte, C., Bennedsen, J.: What do teachers teach in introductory programming? In: Proc. 2nd International Workshop on Computing Education Research, pp. 17–28 (2006)
13. Sung, Y., Chang, K., Chiou, S., Hou, H.: The design and application of a web-based self- and peer-assessment system. Computers & Education 45(2), 187–202 (2005)
14. Tenant, J., Crawford, A., Wilkinson, N.: Supplementary information about self and peer assessment, http://staffcentral.bton.ac.uk/
15. Loughborough University. WebPA, http://www.webpaproject.com/

Uncertainty in Sequential Pattern Mining

Muhammad Muzammal and Rajeev Raman

Department of Computer Science, University of Leicester, UK
{mm386,r.raman}@mcs.le.ac.uk

Abstract. We study uncertainty models in *sequential pattern mining*. We discuss some kinds of uncertainties that could exist in data, and show how these uncertainties can be modelled using probabilistic databases. We then obtain *possible world semantics* for them and show how frequent sequences could be mined using the *probabilistic frequentness* measure.

Keywords: Mining Uncertain Data, Sequential Pattern Mining, Probabilistic Databases, Theoretical Foundations of Data Mining.

1 Sequential Pattern Mining

Sequential pattern mining [2] is an important data mining problem: it is concerned with databases that contain sequences of *events*, each of which is associated with a *source*. For example, a transaction database of a store may contain sequences of purchases (events) made by individual customers (sources), and the objective is to find patterns of customer purchasing behaviour in successive visits. This has applications in various domains including transaction databases, web access patterns and biological sequences, and is formally defined as follows. Let $\mathcal{I} = \{i_1, i_2, \ldots, i_q\}$ be a set of *items* and $\mathcal{S} = \{1, \ldots, m\}$ be a set of *sources*. An *event* $e \subseteq \mathcal{I}$ is a collection of items. A *database* $D = \langle r_1, r_2, \ldots, r_n \rangle$ is an ordered list of *records* such that each $r_i \in D$ is of the form (eid_i, e_i, σ_i), where eid_i is event-id, e_i is an event and σ_i is a source. A *sequence* $s = \langle s_1, s_2, \ldots, s_a \rangle$ is an ordered list of events. Let $s = \langle s_1, s_2, \ldots, s_q \rangle$ and $t = \langle t_1, t_2, \ldots, t_r \rangle$ be two sequences. We say that s is a *subsequence* of t, denoted $s \preceq t$, if there exist integers $1 \leq i_1 < i_2 < \cdots < i_q \leq r$ such that $s_k \subseteq t_{i_j}$, for $k = 1, \ldots, q$. The *source sequence* corresponding to a source i, denoted by D_i, is just the multiset $\{e | (eid, e, i) \in D\}$, ordered by eid. For a sequence s and source i, let $X_i(s, D)$ be an indicator variable, whose value is 1 if $s \preceq D_i$, and 0 otherwise. The objective is to find all sequences s whose *support* (*Supp*) is at least some user-defined threshold $\theta, 1 \leq \theta \leq m$, where $Supp(s, D) = \sum_{i=1}^{m} X_i(s, D)$.

2 Modelling Uncertainty

Traditionally, it is assumed that data is deterministic. However, it is now recognized that data is often inherently noisy or uncertain. *Probabilistic* databases are one way to model such uncertainties [1,7]. Recently, many data mining problems

L.M. MacKinnon (Ed.): BNCOD 2010, LNCS 6121, pp. 147–150, 2012.

have been studied in probabilistic databases including frequent itemset mining [1,3]. We focus on sequential pattern mining and our interest is in situations where there is uncertainty either about a source or in the associated events.

Source-Level Uncertainty. In a retail transaction database, a customer's details may be incomplete or incorrect, or the database may itself be uncertain as a result of "deduplication" or cleaning [4], leading to ambiguity in the customer's identity. A person/vehicle may be detected by a sensor/camera, but identification methods may be noisy, leading to uncertainty (take the UK police's automatic number plate recognition database [9] for example). In such scenarios, it is certain that an event occurred (e.g. a customer bought some items, a vehicle/person entered an area) but there is uncertainty about the source associated with that event. Situations like this can be modelled using *attribute level* uncertainty [7], when the 'source' attribute is a probability distribution over sources.

A *probabilistic database* D^p is an ordered list $\langle r_1, \ldots, r_n \rangle$ of records of the form (eid, e, W) where eid is an event-id, e is an event and W is a probability distribution over $\mathcal{S}$. The distribution W contains pairs of the form (σ, c), where $\sigma \in \mathcal{S}$ and $0 < c \leq 1$ is the confidence that the event e is associated with source σ; we assume $\sum_{(\sigma,c) \in W} c = 1$. A *possible world* D^* of D^p is generated by taking each event e_i in turn, and assigning it to one of the possible sources $\sigma_i \in W_i$, where $\sigma_i \in \mathcal{S}$. Thus every record $r_i = (eid_i, e_i, W_i) \in D^p$ takes the form $r_i' = (eid_i, e_i, \sigma_i)$, for some $\sigma_i \in \mathcal{S}$ in D^*. By enumerating all such possible combinations we get the complete set of possible worlds. Assuming that the distributions associated with each record r_i in D^p are stochastically independent, the probability of a possible world D^* is $\Pr[D^*] = \prod_{i=1}^{n} \Pr_{W_i}[\sigma_i]$.

Table 1. A source-level uncertain database (L) and one possible world D^* (R) showing sources and associated events (here, $\Pr[D^*] = 0.6 \times 0.3 \times 0.7 = 0.126$)

eid	event	W
e_1	a	$(\sigma_1{:}0.6)(\sigma_2{:}0.4)$
e_2	b	$(\sigma_1{:}0.3)(\sigma_2{:}0.2)(\sigma_3{:}0.5)$
e_3	c	$(\sigma_1{:}0.7)(\sigma_3{:}0.3)$

source	event(s)
σ_1	$(a)(b)(c)$
σ_2	$\langle\rangle$
σ_3	$\langle\rangle$

Table 2. An event-level uncertain database (L), all possible worlds for D_2^p (C) and a possible world D^* for D^p (R) containing one world each from possible worlds of every D_i^p. (here, $\Pr[D^*] = 0.126 \times 0.48 \times 0.35 = 0.021$)

	p-sequence
D_1^p	$(a:0.6)(b:0.3)(c:0.7)$
D_2^p	$(a:0.4)(b:0.2)$
D_3^p	$(b:0.5)(c:0.3)$

$\langle\rangle$	$0.6 \times 0.8 = 0.48$
(a)	$0.4 \times 0.8 = 0.32$
(b)	$0.6 \times 0.2 = 0.12$
$(a)(b)$	$0.4 \times 0.2 = 0.08$

source	possible world
σ_1	$(a)(b)(c) = 0.126$
σ_2	$\langle\rangle = 0.48$
σ_3	$\langle\rangle = 0.35$

Event-Level Uncertainty. In some cases, the 'source' of the event is known but the 'event' itself is uncertain. Consider a scenario where employees movements are tracked in a building using RFID sensors [5]. A typical relation SIGHTING(t, tID, aID) in PEEX system [5], denotes that the RFID tag tID was detected by antenna aID at time t. Consequently, PEEX processes the SIGHTING relation to output a higher-level *uncertain* relation such as MEETING(time, person1, person2, room, prob). An example tuple such as (103, 'Alice', 'Bob', 435, 0.4) in MEETING means that at time 103, PEEX believes that Alice and Bob are having a meeting (event) with probability 0.4 in room 435 (source) [5]; since antennae are at fixed locations, the source is certain but the event is uncertain.

A *probabilistic database* D^p is a collection of p-sequences $D_1^p, \ldots, D_m^p$, where D_i^p is associated with source $i \in \mathcal{S}$, $D_i^p = \langle (e_1, c_1) \ldots (e_k, c_k) \rangle$, where the events e_j are ordered by eid and c_j is the confidence that e_j actually occurred. The *possible worlds* semantics of D^p is as follows. For each event e_j in a p-sequence D_i^p there are two kinds of worlds; one in which e_j occurs and the other where it does not. Let $occurred = \{x_1, \ldots, x_l\}$, where $1 \le x_1 < \ldots < x_l \le k$, be the indices of events that occur in D_i^*. Then $D_i^* = \langle e_{x_1}, \ldots, e_{x_l} \rangle$, and $\Pr(D_i^*) = \prod_{j \in occurred} c_j * \prod_{j \notin occurred} (1 - c_j)$. The set of all possible worlds of D_i^p, denoted by $PW(D_i^p)$ is obtained by taking all possible 2^l alternatives for $occurred$, and we say $PW(D^p) = PW(D_1^p) \times \ldots \times PW(D_m^p)$. For any $D^* \in PW(D^p)$ such that $D^* = (D_1^*, \ldots, D_m^*)$, the probability of D^* is given by: $\Pr[D^*] = \prod_{i=1}^{m} \Pr(D_i^*)$.

3   Probabilistic Frequentness

For Frequent itemset mining in probabilistic databases, measures like *expected support* [1] and *probabilistic frequentness* [3] have been used. An expected support based approach for mining sequential patterns in probabilistic databases was proposed in [6]. Here, we focus on *probabilistic frequent* sequential patterns.

Definition 1. *Given a probabilistic database D^p and its set of possible worlds $PW(D^p)$, the* support probability *for a sequence s is denoted by:* $\Pr_i(s) = \sum_{D^* \in PW(D^p),(Supp(s,D^*)=i)} \Pr(D^*)$, *where $Supp(s, D^*)$ is the support of s in D^*. Note that $\Pr_i(s)$ is the probability that the support of s is exactly i. Further, define the* support probability distribution *(SPD) as the vector* $\langle \Pr_0(s), \ldots, \Pr_m(s) \rangle$.

Denote by $\Pr_{\ge \theta}(s) = \sum_{k=\theta}^{m} \Pr_k(s)$ the probability that the support of s is at least θ. Given D^p and two user-specified thresholds namely *support* θ, $1 \le \theta \le m$ and a *confidence* $\tau \in (0, 1]$, the objective is to find all *probabilistic frequent sequences (PFSes)* s s.t. $\Pr_{\ge \theta}(s) \ge \tau$ (i.e. all s with probability $\ge \tau$ of having support $\ge \theta$). Next, we show that we can obtain PFSes by *dynamic programming* (DP) for event-level uncertainty. By contrast, we show the computational intractability of finding PFSes for source-level uncertainty. We consider the fundamental question "is s a PFS", i.e. given D^p, s, θ and τ, is $\Pr_{\ge \theta}(s) \ge \tau$?

PFSes for Event-Level Uncertainty. First, we compute the probability with which a source supports a sequence s i.e. we compute $\Pr(s \preceq D_i^p) \, \forall \, i, 1 \le i \le m$, as done by [6]. Then, we compute $\Pr_{i,j}(s)$, for $0 \le i, j \le m$, which is the probability that exactly i of the first j sources support s, by DP using the recurrence:

$$\Pr_{i,j}(s) = \Pr_{i-1,j-1}(s) \cdot \Pr(s \preceq D_i^p) + \Pr_{i,j-1}(s) \cdot (1 - \Pr(s \preceq D_i^p)), \quad (1)$$

where $\Pr_{0,j}(s) = 1$, $0 \leq j \leq m$ and $\Pr_{i,j}(s) = 0, \forall\, i > j$. Clearly, $\Pr_{i,m}(s) = \Pr_i(s)$, for all i, and we can use this to determine if s is a PFS.

PFSes for Source-Level Uncertainty. In source-level uncertainty, an event may potentially be associated to more than one sources as shown in Table 1. Note that the DP computation in Eq. 1 computes the value $\Pr_{i,j}(s)$, which does not help in this case. For example, in Table 1, event 'b' is confused between sources σ_1, σ_2 and σ_3, but it could only be associated to one of the three in a real world, which is ignored when using Eq. 1. For example, for $s = (b)$, $\Pr_{2,2}(s) = 0$, as only one of the sources can support s. However, using Eq. 1, we obtain: $\Pr_{2,2}(s) = \Pr_{1,1} \times \Pr(s \preceq D_2^p) + \Pr_{2,1} \times (1 - \Pr(s \preceq D_2^p)) = 0.3 \times 0.2 + 0 \times 0.8 = 0.06$, which is not correct. So, Eq. 1 does not work for source-level uncertainty. We further note that it is not possible to compute the value $\Pr_{i,j}(s)$. As mentioned above that $\Pr_{k,m}(s) = \Pr_k(s)$, for all k, we say that computing $\Pr_k(s)$ (i.e. the probability that exactly k sources support s) as *Exact-k-Support* problem.

Theorem 1. *Given a probabilistic database D^p, a sequence s and a number $k, 0 \leq k \leq m$, computing the Exact-k-Support for s in D^p is $\sharp P$-complete.*

Theorem 1 is shown by reducing the problem of computing the number of perfect matchings in a bipartite graph, a $\sharp P$ complete problem [8], to the Exact-k-Support problem.

4 Conclusions and Future Work

We studied uncertainty models for sequential pattern mining and discussed *probabilistic frequentness* computation for source-level and event-level uncertainties. An empirical evaluation and comparison with *expected support* in computational cost and in quality of the solution should be an interesting direction to explore.

References

1. Aggarwal, C.C. (ed.): Managing and Mining Uncertain Data. Springer, Heidelberg (2009)
2. Agrawal, R., Srikant, R.: Mining sequential patterns. In: ICDE, pp. 3–14 (1995)
3. Bernecker, T., Kriegel, H.P., Renz, M., Verhein, F., Züfle, A.: Probabilistic frequent itemset mining in uncertain databases. In: KDD, pp. 119–128 (2009)
4. Hassanzadeh, O., Miller, R.J.: Creating probabilistic databases from duplicated data. The VLDB Journal 18(5), 1141–1166 (2009)
5. Khoussainova, N., Balazinska, M., Suciu, D.: Probabilistic event extraction from rfid data. In: ICDE, pp. 1480–1482 (2008)
6. Muzammal, M., Raman, R.: Mining sequential patterns from probabilistic databases. Tech. Rep. CS-10-002, Dept. of Computer Science, Univ. of Leicester (2010), http://www.cs.le.ac.uk/people/mm386/pSPM.pdf
7. Suciu, D., Dalvi, N.N.: Foundations of probabilistic answers to queries. In: SIGMOD Conference, p. 963 (2005)
8. Valiant, L.G.: The complexity of computing the permanent. Theor. Comput. Sci. 8, 189–201 (1979)
9. Wikipedia: http://en.wikipedia.org/wiki/anpr — Wikipedia, the free encyclopedia (2010), http://en.wikipedia.org/wiki/ANPR (accessed April 30, 2010)

A Data Integration Methodology and Architecture with Quality Assessment Functionality

Jianing Wang

Department of Computer Science and Information Systems,
Birkbeck College, University of London, London WC1E 7HX
jianing@dcs.bbk.ac.uk

1 Introduction

Information with various formats are gathered and organised by different parties. Data Integration (DI) aims to eliminate the syntactic, structural and semantic heterogeneities associated with such information [1], combine them, and provide access interfaces to the user. In practice, apart from these heterogeneity issues, other factors also have impact on the design of integrated data resources. Examples of such factors include the users' requirements, domain knowledge of the end-users and data integrators, query capabilities of the available data sources, incomplete information contained in the data sources, etc. This leads data integration a complex and error-prone process [2]. Many DI tools have been designed to (semi-)automatically assist integrators in DI tasks such as similarity matching and mapping generation. However, the quality of the integrated solutions generated is still difficult to determine and control, especially in reflecting users' requirements in aspects such as completeness, consistency, accuracy, minimality and performance of the integrated resources [3].

Generally speaking, the DI task can be achieved in four steps: *preintegration, schema comparison, schema conformance* and *schema merging and restructuring* [4]. 1) The preintegration step focuses on the analysis of schemas in order to decide the integration policy, including the integration approach to adopt and the integration strategies to use. 2) The schema comparison step focuses on detecting the relationships between the source schemas by undertaking schema matching. Several tools have been developed for this, such as COMA++ (http://dbs.uni-leipzig.de/en/Research/coma.html). 3) The schema conformance step focuses on aligning schemas to make them compatible for integration. Generally, this step is merged with the next step. 4) The schema merging and restructuring step focuses on creating a simple superimposition of common concepts and restructuring this in order to meet users' requirements. Transformations are created during this step to link the source schemas and the integrated schema. However, this schema may not be complete, consistent and may have redundancies and it may also not fully meet the users' requirements. Therefore, a restructuring phase also needs to be performed with the aim of generating a schema that is closer to the users' requirements [4]. The schema conformance, merging

L.M. MacKinnon (Ed.): BNCOD 2010, LNCS 6121, pp. 151–154, 2012.

and restructuring phases can be supported by DI tools that have functionalities for creating and storing the integrated resources and for global query processing. Such tools include Clio (`http://queens.db.toronto.edu/project/clio/`) and AutoMed (`http://www.doc.ic.ac.uk/automed/`), etc.

This paper proposes a DI methodology that supports quality assessment of the integration resources (by 'integration resources', we mean here the data sources, the intermediate schemas, the global schemas, mappings and other metadata), and a DI architecture for the realisation of this methodology. In this architecture, off-the-shelf DI tools can be used to perform standard data integration tasks, and a new quality assessment tool measures and analyses the quality of an integrated resource. This quality assessment functionality is based on the quality framework and quality criteria proposed in [3].

2   The DI Methodology and Architecture

In this section, we introduce a DI methodology that improves the existing DI processes discussed in Section 1. Our DI methodology includes three integration processes *matching/mapping, mapping revision* and *quality control*. We discuss it in detail by walking through the DI architecture that implements this methodology as illustrated in Figure 1. This architecture is composed of four main components a pre-existing schema matching tool, a data integration tool, an ontology matching tool and the new quality assessment tool. In this architecture, three heterogeneous data sources are being integrated and the data integrator has access to basic information stored in data sources, such as schemas and data. We also assume there is no existing global schema to start off with. The three DI processes are as follows. The whole process is iterative, and steps 3 onwards below may be applied multiple times.

The **matching/mapping** phase focuses on understanding the data sources by using a schema matching tool and creating the intermediate schema if necessary, the global schemas and mappings as the initial integration resources using the integration tool. This phase is demonstrated as steps 1-5 in Figure 1. We use COMA++ and AutoMed as the schema matching and integration tool respectively, and they can be replaced by other tools that provide similar functionalities, such as GLUE and Clio.

The **mapping revision** phase focuses on refining the initial integration resources by using ontology techniques[1]. This phase is demonstrated as steps 6-8 and then repeating steps 3-5 in Figure 1. In step 6, we translate all the local, intermediate and global schemas into their corresponding OWL representations, in order to not only align such schemas to be compatible for integration since we are integrating heterogenous data sources, but also to enrich the semantics in the integration resources. Such semantics can be enriched in two ways. Some semantics can be added during the translation from the schemas to their OWL representations with the assistance from the domain and upper-level ontology.

---

[1] We use OWL (`http://www.w3.org/TR/owlref/`) as the ontology language in our discussion of the architecture.

The integrator could also define assertions on the OWL schemas in order to express their own domain knowledge and information provided by the users (step 8). We then apply the ontology matching tool to such OWL schemas and more precise correspondences between schemas are expected to be discovered (step 7-8). The integrator examines the matching results and refines the initial integration resources (step 3-5).

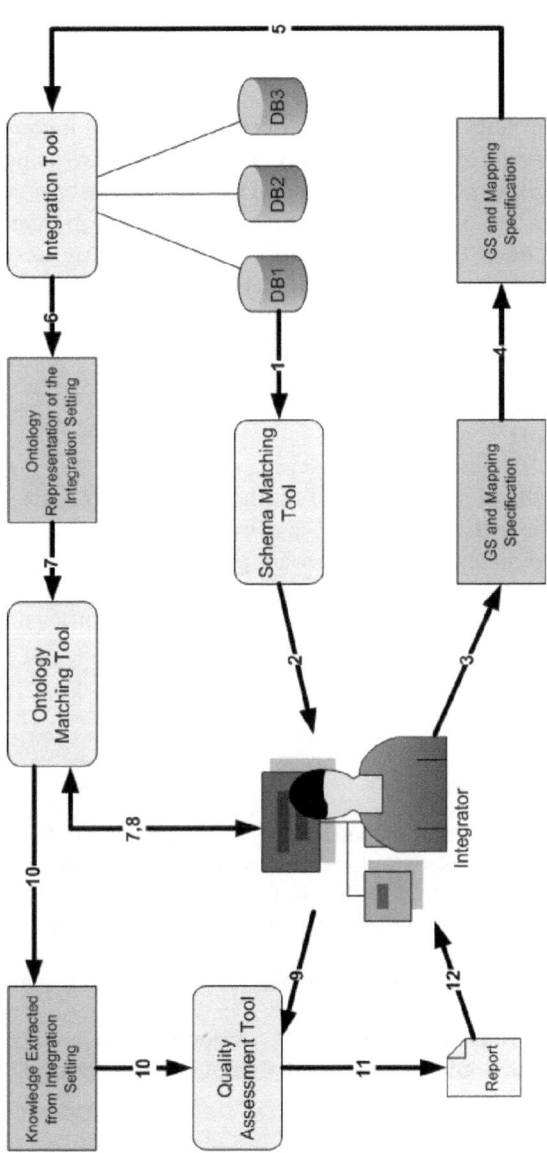

Fig. 1. Integration Architecture with Quality Assessment

The *quality control* phase focuses on assessing the quality of the integration resources with respect to users' requirements. This phase is demonstrated as steps 9-12 in Figure 1. First, the integrator sets up the quality framework discussed in [3], and establishes relationships between different quality factors with respect to the role users play and their corresponding quality requirements (step 9). Then the integration knowledge base is built by automatically translating the integration resources into their OWL representations that are suitable for the quality assessment purpose (step 10). For each quality factor of interest, the integrator uses the quality assessment tool to measure that quality factor using the associated quality metrics and populate the quality framework with the results. After all quality factors have been measured with appropriate quality metrics and the quality framework has been populated, inconsistencies between the various quality criteria/factors may be discovered by using an ontology reasoner, such as Pellet (`http://clarkparsia.com/pellet/`) (step 11). A quality report presenting the quality measurement results will be generated. The integrator then examines the quality report and makes any necessary changes to the integration resources e.g., modifying the schema and mapping specifications, modifying the assertions, changing the quality requirements (repeat step 3 onwards).

3   Conclusion

In this paper, we have proposed a DI methodology and architecture with quality assessment functionality. Our work has two main advantages in supporting the current DI demands. First, it covers DI processes commonly adopted by data integrators. In addition, it also supports mapping revision and quality assessment. Second, it reuses several off-the-shelf DI tools directly because the new quality assessment functionality is separated from these tools. Full details of this DI architecture and the quality aspect can be found in [3].

References

1. Bishr, Y.: Overcoming the semantic and other barriers to GIS interoperability. International Journal of Geographical Information Science 12, 299–314 (1998)
2. Halevy, A., Rajaraman, A., Ordille, J.: Data integration: the teenage years. In: Proceedings of the 32nd International Conference on Very Large Data Bases (VLDB), pp. 9–16 (2006)
3. Wang, J.: Quality assessment in data integration. Technical report, Birkbeck DCSIS (2010)
4. Batini, C., Lenzerini, M., Navathe, S.B.: A comparative analysis of methodologies for database schema integration. ACM Comput. Surv. 18(4), 323–364 (1986)

Author Index